BESTSELLING BOOK SERIES

Buying a Computer For Dummies, 2nd Edition

Cheat Sheet

Where to Spend Extra Money

Buy a faster microprocessor. Nothing beats a fast microprocessor. Also, because it's the most difficult item to upgrade later, it's better to spend more money here first.

Get a bigger hard drive. Although it's easy to add more storage later, most folks typically underestimate their storage needs. Too much space is great!

Maximize your memory! Ensure that as much memory as possible is in one "bank."

Jumbo-size your monitor. Those 19-plus-inch screens are *dreamy*.

Don't Forget to Buy These Items Too

- A mousepad
- A wristpad
- A power strip, or surge protector, or UPS
- A printer cable
- Paper for your printer
- Extra printer toner or ink
- A modem cable
- A few floppy disks or zip disks
- Backup tapes
- A roll of paper towels
- A nice reference book, such as *PCs For Dummies*, 7th Edition (published by IDG Books Worldwide, Inc.)

Words of Wisdom

- Don't dwell on brand names, but rather a solution to your software problem.
- Ignore part numbers: It's an 8GB hard drive, not an 8ZRc4012C-x.
- Avoid untested technology. Unless you see an item in numerous computer ads, it's probably not worth getting.
- Software drives the hardware. Without software to take advantage of a fancy computing device, the device is useless.
- Over the lifetime of your PC, you will spend as much on software as you do on hardware — and maybe more.
- Most PCs have a useful life of about four years. After that, it's cheaper to buy a new PC than to upgrade your existing model.

Questions to Help You Decide What You Want a Computer to Do

- What do you see yourself doing with your computer?
- How do you spend most of your time?
- Which activities are the most repetitive?
- Do you do anything that involves lists or organizing information?
- Do you ever sit with a calculator or typewriter for more than a few minutes each week?

For Dummies®: Bestselling Book Series for Beginners

Buying a Computer For Dummies, 2nd Edition

Cheat Sheet

Important Questions to Ask a Potential Dealer (And Some Ideal Answers)

Q: Where do you fix your computers?

A: Right here or in your home or office!

Q: Can I phone up someone to ask questions?

A: Sure! At any time. Here's our 800 number!

Q: Do you offer classes?

A: Yes, we have our own classroom, and classes are free to anyone who buys our computers!

Important Phone Numbers and Information

My dealer's phone number: _____

My dealer's support number: _____

My dealer's Web page address: _____

My dealer's e-mail address: _____

My computer's make and model number: _____

My computer's serial number: _____

Date of purchase: _____

The Five Steps to Buying a Computer

1. Decide what you want your computer to do.
2. Find the software that will get you the result you want.
3. Find the hardware to run your software.
4. Shop for service and support.
5. Buy that computer!

Types of Support

Vanilla: You pay not only for the phone call but also for the support.

Chocolate: You pay only for the phone call.

Carob: You get free support, but you pay for the phone call for 90 days; after that, you pay for the support.

Fudge: Free phone call, free support, no time limit.

The IDG Books Worldwide logo is a registered trademark under exclusive license to IDG Books Worldwide, Inc., from International Data Group, Inc. The ...For Dummies logo is a trademark, and For Dummies is a registered trademark of IDG Books Worldwide, Inc. All other trademarks are the property of their respective owners.

For Dummies®: Bestselling Book Series for Beginners

TM

References for the Rest of Us! ®

BESTSELLING BOOK SERIES

Are you intimidated and confused by computers? Do you find that traditional manuals are overloaded with technical details you'll never use? Do your friends and family always call you to fix simple problems on their PCs? Then the ...*For Dummies*® computer book series from IDG Books Worldwide is for you.

...*For Dummies* books are written for those frustrated computer users who know they aren't really dumb but find that PC hardware, software, and indeed the unique vocabulary of computing make them feel helpless. ...*For Dummies* books use a lighthearted approach, a down-to-earth style, and even cartoons and humorous icons to dispel computer novices' fears and build their confidence. Lighthearted but not lightweight, these books are a perfect survival guide for anyone forced to use a computer.

> *"I like my copy so much I told friends; now they bought copies."*
>
> — *Irene C., Orwell, Ohio*

> *"Quick, concise, nontechnical, and humorous."*
>
> — *Jay A., Elburn, Illinois*

> *"Thanks, I needed this book. Now I can sleep at night."*
>
> — *Robin F., British Columbia, Canada*

Already, millions of satisfied readers agree. They have made ...*For Dummies* books the #1 introductory level computer book series and have written asking for more. So, if you're looking for the most fun and easy way to learn about computers, look to ...*For Dummies* books to give you a helping hand.

IDG BOOKS WORLDWIDE

1/99

Buying a Computer

FOR

DUMMIES®

2ND EDITION

by Dan Gookin

IDG BOOKS WORLDWIDE

IDG Books Worldwide, Inc.
An International Data Group Company

Foster City, CA ◆ Chicago, IL ◆ Indianapolis, IN ◆ New York, NY

Buying a Computer For Dummies,® 2nd Edition

Published by
IDG Books Worldwide, Inc.
An International Data Group Company
919 E. Hillsdale Blvd.
Suite 400
Foster City, CA 94404
www.idgbooks.com (IDG Books Worldwide Web site)
www.dummies.com (Dummies Press Web site)

Library of Congress Catalog Card No.: 99-66696

ISBN: 0-7645-0632-3

Printed in the United States of America

10 9 8 7 6 5 4 3 2 1

2B/RW/RR/ZZ/IN

Distributed in the United States by IDG Books Worldwide, Inc.

Distributed by CDG Books Canada Inc. for Canada; by Transworld Publishers Limited in the United Kingdom; by IDG Norge Books for Norway; by IDG Sweden Books for Sweden; by IDG Books Australia Publishing Corporation Pty. Ltd. for Australia and New Zealand; by TransQuest Publishers Pte Ltd. for Singapore, Malaysia, Thailand, Indonesia, and Hong Kong; by Gotop Information Inc. for Taiwan; by ICG Muse, Inc. for Japan; by Intersoft for South Africa; by Eyrolles for France; by International Thomson Publishing for Germany, Austria and Switzerland; by Distribuidora Cuspide for Argentina; by LR International for Brazil; by Galileo Libros for Chile; by Ediciones ZETA S.C.R. Ltda. for Peru; by WS Computer Publishing Corporation, Inc., for the Philippines; by Contemporanea de Ediciones for Venezuela; by Express Computer Distributors for the Caribbean and West Indies; by Micronesia Media Distributor, Inc. for Micronesia; by Chips Computadoras S.A. de C.V. for Mexico; by Editorial Norma de Panama S.A. for Panama; by American Bookshops for Finland.

For general information on IDG Books Worldwide's books in the U.S., please call our Consumer Customer Service department at 800-762-2974. For reseller information, including discounts and premium sales, please call our Reseller Customer Service department at 800-434-3422.

For information on where to purchase IDG Books Worldwide's books outside the U.S., please contact our International Sales department at 317-596-5530 or fax 317-596-5692.

For consumer information on foreign language translations, please contact our Customer Service department at 1-800-434-3422, fax 317-596-5692, or e-mail rights@idgbooks.com.

For information on licensing foreign or domestic rights, please phone +1-650-655-3109.

For sales inquiries and special prices for bulk quantities, please contact our Sales department at 650-655-3200 or write to the address above.

For information on using IDG Books Worldwide's books in the classroom or for ordering examination copies, please contact our Educational Sales department at 800-434-2086 or fax 317-596-5499.

For press review copies, author interviews, or other publicity information, please contact our Public Relations department at 650-655-3000 or fax 650-655-3299.

For authorization to photocopy items for corporate, personal, or educational use, please contact Copyright Clearance Center, 222 Rosewood Drive, Danvers, MA 01923, or fax 978-750-4470.

is a registered trademark under exclusive license to IDG Books Worldwide, Inc. from International Data Group, Inc.

About the Author

Dan Gookin got started with computers back in the post-vacuum-tube age of computing: 1982. His first intention was to buy a computer to replace his aged and constantly breaking typewriter. Working as slave labor in a restaurant, however, Gookin was unable to afford the full "word processor" setup and settled on a computer that had a monitor, keyboard, and little else. Soon his writing career was under way with several submissions to fiction magazines and lots of rejections.

His big break came in 1984, when he began writing about computers. Applying his flair for fiction with a self-taught knowledge of computers, Gookin was able to demystify the subject and explain technology in a relaxed and understandable voice. He even dared to add humor, which eventually won him a column in a local computer magazine.

Eventually Gookin's talents came to roost as a ghostwriter at a computer book publishing house. That was followed by an editing position at a San Diego magazine. During this time, he also regularly participated in a radio talk show about computers. In addition, Gookin kept writing books about computers, some of which became minor bestsellers.

In 1990, Gookin came to IDG Books Worldwide with a book proposal. From that initial meeting unfolded an idea for an outrageous book: a long overdue and original idea for the computer book for the rest of us. What became *DOS For Dummies* blossomed into an international bestseller with hundreds of thousands of copies in print and in many translations.

Today, Gookin still considers himself a writer and a computer "guru" whose job it is to remind everyone that computers are not to be taken too seriously. His approach to computers is light and humorous yet very informative. He knows that the complex beasts are important and can help people become productive and successful. Gookin mixes his knowledge of computers with a unique, dry sense of humor that keeps everyone informed — and awake. His favorite quote is "Computers are a notoriously dull subject, but that doesn't mean that I have to write about them that way."

Gookin's titles for IDG Books Worldwide include the best-selling *DOS For Dummies, PCs For Dummies, Word For Windows For Dummies,* and the *Illustrated Computer Dictionary For Dummies.* All told, he has written more than 80 books about computers. Gookin holds a degree in communications from the University of California, San Diego, and lives with his wife and four boys in the wilds of Idaho.

You can e-mail Dan on the Internet: dang@idgbooks.com.

ABOUT IDG BOOKS WORLDWIDE

Welcome to the world of IDG Books Worldwide.

IDG Books Worldwide, Inc., is a subsidiary of International Data Group, the world's largest publisher of computer-related information and the leading global provider of information services on information technology. IDG was founded more than 30 years ago by Patrick J. McGovern and now employs more than 9,000 people worldwide. IDG publishes more than 290 computer publications in over 75 countries. More than 90 million people read one or more IDG publications each month.

Launched in 1990, IDG Books Worldwide is today the #1 publisher of best-selling computer books in the United States. We are proud to have received eight awards from the Computer Press Association in recognition of editorial excellence and three from Computer Currents' First Annual Readers' Choice Awards. Our best-selling ...For Dummies® series has more than 50 million copies in print with translations in 31 languages. IDG Books Worldwide, through a joint venture with IDG's Hi-Tech Beijing, became the first U.S. publisher to publish a computer book in the People's Republic of China. In record time, IDG Books Worldwide has become the first choice for millions of readers around the world who want to learn how to better manage their businesses.

Our mission is simple: Every one of our books is designed to bring extra value and skill-building instructions to the reader. Our books are written by experts who understand and care about our readers. The knowledge base of our editorial staff comes from years of experience in publishing, education, and journalism — experience we use to produce books to carry us into the new millennium. In short, we care about books, so we attract the best people. We devote special attention to details such as audience, interior design, use of icons, and illustrations. And because we use an efficient process of authoring, editing, and desktop publishing our books electronically, we can spend more time ensuring superior content and less time on the technicalities of making books.

You can count on our commitment to deliver high-quality books at competitive prices on topics you want to read about. At IDG Books Worldwide, we continue in the IDG tradition of delivering quality for more than 30 years. You'll find no better book on a subject than one from IDG Books Worldwide.

John Kilcullen
Chairman and CEO
IDG Books Worldwide, Inc.

Steven Berkowitz
President and Publisher
IDG Books Worldwide, Inc.

Eighth Annual
Computer Press
Awards ≥1992

Ninth Annual
Computer Press
Awards ≥1993

Tenth Annual
Computer Press
Awards ≥1994

Eleventh Annual
Computer Press
Awards ≥1995

IDG is the world's leading IT media, research and exposition company. Founded in 1964, IDG had 1997 revenues of $2.05 billion and has more than 9,000 employees worldwide. IDG offers the widest range of media options that reach IT buyers in 75 countries representing 95% of worldwide IT spending. IDG's diverse product and services portfolio spans six key areas including print publishing, online publishing, expositions and conferences, market research, education and training, and global marketing services. More than 90 million people read one or more of IDG's 290 magazines and newspapers, including IDG's leading global brands — Computerworld, PC World, Network World, Macworld and the Channel World family of publications. IDG Books Worldwide is one of the fastest-growing computer book publishers in the world, with more than 700 titles in 36 languages. The "...For Dummies®" series alone has more than 50 million copies in print. IDG offers online users the largest network of technology-specific Web sites around the world through IDG.net (http://www.idg.net), which comprises more than 225 targeted Web sites in 55 countries worldwide. International Data Corporation (IDC) is the world's largest provider of information technology data, analysis and consulting, with research centers in over 41 countries and more than 400 research analysts worldwide. IDG World Expo is a leading producer of more than 168 globally branded conferences and expositions in 35 countries including E3 (Electronic Entertainment Expo), Macworld Expo, ComNet, Windows World Expo, ICE (Internet Commerce Expo), Agenda, DEMO, and Spotlight. IDG's training subsidiary, ExecuTrain, is the world's largest computer training company, with more than 230 locations worldwide and 785 training courses. IDG Marketing Services helps industry-leading IT companies build international brand recognition by developing global integrated marketing programs via IDG's print, online and exposition products worldwide. Further information about the company can be found at www.idg.com. 1/24/99

Author's Acknowledgments

This book has existed in many forms over the past ten years. Originally it was a pamphlet published by *Byte Buyer,* in San Diego, California. My thanks go to Jack Dunning and Tina Rathbone for their assistance with that edition, called *How to Understand and Buy Computers.*

Several years ago, it became another book, *Buy That Computer!* (published by IDG Books Worldwide). I'd like to thank John Kilcullen for picking up the idea. Thanks also go to David Solomon for his input and wisdom.

Other thanks go to Chris Wagner, Jerry Hewett, Al Telles, Ken Jacobson, and Sandy Gookin (wife unit) for various contributions over the years. Thanks also to Takara for the best sushi in northern Idaho. Finally, thanks to all the readers through the years who have written to me or phoned me up on the radio to ask questions about computers. It's those questions that keep me in touch with what people really need. I hope this book doesn't disappoint.

Publisher's Acknowledgments

We're proud of this book; please register your comments through our IDG Books Worldwide Online Registration Form located at http://my2cents.dummies.com.

Some of the people who helped bring this book to market include the following:

Acquisitions, Editorial, and Media Development

Senior Project Editor: Kyle Looper
  (Previous Edition: Rebecca Whitney)

Acquisitions Editor: Andy Cummings

Copy Editor: Suzanne Thomas

Technical Editor: Lee Musick

Editorial Manager: Leah P. Cameron

Editorial Assistant: Beth Parlon

Production

Project Coordinator: E. Shawn Aylsworth

Layout and Graphics: Amy M. Adrian, Karl Brandt, Kate Jenkins, Jill Piscitelli, Brent Savage, Janet Seib, Brian Torwelle, Mary Jo Weis, Dan Whetstine

Proofreaders: Laura Albert, Vickie Broyles, John Greenough, Marianne Santy, Charles Spencer

Indexer: Nancy Anderman Guenther

Special Help
  Amanda Foxworth

General and Administrative

IDG Books Worldwide, Inc.: John Kilcullen, CEO; Steven Berkowitz, President and Publisher

IDG Books Technology Publishing Group: Richard Swadley, Senior Vice President and Publisher; Walter Bruce III, Vice President and Associate Publisher; Joseph Wikert, Associate Publisher; Mary Bednarek, Branded Product Development Director; Mary Corder, Editorial Director; Barry Pruett, Publishing Manager; Michelle Baxter, Publishing Manager

IDG Books Consumer Publishing Group: Roland Elgey, Senior Vice President and Publisher; Kathleen A. Welton, Vice President and Publisher; Kevin Thornton, Acquisitions Manager; Kristin A. Cocks, Editorial Director

IDG Books Internet Publishing Group: Brenda McLaughlin, Senior Vice President and Publisher; Diane Graves Steele, Vice President and Associate Publisher; Sofia Marchant, Online Marketing Manager

IDG Books Production for Dummies Press: Debbie Stailey, Associate Director of Production; Cindy L. Phipps, Manager of Project Coordination, Production Proofreading, and Indexing; Tony Augsburger, Manager of Prepress, Reprints, and Systems; Laura Carpenter, Production Control Manager; Shelley Lea, Supervisor of Graphics and Design; Debbie J. Gates, Production Systems Specialist; Robert Springer, Supervisor of Proofreading; Kathie Schutte, Production Supervisor

Dummies Packaging and Book Design: Patty Page, Manager, Promotions Marketing

◆

The publisher would like to give special thanks to Patrick J. McGovern, without whom this book would not have been possible.

◆

Contents at a Glance

Cartoons at a Glance

By Rich Tennant

page 203

page 3

page 155

page 247

page 39

Fax: 978-546-7747 • E-mail: the5wave@tiac.net

Table of Contents

Introduction

· ·

*W*elcome to *Buying A Computer For Dummies* — a book which assumes that you know *nothing* about a computer but are strangely compelled to buy one. If that's you, you have found your book!

This book is not a buyer's guide. In it, you won't find endless, boring lists of prices and products and useless part numbers. Instead, this book assumes that you need a computer for some reason. You'll discover that reason and then read about how to find software to carry out that task. From there, you'll match hardware to your software and end up with the computer that's perfect for you.

Because this is a *...For Dummies* book, you can expect some lively and entertaining writing — not boring computer jargon. Nothing is assumed. Everything is explained. The result is that you'll have your own computer and actually enjoy the buying process.

About This Book

Buying a computer is a five-step process, which this book fully explains. Along the way, you'll read about computer hardware and software and fill in some worksheets that help you configure a computer just for you.

The five steps to buying a computer are outlined in Chapter 1. After that, the book is divided into several parts, each of which occurs at a different stage in the buying process:

Part I overviews the buying process.

Part II discusses computer hardware and software: what it is and why you need it.

Part III details the buying process: where to buy, how to read a computer ad, and how to find service and support before the sale.

Part IV deals with setting up your new computer.

Part V is the traditional *...For Dummies* "Part of Tens" — various lists for review or to help you get on your way.

This book also has a Q&A appendix for any lingering questions you may have.

And Just Who Are You?

Let me assume that you're a human being who wants to own a computer. You probably don't have one now, or, if you do, it's very, *very* old and you desire a new one. Other than that, your experience with a computer is very limited. You've heard the jargon and know some brand names, but that's about it. If that's you, then this is your book.

This book concentrates on buying a computer, which can be either a PC, Macintosh, hand-held, laptop, or game console. Although all the information does apply to buying *any* computer, the main thrust involves buying a desktop computer.

Icons Used in This Book

Lets you know that something technical is being mentioned. Because it's technical, and written primarily as nerd trivia, you can freely skip the information if you want.

Flags useful information or a helpful tip. When you're visiting the computer store, for example, make sure that you leave with the same number of children you had when you arrived.

Something to remember, like all computers need a monitor or else you'll never see what it is you're doing.

Oops! Better watch out. You have lots of warnings to heed when you're buying a computer. This icon lets you find them right quick.

Where to Go from Here

Steadily grab this book with both hands, and start reading at Chapter 1. Then continue reading. Occasionally, you may be asked to visit a computer store or find a computer advertisement. Do so when asked. Fill in the worksheets that are offered. Then get ready to go out and buy yourself a computer.

Part I
Understanding the Whole Ordeal

The 5th Wave · By Rich Tennant

"WHY DON'T YOU TAKE THAT OUTSIDE, HUMPTY, AND PLAY WITH IT ON THE WALL?"

In this part . . .

*B*uying stuff is easy, even if you don't have the money! You can pay outright for a brand new VCR or a DVD player or you can charge it to your credit card. Figuring out how it works is cinchy, and if you get stuck then any handy 13-year-old kid can help you out. But a computer?

Computers are daunting. They have lots of cables and connectors. There are buttons galore which, unlike the microwave, aren't labeled "Popcorn" or "Baked Potato." Where are the "Word-processor" or "Internet-shopping" buttons? And the 13-year-old? He's no fool, his rates start at $35 an hour.

The whole ordeal of buying a computer can be utterly painless. It's possible to buy a computer that's just right for you, paying the least amount of money for all the stuff you need plus proper service and support. That's why this book was written.

Chapter 1

Buying a Computer (Step-by-Step)

• •

In This Chapter

▶ The five steps to buying a computer

▶ Step 1: Decide what you want the computer to do

▶ Step 2: Find software to get that job done

▶ Step 3: Find hardware to make the software go

▶ Step 4: Shop for service and support

▶ Step 5: Buy that computer!

• •

I'll bet that Steven King could write a really scary book about the typical computer-buying experience. I'm talking true, solid horror here, something everyone could identify with. Of course, buying a computer isn't really that scary. Sure, you can't escape from gruesome (well, tiresome) computer jargon. And technology marches forward like creeping slime, paralyzing you with fear that today's technology will become obsolete quickly.

Buying a computer doesn't have to be a nightmare, however. Just like buying anything, the more you know about what you're buying, the better you can make your decision. The real key to buying a computer is finding one just for you. You can find the right computer by following the five easy steps outlined in this chapter.

✔ I should tell you up front that the biggest mistake people make in buying a computer is shopping for price rather than service. Although lots of places will sell you the cheapest computer in the universe, don't expect them to offer much after-sale support.

✔ Yes, you need support.

✔ The second biggest mistake is shopping for hardware before shopping for software.

✔ Though you can use this book to help you find a nice used computer, I don't recommend buying one as your first computer. Why? No support. (See Chapter 20.)

The Five Steps to Buying a Computer

If you want to buy the perfect computer, the one Santa would have given you had you been good all year, then you should follow these five simple steps:

1. **Decide what you want the computer to do.**

   There are as many reasons for buying a personal computer as people to think up the reasons. And owning a computer brings more benefits than could possibly be listed — even by a computer. So you have no excuse for not completing this step. When you finish this task, the rest of the steps fall nicely into place.

2. **Find the software that will get you the result you want.**

3. **Find the hardware to run your software.**

   Most people confuse the order of Steps 2 and 3, worrying about hardware before software. But the truth is that you buy a computer to get work done, not to support some major brand-name manufacturer. For example, you buy a TV so you can watch what's *on* the TV and not the TV set itself. The software programs in a computer are what get the work done, just like the programs on a TV are what entertain you (not that imitation mahogany cabinet).

4. **Shop for service and support.**

   This is the most important step — more important than buying the computer (which comes last). Too many computer buyers overlook service and support and regret it later. I'll rant about this at length later in the chapter.

5. **Buy that computer!**

   Although this statement seems obvious, I know lots of folks who put off the purchase, holding out for a better deal or newer technology that's just "moments away." Bah! When you're ready to buy, buy. 'Nuff said.

- ✔ If you haven't already decided what a computer can do for you, skim through Chapter 15 to see what the little beasties are capable of.

- ✔ The *software* gets the work done. You buy hardware to support the software you've chosen.

- ✔ "Service" means getting the computer fixed. Support means getting H-E-L-P when you need it. *Everyone* needs service and support with a new computer. Everyone.

Step 1: What Do You Want to Do with Your Computer?

The first step toward buying your own computer is to decide what you want to do with it. You buy a car to avoid the burden of walking long distances. You buy a phone so that you don't have to live near everyone you know. And you buy dental floss because you're over 30. But a computer?

Well? What do you see yourself doing on a computer?

Computers aren't like aquariums or the television: They come with no prepackaged entertainment value (though the fish on a computer screen require no food and never seem to die). Instead, it's up to *you* to figure out what it is you want the computer to do. Only when you know what the computer will do for you do all the other steps in the buying process fall into place.

- ✔ Some people know instantly what they want a computer to do. I want a computer to help me write. My son wants a computer to play games. My grandmother doesn't have a computer, although she could use one to help her with her church flock and to write up her meeting notes.

- ✔ Not every "computer" looks like an IBM PC. Chapter 3 discusses the various makes, models, and types of computers you can buy.

- ✔ The number one reason to buy a computer today is "to do the Internet." With your computer you can communicate with others on the Internet, browse the Web, view news and sports, entertain yourself, chat, shop, trade stocks, mind your finances, or just plain goof off.

- ✔ It helps to picture yourself in the future, working on a computer. What are you doing (besides swearing at it)?

- ✔ If you ever work with lists, numbers, 3-x-5 cards, home finances, stocks, bonds, or Swiss bank accounts or if you trade in plutonium from the former Soviet Union, you need a computer.

- ✔ If you're buying a computer to complement the one at your office, you probably need something similar at home.

- ✔ If you're buying a computer for your kids in school, ask their teachers what types of computers best run the software the school uses. Buy something similar for home.

- ✔ If you still don't think that you need a computer, you probably don't. The biggest excuse people give for not having a computer is that they can't figure out what to do with it. (Price is the second excuse.) Those people probably have lists, write letters, do home finance, pay bills, and buy and sell Soviet plutonium on a weekly basis. Face it: Those folks are going nowhere fast.

Step 2: Looking for Software

After you know what you want the computer to do, you go out and look for software to get the job done. This task involves going to the software stores and seeing what's available or asking friends who have computers what they recommend.

When you've found the software you need, take notes. On each software package, on the side, are its hardware requirements — like the nutritional contents on a box of cereal. Write that information down, using a form similar to the one shown in Figure 1-1.

Software Worksheet

Category:	Office	Word processing	Spreadsheet
	Recreation	Database	Graphics
	Utility	Communications	Internet
	Education	Programming	Personal Finance
	Multimedia	Reference	Productivity

Product Name: _____

Developer: _____

Price: _____

Type of support: Vanilla   Chocolate   Carob   Fudge

Operating System:	Windows 98	Windows NT	Version: _____
	Windows 95	Windows 2000	
	Macintosh	DOS	Other: _____

Microprocessor: 486/better   Pentium MMX   Pentium: _____

Speed: _____ MHz

Memory needed: _____ Megabytes

Hard disk storage: _____ Megabytes

CD-ROM: Yes   No

DVD: Yes   No

Graphics: Graphics memory: _____ Megabytes

Other: _____

Sound: SoundBlaster   AdLib   None   Other: _____

Special printer: Nope   Recommended:

_____

Special peripherals:	Scanner	Modem	Microphone
	MIDI	Joystick	Special Mouse: _____

Other Stuff: _____

Figure 1-1:
The For
Dummies
software
require-
ments
worksheet.

Chapter 16 shows you how to fill out the form. That's your ticket for the next step: buying hardware to run your software.

✔ It's best to try software before you buy it. Just about any computer store lets you try it: Sit down at the computer and play with the software you plan to buy. See how much you like it. See whether it works the way you expect it to. Does it make sense? If not, try something else.

✔ You're not buying anything in this step. You're just looking at various software packages you'll purchase later and jotting down their hardware appetite. That information — the stuff on the side of the box — helps you assemble your perfect computer system.

Step 3: Finding Hardware

After assembling your software lineup, your next step is to match your computer's hardware to the software's requirements. The idea is to find a computer that can run your software. The software knows what it needs (on the side of the box); you simply have to fill the order.

The task is simple: Gather all the forms you filled in for the software you plan to buy (the various copies of the forms you filled out in Step 2 above), then work the Hardware Worksheet, as shown in Figure 1-2.

Thanks to the worksheet, you will know exactly what type of computer hardware you need. You'll never be steered to the wrong machine.

But don't buy anything yet!

✔ Most people make the mistake of shopping for hardware first and software second. After all, what you're buying is a *computer.* What the computer *does,* however, is more important.

✔ As another example, you may go shopping for a car when what you're really buying is transportation.

✔ If you match your software to your hardware, you won't be one of the sorry people who has to return to the computer store weeks later to upgrade your memory or hard drive or something else you should have had in the first place.

```
                            Hardware Worksheet


Operating System:   Windows 98          Windows NT          Other: _____
                    Windows 2000        Macintosh

Microprocessor:     Pentium_____       Speed: _____      MHz

Memory:     _____     Megabytes

Hard drive storage:     _____     Gigabytes

SCSI:     YES        NO

Floppy drive(s):   3 1/2-inch     1.44M     LS-120 SuperDisk

CD-ROM:   Standard      CD-R         CD-R/W
          DVD           DVD-RAM

Removable:   ZIP drive      JAZ drive     Other:_____

Tape backup:  Capacity: _____        DAT

Graphics:   Graphics Memory: _____     Megabytes

Monitor:   Diagonal: _____ inches   Dot pitch: _____ mm
           Flat-screen

Modem:   Internal    External
         v.90    ISDN    xDSL    Satellite
         Speed:_____ bits per second

Mouse:   Standard mouse      Trackball    Other: _____
         "Wheel" mouse

Sound:   Soundblaster    AdLib      Other: _____
         External speakers          Sub-woofer

Ports:   Serial:    COM1  COM2  COM3  COM4
         Parallel:  LPT1    LPT2
         USB        Firewire
         Joystick   MIDI

Other Options:   _____

Printer:   IBM/Lexmark   Hewlett-Packard  Epson  Canon
           Other: _____
           Laser      Inkjet
           Color
```

Figure 1-2:
The ...For
Dummies
hardware
require-
ments
worksheet.

Step 4: Shopping for Service and Support

Crazy Omar and Discount Dave may have deals on computers, and you can pick up a computer at the massive warehouse/membership store along with a case of pop and a vat of peanut butter — but what kind of support do those places offer? Especially if you're a first-time buyer, there's no substitute for after-sale support. The support consideration far outweighs getting a deal or finding the cheapest computer in the land.

Have a little class

I won't steer any of my friends to a local computer store unless there is a classroom attached. It's wonderful to know that a store is so dedicated to happy users that it devotes floor space to a classroom.

Some people take classes *before* they buy their computer. I recommend buying the computer first and taking the classes later. That way, you have something to go home and practice on. Also, with the computer in your possession, you'll be able to ask more detailed and useful questions than if you've never used one.

- ✔ It's easy to forget service and support because it's not mentioned prominently in the ads. Instead, you see prices and deals and sales. Ignore them!

- ✔ *Service* is the ability to fix your computer if something goes wrong with it. The best service is on-site, where someone comes to you and fixes your little electronic friend right where it lives. The worst service is when you have to box up your computer and ship it to some overseas factory.

- ✔ *Support* is help. It can be in the form of classes, phone support, or training.

- ✔ The trade-off for a cheap computer is little service and no support.

- ✔ Chapter 20 goes into more detail about shopping for service and support. This is very important! Read it! I'm not being funny!

Step 5: Buying Your Computer

When you're ready to buy your computer, buy it. You know what you need the computer for, you know what software to buy, you know what hardware to buy, and you've found a proper dealer with service and support. *So buy it!*

- ✔ The buying process is covered in Part IV of this book.

- ✔ I'd like to tell you that lousy computer dealers don't exist, but they do. Never put money down on a computer. Always pay by credit card — never with cash or a check. Always make sure that you get what you paid for: Check the invoice and, if you're suspicious, have a third-party repair place check your computer.

Don't Sit Around Waiting to Buy!

WARNING!

It's only natural to hesitate a bit before buying a new computer. In fact, Step 5 (buying your computer) is the hardest of all the steps.

Money isn't the main thing that keeps people from buying a new computer. No, it's the rapid advancement of technology that halts computer buyers. Computer technology zooms forward like a rocket sled on a frozen lake. A computer you buy today is guaranteed to be obsolete in three years and nearly useless in five. People see this situation as a warning: Don't buy today's computer; wait for the next generation!

Oh, pish. . . .

Although it's true that the next generation of computers will be better, faster, and probably less expensive, it's also true that waiting . . . gets you nowhere. It's like not catching a bus because you assume that the next bus will have fewer people on it or be cleaner. That may be the case, but while you're waiting, you're going nowhere.

The bottom line is when you're ready to buy, then buy.

Chapter 2

Basic Training

- -

In This Chapter

▶ The basic parts of the computer

▶ The console

▶ The monitor

▶ The keyboard

▶ Other parts

▶ The mouse

▶ Speakers

▶ The modem

▶ The printer

▶ Various other peripherals and options

- -

*P*sychologists claim that we all keep basic images in our heads, images we use to identify things in the world. For example, everyone stores an image of a "dog" in his head. Say "dog" and this image comes up, which you use to identify things dog in the world. The same is true with "computer."

When you think "computer," an image comes into your head, a prototype computer by which you can judge other objects in the world, identifying them properly as a computer or a looks-like-a-computer rather than looks-like-a-dog.

The sections that follow describe the various pieces of a computer, some of which you may be familiar with and some of which you probably don't know. This is your basic training for tagging the most elementary parts of a computer.

Basic Parts

The basic parts of all computers are:

- ✔ The console
- ✔ The monitor
- ✔ The keyboard

The following sections help familiarize you with each.

The console

The main part of any computer system is the *console*. This is a box that contains the computer's innards — all the electronics that make the computer go. Figure 2-1 illustrates a typical PC console.

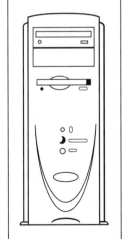

Figure 2-1:
A typical
computer
console.

Some consoles are mere boxes, usually with slots for inserting disks plus a host of buttons. Other consoles, such as those used in computer laptops, may contain *everything*. Whatever. The name of the box is "console."

✔ That's *CON*-sole, not con-*SOLE,* which means to express sorrow or grief.

✔ The console is where the computer *really* is. My aunt thinks the computer is in the monitor (covered next). But that's just where you look. The real computer is in the console. Everything else is an add-on.

✔ A palm-top computer is basically its own console. Ditto for game machines, which are merely computer consoles you plug into a TV set.

The monitor

To see the computer's output you need a monitor. In the old days, and still true for some game consoles today, a TV set was used instead of a "monitor." But as computer graphics grew more and more sophisticated, separate computer monitors were preferred (see Figure 2-2).

Figure 2-2:
A computer
monitor.

The monitor displays information on a screen, which is the glassy part of the monitor. (The monitor itself is the entire box.) The screen shows information generated by the computer, usually telling you what the computer is up to or giving you some other form of entertaining (or frustrating) feedback.

Most computers have a separate monitor. Some models, such as the iMac and all laptops, have built-in monitors. Chapter 9 discusses monitors at length, where you can decide if a built-in model or stand-alone monitor is better for you.

✔ Because laptop and palm-top computers don't have a separate monitor box, the monitor is often just referred to as "the screen" on those systems.

✔ Game consoles produce sophisticated graphics, yet don't display text as much as a desktop computer would. Therefore, a TV set is okay for a game console's monitor, but for a full-on computer, a TV set has too low a resolution to make it practical.

✔ The future digital televisions will, most likely, be fully compatible with your computer, allowing you to use your TV as an alternative form of computer monitor.

Keyboard

Most computers lack ears. You'd never know this by the way people constantly yell at them. Even so, that's not the main way you communicate with a computer. For most of us, typing is the key. And for that, you need a keyboard.

The type of keyboard a computer has depends on the computer's purpose. Most computers have a full, typewriter-sized keyboard either built-in or as its own unit connected to the console with a curly cable.

Some computers, laptops, and hand-held have a built-in keyboard. And some computers, such as the palm-tops and game consoles, have no keyboards.

✔ If the computer lacks a keyboard, you generally communicate with it in some other way. For palm-tops, you use a pen (or your finger) to enter information, either by punching buttons or by touching the screen directly. For game consoles, you use a game pad or high-tech joystick for input.

✔ Chapter 9 has more information on keyboards.

Beyond the Basic Parts

Now that you think you have a grip on the basic parts, say hello to the whole hoard of external add-ons. Many of these were once considered "bonuses" for a computer. Today they're more-or-less standard.

Mouse

The keyboard's pal is the mouse.

No, not that kind of mouse. It's a computer mouse (see Figure 2-3), used with PC and Macintosh computers to help you mess with graphical information. (And everything is graphics these days.)

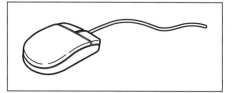

Figure 2-3:
The typical
computer
mouse.

Most computers sold today come with their own mouse, though the type of mouse may be optional/extra on some PCs. (All Macintosh computers come with a mouse.) Chapter 9 explains more about the mice and your choices, depending on which type of computer you have.

> ✔ Laptops have various mouse alternatives, devices that perform the same function but which aren't exactly mice. (More on this in Chapter 13.)

> ✔ Palm-top and game consoles generally do not need computer mice.

Speakers

All computers make noise. They hum. They chirp. They warble. But the real sounds a computer makes are only possible through speakers. Sometimes these speakers are buried inside the console; other times they're external left and right speakers just like a stereo.

Fortunately, unlike a visit to the stereo store, you don't need to bone-up that much on computer speakers. Generally, speakers are options only for some types of computers. Even then, the options are "basic," "very good," and "over-priced." And if you're into audio in any way, then you'll probably care enough to know the proper terms, so this part of the computer won't be an issue to you. Otherwise, Chapter 12 goes into all the detail you should care to know.

> ✔ Almost all desktop computers have the option of having external speakers.

> ✔ Some laptops have external speaker options, but most laptop computers have a tiny built-in speaker, one that's merely designed to scare your seatmates when you play *Doom* on an airplane.

✔ Smaller, hand-held, and palm computers lack true speakers, though they do have the ability to beep and bleep and may, in some cases, be able to play music. (The point is that you don't buy that type of computer specifically to hear opera.)

✔ Game consoles usually have left and right sound outputs, which you can either plug into a TV or directly into your home stereo.

Modem

Once an option on most computers, modems are now pretty much standard. What they do is allow your computer to use the phone lines to communicate with another computer or the Internet. How they do this is covered briefly in Chapter 11, but that's not important. The issue is that modems are necessary if you want to use your computer to cruise the Internet.

✔ Chapter 11 covers everything you need to know about buying a modem.

✔ Modems are still options on some computers. Make sure that you get one if you want to do the Internet.

✔ Modems are generally included in laptop computers, though some of the less-expensive models may not have them. It's best to ask.

✔ Smaller computers do not have modems and may not even have any way to connect them. Again, it's best to ask (or even to consider why you need such a small computer if a modem is that important to you).

✔ A modem is not the same thing as a "network card." The network card allows two computers to talk to each other directly through a special network cable. This happens in office settings mostly; though you can network computers in your home or small office if you like — but it has nothing to do with modems.

Printer

A final device that's often not thought of as part of a computer, but that's still necessary, is the printer. The printer is used to put information down on paper, to create a "hard copy" of the stuff you see on the screen. It's the final result of your computing efforts.

Computer printers come in a variety of styles, sizes, and abilities, all of which are covered in Chapter 23.

✔ Most computers need a printer, but keep in mind that printers do not come with computers. They must be purchased separately.

> ✔ You can use a printer with a laptop computer, providing the laptop computer has a printer connection (a printer *port*) or the laptop connects to a docking station that has a printer connection.
>
> ✔ Printers are generally not required for small computers or game machines.

Peripherals and other expansion options

The list of devices you can add to your computer system is endless. You'll probably pick up most of these items after you buy the computer, but you may want to have some installed at the time of the purchase, especially if they're necessary to run your software.

Anything beyond the basic computer unit (console, monitor, keyboard, mouse) is considered a *peripheral.* These are devices that expand or enhance your computer and what it can do.

For example, the printer is really a peripheral device. Another common peripheral would be a scanner or a digital camera.

Beyond peripherals, *expansion options* are options that are added to the inside of the computer. For example, you could add a special TV card that lets you view TV or edit video tape on your computer. The possibilities are limitless.

> ✔ Just about anything hanging off a computer's main box is a peripheral. *Peripheral* is a term you can use to impress the people at the computer store.
>
> ✔ Peripherals are usually found in the domain of the desktop computers. Laptops and smaller systems lack the expansion options of their larger cousins.

Chapter 3

Computers from A to Z

• •

In This Chapter

▶ Traditional PC computers

▶ The Macintosh

▶ Laptops

▶ Hand-held and palm computers

▶ Game machines

▶ Workstations, servers, and mainframes

▶ The so-called "free" computers

• •

*Y*ou think nothing today of having a telephone that looks like Elvis Presley, Mickey Mouse, or the Starship Enterprise. But 50 years ago? No way! Phones back then were black, heavy-desktop models. Some mounted on the wall, but basically all phones were alike. Choices were few.

Computers don't all look alike any more, either. There are different makes and models, from the ancient, boxy, dinocomputers weighing several tons each down to the slender Palm Pilot weighing 4 ounces. This chapter provides a swift introduction to the various makes, models, and styles of computers, from A to Z.

> ✔ Refer to Chapter 2 for information on what the various computer components are.

What Is a Computer?

I suppose in the book *Brain Surgery For Dummies* (IDG Books Worldwide) one of the first chapters is called "What is a brain?" The idea is that not everyone attempting to buy a computer (or slice into a brain) is really all that comfortable with the concept. And that's why *...For Dummies* books are written: to remove the fear and put some fun into understanding difficult concepts!

A computer is an electronic device. It consists of two parts, hardware and software. Say that out loud: *hardware* and *software.*

The hardware is the physical part of the computer, the console (as I describe in Chapter 2), plus all the electronics inside and outside the console.

The software is the brains of the operation. It consists of special instructions (programs) that tell the hardware exactly what to do.

When you buy a computer, you buy both hardware and software. Even though the emphasis is usually on the hardware (IBM-this, Dell-that), it's the software that's more important.

I'll discuss hardware and software in more detail in Part II of this book (and specifically in Chapter 5). For now, however, know that a computer or any number of similar computing devices consist of hardware and software. You need both to have a computer.

The traditional PC

The original IBM PC (see Figure 3-1) was what's known as a *desktop* computer. The main box, the "console," sits flat and square on the desktop. The monitor perches on top of the console, and the keyboard sits in front.

The most popular PC configuration today is the mini-tower model, which is like a desktop model turned on it's side (see Figure 3-2). This type of desktop model, primarily because you can set the mini-tower console on the floor if you like.

- ✔ PC is an acronym for Personal Computer. This name comes from the first IBM model, the IBM PC.

- ✔ Before the IBM PC, personal computers were called *microcomputers.* It was a disparaging term because other computers of the day were much larger.

- ✔ The "mini-tower" is named that way because the original on-its-side PC was dubbed the "tower model." Mini-towers are more compact, though they lack a lot of the internal expansion room that tower models have.

- ✔ Smaller desktop models are still available. They're usually called "small footprint" PCs, the footprint being the amount of space the computer occupies on your desk.

- ✔ There are some new model PCs that have both the console and monitor in the same box. These systems don't have an official nickname as of yet.

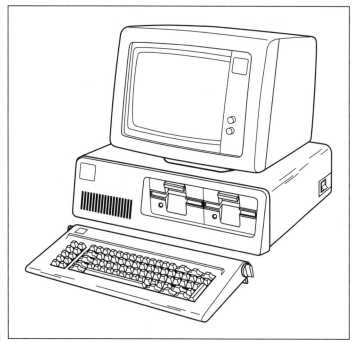

Figure 3-1:
The original
IBM PC.

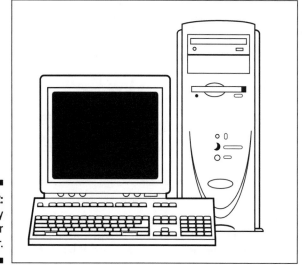

Figure 3-2:
A modern-day
mini-tower
computer.

The Macintosh alternative

Beyond the PC world lives the Macintosh, a popular alternative to the traditional, stodgy IBM-type computers. Macs (as they're called) are known to be the irreverent computer, usually adored by creative types or people just wanting to be different. And while they are fun and easy to learn and use, the only downside is that the Macintosh computer is more expensive than its PC cousin.

The most popular Macintosh model sold today is the iMac (see Figure 3-3), where the I might stand for Internet or Intelligent or any of a number of Interesting things. The iMac is an all-in-one package, monitor and console, and comes with everything you need to get started computing or use the Internet. It's currently the top-selling individual computer model, plus it comes in assorted yummy colors.

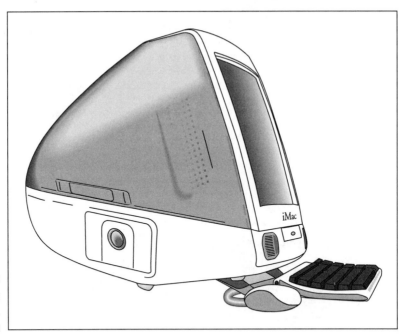

Figure 3-3:
The iMac.

A more powerful and expandable alternative to the iMac is the G3 Macintosh (see Figure 3-4), which is more on a par with a high-end mini-tower PC. The G3 Mac is much more expandable than the iMac, which makes it well-suited to "power users."

✔ Truly, the iMac is the easiest computer to set up and use.

✔ Generally speaking, the Mac excels at doing graphics. Most graphic production facilities use Macintoshes over PCs. In Hollywood, the Mac is
the most popular computer model for just about everything.

✔ Other Macintosh makes and models exist. If you want the complete list, I
can recommend the book *MacWorld Mac Secrets,* by David Pogue and
Joseph Schorr (published by IDG Books Worldwide). They list every
Mac make and model ever produced.

✔ I know Mac people like to boast that their computers are *not* more
expensive than PCs. These people go into trivial details and discuss
technological minutial to justify the Mac's pricing. Even so, the cheapest
computer you can buy in the store is not a Macintosh.

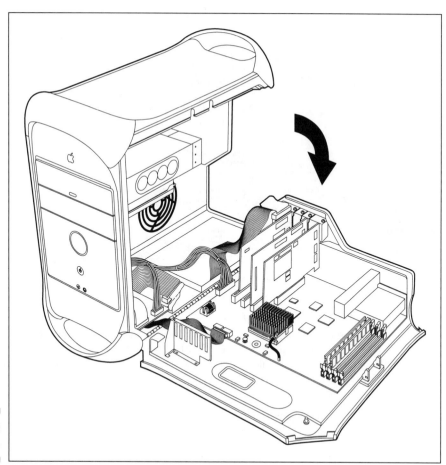

Figure 3-4:
The G4 Mac.

Laptops for every kind of lap

Portable computers are available for people on-the-go or just anyone who wants a smaller computer than the traditional desktop model. For example, if you take your work home with you, it's just easier to have a laptop you can lug back and forth than to try and share information between a home and office computer.

Laptops have the same features as desktop computers, but smaller. Figure 3-5 shows a typical PC laptop, which has everything a desktop PC has but all shoved into the space of a typical notebook. Because of the smaller components, laptops usually run more than twice the cost of a comparable desktop system.

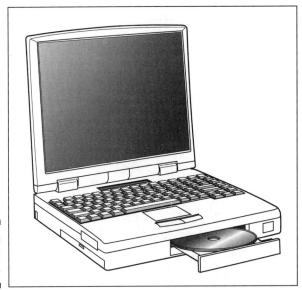

Figure 3-5:
A typical PC
laptop.

On the Macintosh side, the PowerBook is the laptop of choice (see Figure 3-6). It's essentially a Macintosh all crammed into a tiny space. The newest variation is the iBook, which is like a mini-version of the iMac — and very price competitive with PC laptops.

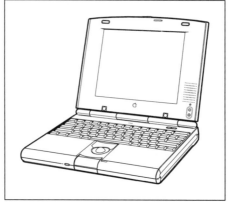

Figure 3-6:
A
Macintosh
PowerBook.

✔ Laptop computers are also known as *notebooks*. (In the olden days, the term "notebook" used to imply a lightweight laptop, but today all laptops are light enough to be notebooks.)

✔ I don't generally recommend laptops as your first computer purchase. Even so, there are circumstances when a laptop will suit you far better than a desktop could.

✔ Also see Chapter 13, which covers the issues involved with buying a laptop computer.

Palm-top computers

The latest rage is the palm-top computer. In this case, the typical computer and its monitor are shrunk down to wallet-size (men's or women's). Yes, these are real computers, but within the ranks of the palm-tops, you'll find a wide variety of types.

The most popular palm-top device is the Palm computer, also known as the Palm Pilot (see Figure 3-7). It's not a real computer nor an electronic organizer, but more of a "data gather." While you can play games with it, write notes or doodle, it's more of a supplement to a desktop computer than a full-on replacement.

Another palm-sized computer, one step down from a laptop, is the Windows CE system, as shown in Figure 3-8. These are palm-size (or large) computers that have a real operating system and many of the features and software found in a full laptop. Granted, they cost more than Palm Pilots, but for that extra price you get a fully functional computer you can slip into your pocket.

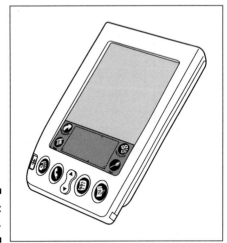

Figure 3-7:
The Palm V.

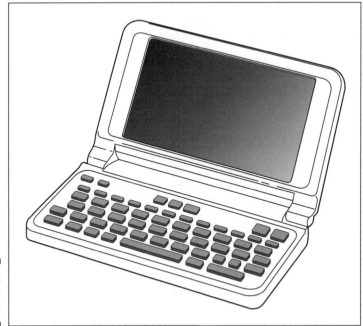

Figure 3-8:
A Windows
CE system.

  ✔ The Palm Pilot is a revolutionary computer because it doesn't pretend
     to be a mini-version of a full-on computer. It serves as a notepad,
     address book, and scheduler, and it has lots of unique software. The
     Palm Pilot never pretends that it's a big computer squished into a little
     box; it does specialized tasks and does them very well.

✔ The Palm Pilot can talk with both Macintosh and PC computers, making it an ideal supplement to a desktop system.

✔ Windows CE computers attempt to offer many of the features of a desktop or laptop PC, but in a smaller package. Some people prefer these tiny PCs, which have longer battery life than a laptop but with many of the same features.

✔ There is another class of palm-top computer, which are neither the Palm Pilot nor Windows CE systems. These are hand-held organizers or day planners.

The gaming consoles

Though often sneered at by "real" computer owners, the so-called gaming consoles are also viable computers in their own right. This was even true back in the days of the early Atari machines. If it has input and output, uses hardware and software, and you can manipulate it, it's probably a computer.

There are several manufacturers of home game consoles: there's the Sony Playstation (see Figure 3-9), Nintendo 64, Dreamcast, 3DO, and quite a few more. Each of these consoles has lots of technology built into them. Sure, they may not crunch numbers or process words, but they do one thing and do it very well: play games.

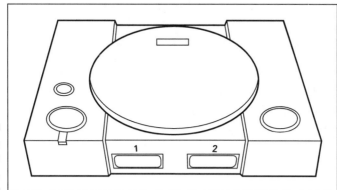

Figure 3-9:
The Sony
Playstation.

✔ As with buying any computer, the key here is *software*. Your choice of one of the game consoles will most likely depend on which games you want to play — not on the technical specs of the console itself. (This is a lesson very obvious for game consoles, but one that people buying PCs and Macintoshes need to learn.)

✔ Some game consoles have graphics and computing technology that blow away anything you'll find in a desktop computer.

Workstations and servers

The term *workstation* is loosely defined when it comes to computers. In one point of view, a workstation is any high-power computer with the latest microprocessor, lots of memory, tons of hard disk storage, and a huge price tag.

Workstations can be targeted to people doing specific tasks that require a lot of computing power. For example, you could configure a standard PC with lots of memory and graphics horsepower, stir in the proper software, and you'd have a graphics workstation. Or you could buy a computer made by Silicon Graphics, one that's specifically designed to be a graphics workstation.

On the other end of the spectrum, workstations can also be dumb old computers. For example, a PC slaved to a network where some minion enters orders is a type of workstation. (The term is vague, but don't blame me!)

Then there is the *server.*

A server is yet another high-end computer that works as the center of a computer network. For example, most large offices (and many small ones) have a central computer called the "server" (or the "file server"). It contains the programs and information used by all the other computers on the network. Again, this would be a high-end, technology-packed PC or Macintosh that merely runs the network.

 ✔ Silicon Graphics is the company that makes the computer most often used to create computer animation in the movies or on TV.

 ✔ Most people reading this book will not be buying themselves a server. These systems are usually installed by networking consultants or professionals who configure an entire office with computers. (Still, the information in this book does apply to servers as well as regular computers.)

 ✔ See Chapter 5 for more information on microprocessors.

Mainframes

The final computer category is the most ancient: the mainframe or "big iron" that used to do all the computing work before personal computers became popular in the late 1970s.

 ✔ Yes, you can still buy mainframe computers today. They still make them. Unfortunately, the information in this book will not help you choose the proper mainframe for your business (or home if you're that eccentric).

 ✔ The typical home computer sold today has far more power than all the mainframes of 30 years ago.

✔ Smaller mainframes were known as mini-computers. They were used, for example, to run a small office back in the '70s and '80s. As PCs became more sophisticated, they took over the role of the mainframe.

✔ Supercomputer is another classification of computer, though they're really like mainframes. A supercomputer is specifically designed to do many tasks quickly. Most of the jobs delegated to the supercomputers of the past decade are now accomplished by a team of regular computers working together.

How Much Will This Cost?

You're probably curious as to how much this machine will cost you? Honestly, in the big picture, price isn't important right now. (Refer to the five steps in Chapter 1). Still, you're probably curious, so why not toss out some numbers.

Remember, these numbers have no value until you're ready to buy a computer. (You'll understand why at the end of Part III.)

If you want a nice, state-of-the-art computer capable of handling most of the software out there, plan on spending about $1,500, maybe a few hundred less.

Some computers, such as workstations, high-end PCs, or Macintoshes, cost more. You could pay, for example, $3,000 or higher for the latest computer model with the fastest microprocessor and all that techy stuff.

Then there's the cost of software, which is rarely added into the purchase price. Most people spend as much — if not more — on software than they do on the computer hardware.

There. Now you know.

But what does it all mean . . . ?

✔ The iMac is about the most affordable computer considering the technology you get for that price. Ditto the iBook Macintosh laptop.

✔ Most laptops cost two to three times as much as their desktop counterparts. The reason? Miniaturization. That huge miniaturizing computer in Utah costs a lot to rent.

✔ Most game consoles run between $150 to $300.

✔ Hand-held computers and palm-tops run from under $100 for the very specific, daybook models to around $1,000 for the most recent stuff.

> ✔ Cost should *not* be the most important factor when buying a computer. Keep in mind the five steps from Chapter 1! Software availability and, especially, service and support can affect price beyond what they print in the newspaper.

The "free" computer

Some PCs are sold free. Does that make sense? No, they aren't really given way. They're sold for nothing; after you buy the computer, you get rebate coupons for the purchase price, which means you pay nothing. But do you?

Nothing is free, of course. What you get free is the computer hardware. What you pay for is Internet service. For example, you're given a $700 computer, but you must sign up for *four years* of Internet service at $20 a month. (That's $960.)

That may sound like a deal, considering that you want to do the Internet and would have to pay for it anyway. But consider this: If the computer breaks, is lost, stolen, or explodes, you still pay the $20 a month. Even if you replace the computer in a few years (since it will become obsolete before 4 years is up), you cannot stop paying. And you pay for the Internet service whether you move or die, or whether you choose another Internet service in the meantime. Yes, you're stuck.

I rarely recommend the "free PC" scheme for anyone. As you read this book, you'll discover for yourself why this may turn out to be a not-so-free PC after all.

Chapter 4

Introduction to Hardware and Software

*T*he old alchemists believed that everything was composed of water, air, earth, or fire. To me that means "warm mud," but on the upside, the alchemists also believed that you could turn lead into gold. Oh, well.

Computer scientists, looking much like alchemists but without the funny hats, believe that all computers are composed of two parts: hardware and software. If you can figure out how those two elements work, you can use a computer to turn silicon into gold.

This chapter covers the basics of all computer systems: hardware and software. You gotta know which is which because one is far, far more important than the other. It's when you don't know which is more important that you end up buying a computer that may not be right for you.

Hardware: The Hard Stuff

Computer hardware is easy to identify: It's anything you can touch. The monitor, computer box (console), keyboard, printer, modem, and the doodads inside the box — it's all hardware.

✔ If you can touch it, it's hardware.

✔ If you drop it on your foot and you say "ouch," it's probably hardware.

✔ Here's one that baffles most people: Floppy disks and CD-ROM disks are hardware. Even though they store software, the disks and themselves are hardware. The software — like music on a cassette tape — is not the hardware on which it is stored.

✔ The most important piece of hardware is the computer's microprocessor.

The microprocessor (the main piece of hardware)

All hardware in any computer is geared to work best with a single chip. That chip is the computer's *microprocessor.*

The entire computer, no matter how big it is or who makes it, is designed around a single type of microprocessor. The microprocessor determines the design and potential of the rest of the computer.

In keeping with years of computer industry tradition, microprocessors are given silly names: Pentium, Power PC, Alpha, and Athlon for example. Also, microprocessor names look like numbers: 80386, 486, and 68040. You also see combinations of the two: K6, Pentium II, G3. The names do have some significance, although they're nothing to fret over now. Just know that Pentium is the name of a microprocessor chip and not some building to visit when you're in Rome.

All the details of the microprocessor are presented in Chapter 5. At this point, all you need to know is that the microprocessor is the most important piece of hardware in a computer.

✔ The microprocessor is not the computer's brain; the brain part (if it has any) is the software, which is covered in the latter part of this chapter.

✔ The microprocessor is also called the CPU, or central processing unit.

✔ Some folks call the microprocessor "processor," for short. They're probably the same folks who call McDonald's "Mickey Dee's," even though they're not saving any syllables.

Basic hardware

The microprocessor isn't the computer. Though the type of microprocessor used in a computer tells you a great deal about the computer and the rest of the hardware, it's merely the center of attention. Supporting the microprocessor are many other items inside and outside the computer's box. Here's the short list:

- ✔ **BIOS:** The BIOS *(bye-oss)* is the computer's personality. It rules over the computer's basic parts, such as the printer, keyboard, monitor, memory, and so on. The BIOS exists as a special program burned onto a silicon chip. BIOS stands for Basic Input/Output System. Sometimes it's called *firmware.*

  Although the BIOS controls the basics of the computer, it doesn't run everything. For that, the computer needs an operating system.

- ✔ **Memory:** By itself, the microprocessor doesn't remember much. It's like an absentminded professor: smart and quick but forgetful. To help the microprocessor store information to manipulate, RAM, also known as *memory,* is used. Chapter 6 discusses memory.

- ✔ **Storage devices:** Computer memory is short-term memory; its contents are erased when you turn off the power. For long-term storage, other devices are used, including hard disks, CD-ROMs, floppy disks, and other media and storage devices. Chapter 7 covers this topic.

This basic hardware (microprocessor, BIOS, memory, and storage devices) lives inside the console for the most part. Other basic hardware surrounds the computer, like supplicants worshiping a shrine:

- ✔ The monitor
- ✔ The keyboard
- ✔ The mouse or "pointing device"
- ✔ The printer
- ✔ The modem (which is sometimes inside the console)
- ✔ Other gizmos

All this stuff is hardware, and all of it works with the microprocessor to create the hardware side of your computer system. By itself, hardware is unimportant. Only with the proper software driving everything do you get the most from your hardware.

- ✔ About half the computer hardware lives inside the computer box, officially known as the *console.* The other half sits outside, connected to the box with cables. In fact, cables are a very big and ugly part of any computer — something they don't show you in the ads.

- ✔ Review Chapter 2 for information on specific pieces of hardware in a computer system.

- ✔ Some external devices are called *peripherals.* For example, the printer is a peripheral. Although the keyboard and monitor could be considered peripherals, they're too important to the computer's basic operation to be called that. (It's a thing for semanticists and college professors to debate.)

✔ You'll notice that all computer hardware either produces input (sends information to the microprocessor) or generates output (receives or displays information from the microprocessor). Some devices, such as a modem, do both. This process is all part of something called I/O, or Input/Output, which is the basic function of all computers. It's nerdy stuff.

Software, the Other Hard Stuff

Software is the brains of the operation. Some people claim that the microprocessor is the computer's brain. No. No. No. No. No. The microprocessor is just a big, flat, expensive piece of technology — like a Keebler fudge cake with metal legs. You need software to make the microprocessor seem like it has any sort of intelligence.

The operating system

The main piece of software controlling your computer is called the *operating system*. It's the operating system — not the microprocessor — that tells the whole computer what to do. All hardware, including the microprocessor, must obey the operating system. And all software must work with the operating system.

The operating system has three important jobs: controlling the hardware, controlling the software, and giving you (the human) a way to ultimately control everything yourself.

Control that hardware! The operating system tells the computer what to do and how to do it. Although the microprocessor inside the computer may be doing the work, the operating system is giving the orders.

Closely linked to the operating system is the BIOS (see the section "Basic hardware," earlier in this chapter). The operating system gives instructions, in the course of its duties, to *both* the microprocessor and the BIOS.

Supervise that software! All the software you use (everything — all the applications, programs, utilities, and games) must work with the operating system. In fact, software is written for the operating system, not for the computer or microprocessor. Only a few games are written directly to the computer's hardware. Just about every other program is designed for a specific operating system.

The key to a successful operating system is a large software base (lots of computer programs that work under that operating system). That base is what makes the traditional operating systems so successful. Even though everyone hated DOS, it could run millions of programs. That's what made it so popular (albeit infamously so).

Work with humans! Finally, the operating system has to present you, the person ultimately in charge of the computer, with a reasonable method of controlling things. Most computers today do so using a graphical interface, showing you pictures and images to represent computer concepts.

The operating system has to show you ways to run programs and ways to control the computer's hardware. Chapter 13 discusses various operating system types in detail and shows why some operating systems do this final job better than others.

- The operating system and the microprocessor must work together to give you the best possible computer. When they work together, they're said to be *compatible*.

- You'll likely be using only one operating system. Some computers can have more than one, but that's rare.

- Even hand-held computers and game consoles have operating systems. They may not be as complex as a desktop computer's operating system, but the operating system is there nonetheless.

- DOS stands for Disk Operating System, which seems rather silly until you consider that when it was developed, not every computer came with a disk. In fact, early microcomputers had no disk drives; their operating system was merely the BIOS plus maybe a built-in version of the BASIC programming language.

Applications and other programs

Like a general without an army, an operating system by itself merely looks impressive. The operating system's army in this case is all the programs you have on your computer, which is how you get work done. (Operating systems merely control things; they don't do any real work for you.)

In the Big Picture, the application programs are the reasons you buy your computer. You find yourself a nice and tidy word processor, which runs under a specific operating system, which requires a certain amount of hardware to help it do your stuff. That's the true chain of command.

Putting It All Together

Everything in your computer must work together if you ever expect to get anything from it. Operating systems are written toward specific microprocessors, BIOSes, and other hardware. Programs are written toward specific operating systems, as well as specific hardware. It all works together.

When hardware doesn't work with software, you have an incompatibility. (That's bad.) For example, you cannot run the Macintosh operating system on a PC. Why? Because the Macintosh uses a different type of microprocessor and has an utterly different BIOS. Different hardware and software just don't work together.

The hardware must obey the software. The software must work under the operating system. And everything has to work well with you. Figure 4-1 illustrates this concept graphically.

✔ Remember that *you* are in charge. You pick the software, which then tells you which hardware to get. That's the best way to buy a computer.

✔ All the pieces must fit together well for you to end up buying the best computer you can.

✔ What's the most important piece (besides you)? The software. That's why Step 2 in the buying process (see Chapter 1) is looking for software. When you find it, the rest of the pieces fall naturally into place.

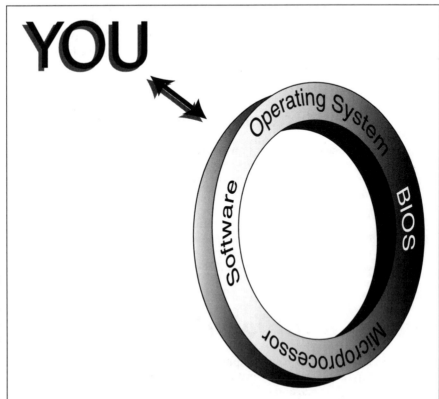

Figure 4-1:
The "how your computer system works" donut.

Part II

Hardware and Software Overview

The 5th Wave   By Rich Tennant

"NAAAH - HE'S NOT THAT SMART. HE WON'T BACK UP HIS HARD DISK, FORGETS TO CONSISTENTLY NAME HIS FILES, AND DROOLS ALL OVER THE KEYBOARD."

In this part . . .

*I*t's the software that drives the hardware, which should have been drilled into your skull by now if you've read through Part I of this book. Yet, to understand the buying process, you must first know about some computer hardware. After all, if you buy software that says "Non-SCSI compatible," it helps to know what that phrase means before deciding whether it's for you. It's like being able to understand the devastating effects of water before you buy a boat.

The chapters in this part of the book cover computer hardware and software. The part has three purposes. The first is to familiarize you with various hardware doodads, especially items you find in a computer ad. The second is to let you know how to buy those items, in case you want to upgrade your hardware and software in the future. The third is to familiarize you with the software and applications that the hardware supports. Read this stuff lightly first and then get into the dirty details later, if the urge strikes you.

Chapter 5

All about Mr. Microprocessor

*A*t the center of everything in your computer's hardware is the micro-processor. It's your PC's traffic cop, the conductor for a mad electronic orchestra. Because all the other hardware in your computer depends on the capabilities of the microprocessor, your computer needs a good, fast micro-processor to make everything run smoothly and sweetly.

The Microprocessor Rules

As your computer's main chip, the microprocessor rules over all other hard-ware in the computer system. Truly it is the center of the hardware universe: All hardware is geared to perform well with the microprocessor, and all soft-ware is written to be understood by the microprocessor.

Knowing how the microprocessor works isn't crucial. More important is being able to compare microprocessors to ensure that you get the best one you can afford in your new computer.

The following sections will help you cope with the various measurements of a microprocessor.

The name game

Microprocessors are given unusual names and numbers, much like charac-ters in the cheesy science fiction movies of the 1950s. Before you understand anything about a microprocessor, you must know its name. After that, I'll introduce you to the various yardsticks by which a microprocessor is judged.

✔ Another term for microprocessor is CPU, which stands for Central Processing Unit. Many ads use CPU instead of "microprocessor" for space reasons.

✔ CPU is also improperly used to describe the computer box or console. Beware of the double usage when shopping.

✔ The microprocessor can also be referred to as a "processor."

✔ Microprocessors are rarely referred to as "Stanley."

Families, names, and flavors

There are two main families for computer microprocessors: the Mac and PC. The Mac is easier, so I'll start there.

G3/G4. All Macintosh computers sold today have the nifty G3 or niftier G4 microprocessor in their hide. It's that simple: If it has the Apple logo on it, it has a G3 or G4 CPU somewhere inside (with the more recent, expensive models sporting the G4).

Pentium. All PC computers sold today have some variation of the Pentium microprocessor in their bosom.

The Pentium has various flavors and names (see Table 5-1 for the full menu). If the chip is made by Intel, then it's called a Pentium. The current model is the Pentium III, though there are still a few Pentium IIs available at discount prices.

Pentium-compatible microprocessors made by other companies are given other names: K6, Athlon, Cyrix, and other names are used to describe non-Intel microprocessors that work and act like Pentiums but are generally cheaper.

Even Intel has it's own Pentium knock-off called the Celeron. Essentially the Celeron is an inexpensive version of the Pentium minus some of the more advanced (expensive) technology.

The little x in a microprocessor number means that another number goes there, depending on the microprocessor's version.

✔ If the computer is a hand-held or laptop, then it uses a Pentium or G3 microprocessor as well, albeit a specially-designed low-power version.

✔ Some specific-purpose computers, such as game consoles and the Palm Pilot, use their own unique microprocessors. For those systems, selecting a microprocessor isn't a major consideration as part of the purchase.

✔ Before the Pentium II there was the Pentium Pro and before that the Pentium (all by itself).

✔ Prior to the Pentium, PC microprocessors were given numbers. You might hear the terms 486 or 386 tossed around by old-timers. (Of course, in the computer biz, an "old timer" might be a 12-year-old.)

✔ Yeah, the Pentium could be called a 586, 686, or 786 — depending on whom you talk to.

Table 5-1	Microprocessor Madness	
Name	*Manufacturer*	*Notes*
6x86 MX	Cyrix	A P2-class microprocessor with it's own MMX-like instructions included
Athlon	AMD	P3-class, formerly dubbed the K7, that's designed to rival the Intel Xeon processor
K5	AMD	The original Pentium competition
K6	AMD	P2-class
M II	Cyrix	A faster P2-class microprocessor
P2	-	Nickname for Pentium II-class microprocessors
P3	-	Nickname for Pentium III-class microprocessors
Pentium II	Intel	A faster Pentium Pro, a P2-class
Pentium III	Intel	Currently the top-of-the-line, P3-class
Pentium Pro	Intel	A processor developed in 1995 that's faster than the original Pentium.
Pentium Xeon	Intel	A super-dooper Pentium designed for high-end network servers.
Pentium	Intel	The original, almost called the 586 or 80586

The measure of power

The power of a microprocessor is measured in bits. How many bits can the microprocessor swallow in one gulp? The more bits, the more information (data) the microprocessor is capable of bandying about.

✔ Early microprocessors dealt with only 8-bits or 16-bits at a time.

✔ Today's microprocessors all handle information in 32-bit chunks.

✔ The G4 found in the Macintosh can process information in 128-bit chunks. It is the first widely-available computer to have such a microprocessor.

- Both the Pentium and G3 microprocessors are 32-bit models.

- In a way, the number of bits can be compared to lanes on a freeway. If you have only two lanes, then too many cars congest traffic, and things slow down. But a six-lane freeway has plenty of room for lots of cars, and traffic flows smoothly.

Zooooom! (Microprocessor speed)

The only technical microprocessor most folks pay attention to is its speed, which is measured in megahertz and abbreviated MHz. The higher a MHz value, the faster the chip. The faster the chip, the more expensive it is.

Fast microprocessor = Better ☺ = More expensive ☹

Speed, of course, is all relative. My first Pentium moved along at 90 MHz. That's a heck of a lot faster than my first IBM PC, which plugged along at just under 5 MHz. Today's systems zoom out at over 550 MHz. Tomorrow's will move even faster.

Even though some microprocessor speed values may look like they're 5 or 100 times faster than others, the speed is relative. For example, a 550 MHz Pentium III is only slightly faster than a 400 MHz Pentium II. You may pay a lot more for that tiny difference.

Also, avoid comparing speeds between different microprocessors; the true test lies in how fast the *software* runs. A graphic image may load faster on a Macintosh with a 444 MHz G3 than it does on a PC with a 550 MHz Pentium III.

- The larger the MHz value, the faster the microprocessor.

- Buy the fastest microprocessor you can afford!

- Never wait for next year's model, which *will* be faster. While you're waiting, you're not going anywhere.

- Your brain has a speed rating of only about 2 MHz. (Not *you* individually — everyone in general.) The human brain can do several million things at a time, however, whereas the microprocessor does only one thing at a time, which is one reason why humans consider themselves to be superior to computers.

Bonus acronyms and ratings

Not being satisfied with mere microprocessor speed and power, manufacturers often devise "bonus" ratings for their chips. These chips are given wondrous new terms boasting of their abilities. And, of course, you pay more for this.

My computer's faster than yours! Nya! Nya! Nya!

Computer nerds aren't satisfied with the mere megahertz rating of a microprocessor. No, they've devised several tests — like a micro-processor SAT — to determine exactly how fast a computer can whiz along.

Computer speed ratings are a complete and total joke, of course, because any "test" they try to pull can be fooled into giving a faster result (as long as you know which switches to throw). Yet this fact doesn't stop the advertisers from boasting how much faster their model is than the competition.

Oh, you see bar graphs and charts in the maga-zines when they compare computer speeds. The truth is that speed is relative because the com-puter sits around idle most of the time waiting for you to type something or for information to float in from the (relatively slow) modem. The following list of various speed-rating tests explains what they mean, if anything:

Norton SI. The original computer speed rating, where a 1.0 equals the speed of the first IBM PC. The bigger the number, the faster the computer; the speed rating, however, depends directly on the microprocessor's horsepower and not on the computer's actual performance (which means that this test can be fooled).

Whetstones. A speed test that measures how fast a computer can do math (which the nerds call "floating-point operations"). Because this test is somewhat inconsistent, the Dhrystone (a pun on Whetstone) test is often used instead.

Dhrystones. A real-world test of a computer's performance. Rather than measure just proces-sor speed (like Norton SI), this test is a much better judge of how fast a computer performs. Unfortunately, it too can be fooled.

Winstones. Another "punish" name, this one dealing with specific computer speeds in Windows. As with every other test, it can be fooled.

The bottom line: Who cares! As long as you match your microprocessor's speed to what your software needs, you'll do nifty-keen.

The first breakthrough term was MMX. Pentium computers boasted that they had MMX ability, which was nothing more than special instructions for game programmers. As long as the game you bought took advantage of the MMX instructions, cool. Otherwise, MMX was merely a one-up on the competition, not adding any real value to the microprocessor.

Another trick is the "3-D graphics" moniker. These microprocessors have spe-cial instructions that supposedly let programmers easily create a 3-D graphic image. Providing you buy software that takes advantage of the 3-D instruc-tions, nifty. Otherwise, the microprocessor is the same as any other — albeit more expensive.

The key, as with all hardware, is whether or not your software will use the newfangled feature. If so, grand. Ensure that you buy a PC with such features so you can use them. Otherwise, you pay a lot for something your software will never specifically take advantage of. Those are the kinds of mistakes this book helps you avoid.

- ✔ MMX doesn't really stand for anything. If it did, then Intel couldn't copyright the term. So instead, they copyrighted "MMX Technology" (which is a trademark). MMX does not specifically stand for *multi*media *ex*tensions, but it should!

- ✔ All Pentiums sold today (IIs and IIIs) come with built-in MMX technology.

- ✔ Software that takes advantage of MMX technology includes a number of games and also some multimedia stuff, educational software, and anything with animation or intense graphics.

- ✔ MMX and other advanced "3-D" features offered by some microprocessors are only well-suited for games. This brings up the obvious point: If you're that much into games, why not get a gaming console instead of a PC and save yourself some money?

Some Microprocessor Q&A for You

The following common questions crop up when normal people attempt to understand computer microprocessors. The answers provided in this section educate you without converting you into a Jolt-cola-swilling computer geek.

What does "386 or greater" mean?

Computer hardware is always developed before computer software. As an example, consider that someone had to invent the bassoon before anyone could write music for it.

To deal with the lag time, software developers take advantage of the fact that older PC microprocessors are compatible with the recent stuff. Software that ran on an archaic IBM PC with an 8088 microprocessor still runs now on a Pentium II. (It runs very fast.)

The common denominator of today's PC microprocessors is the old 80386 (or 386) chip. All the stuff written for that chip works on all later 486 and Pentium microprocessors. This capability is described on a software box by using the term "386 or greater" or "386 or later."

- ✔ Yes, the term "386 or greater" is often used even though it's been years since you could buy a 386 PC.

- ✔ You might also see the term "486 or greater." Or even "Pentium or greater."

> ✔ My nerdy side just wants to blurt this out: Technologically speaking, a Pentium is really nothing more than a very fast 386. Design wise, the chips operate identically; the latest Pentiums merely sport various speed-enhancing additions.

Can I run Power PC programs on my G3/G4 Mac?

As a rule, probably. Because the Mac has sported so many processors over the years, you really must be careful when buying software. Always make sure the software is specifically designed to work with the computer you own.

If it says either "G3" or "iMac" on the box, then it should work on either of those systems, as well as all G4 systems. However, software specifically designed for the G4 (and it will say so on the box), will run only on a G4.

Avoid buying older 680x0 software for your new Mac. It just won't work.

Are all Pentium processors the same?

No. Some software programs require a Pentium II microprocessor. It says so right on the box. If you have anything less, the program does not run or runs painfully slow. This situation rarely happens, but because you're a smart shopper, it's a mistake you'll never make.

Should I buy an upgradable microprocessor option?

Some manufacturers boast that you'll never have to buy another computer because their model enables you to "plug in" a new microprocessor. Golly, that sounds nice. . . .

My advice is to skip paying extra for a computer with an upgradable microprocessor. The reason is simple: When it comes time to upgrade to a new microprocessor, it's just better to go ahead and buy a whole new computer. Why? Because other computer components are built to take advantage of the new microprocessor.

Another reason: It's often cheaper. A new microprocessor may cost 50 to 70 percent of the cost of a whole new computer. PC manufacturers buy microprocessors by the truckload, which means that the microprocessors are cheap. One microprocessor at a time is expensive.

(Also see Chapter 21, about upgrading your equipment, for more ranting on this topic.)

What happened to the "math coprocessor"?

A *math coprocessor* is a special companion chip for the microprocessor, kind of like a pocket calculator. Its job is to do mathematical computations, and it's engineered to do them more swiftly than the microprocessor can do on its own.

All of today's microprocessors have built-in math coprocessors. If your software demands a math coprocessor, you're all set. Only if you somehow buy a used computer would you otherwise have to question whether it had a math coprocessor.

- ✔ The math coprocessor is often called an FPU, or floating-point unit. Same thing.
- ✔ All Pentium compatible and G3 microprocessors come with a built-in math coprocessor.
- ✔ If, for some bizarre reason, you get a 486 PC, note that the 486SX version of that microprocessor lacks a math coprocessor.

What's the cache?

An obscure attribute of a microprocessor is something called the cache (pronounced "cash"). A *cache* is a storage place. In a microprocessor, the cache is used to store instructions a software program gives the computer. The larger that cache storage area, the faster the microprocessor goes.

You may occasionally see a cache value used in describing a microprocessor. For example, a salesperson may boast that his Pentium computer has a "2MB L2 cache." This abbreviation means that the microprocessor has two million bytes of memory to help speed it up.

What's the point? The larger the cache, the better the microprocessor performs. Use the cache size for comparison when you get around to shopping — if you care to; most of the time, my eyes gloss over when salespeople get technical.

L2 means "level two." You'd have to be a scientist in a white lab coat to want to know any more information than that.

Is the Celeron a good Pentium compatible?

The Celeron is made by Intel, so it's the closest thing you can get to a Pentium without the Pentium name.

Essentially, a Celeron is a Pentium II with MMX, but with either no L2 cache or a very small L2 cache. This subtracts significantly from its speed, but reduces the price enough to make it an attractive processor for so-called "home" systems.

I don't recommend getting a PC with a Celeron microprocessor unless it's all you can afford.

Intel is aiming this processer squarely at the low cost PC market. The performance of the initial 266 MHz and 300 MHz 0K L2 versions of the Celeron was compared to that of a plain Pentium with MMX 200-233. That's not so great. However, the 300A and 333A chips offer decent performance, since their L2 cache runs at the same speed as the processor. In fact, all Celeron "A" chips with built-in 128KB of L2 cache beat Pentium II processors at equal clock speeds. Ironic, isn't it?

Intel offers its 300 MHz and faster Celeron chips with 128KB on-chip in two different form factors. One version fits into standard Slot 1 motherboards; the other will fit into Intel's new 370-pin socket. Intel made their Celeron chips socket 370-only, starting with the 466 MHz version. Don't fret, though, if you have a Slot 1 motherboard. Many companies offer adapters.

Should I buy a non-Intel CPU if it saves me money?

Absolutely. The days of flaky, wanna-be microprocessors are in the past. Any non-Intel microprocessor will do the job and save you some money. Two points to remember:

- ✔ Generally speaking, the Intel microprocessors are the fastest. They tend to come out first, and it takes a while for the non-Intel stuff to play catch-up.

- ✔ An exception to the above point is AMD's Athlon chip, which was the first chip AMD had made in quite a while that leapfrogs anything Intel has.

- ✔ If buying an Intel microprocessor would make you sleep better at night, then get one.

What is Socket 7?

Socket 7 is a real-live socket inside your computer's box into which the microprocessor is plugged. This allows you to upgrade your microprocessor later, providing you have a Socket 7 computer and buy a replacement Socket 7 microprocessor.

- ✔ I do not recommend upgrading microprocessors, which is discussed earlier in this chapter.
- ✔ There is also the Slot 1 standard, which is an Intel-specific standard for upgrading microprocessors.

Which is faster, a 400 MHz Pentium or a 400 MHz G3?

It depends on whom you ask. Macintosh people will definitely claim it's the G3 whereas PC people will boast it's the Pentium, hands-down. Who is correct? As you may suspect, they both are. . . .

Seriously, speed is trivial across microprocessor platforms. While you can compare, say, a 500 MHz Pentium to a 500 MHz K5, which are both similar microprocessors, comparing Mac and PC stuff is an annoying waste of time. A better comparison would be to discover which software you like better. After that, the microprocessor's speed will truly be a trivial sideshow.

Chapter 6

Memory Stuff (Temporary Storage)

● ●

In This Chapter

▶ Measuring computer memory

▶ Sizing up a memory chip

▶ Gauging memory speed

▶ Using SIMMs and DIMMs

▶ Understanding memory terms

▶ Filling your memory banks

● ●

*T*wo types of storage are in every computer: temporary and permanent. It's like your brain: You can remember lots of things right away, using its temporary storage. But unless you commit the information to memory, you better write it down, which is permanent storage.

In a computer, temporary storage is provided by memory or RAM (Random Access Memory). The more RAM your computer has, the smoother it operates and the more information you can "play" with at once. How much RAM you'll need in your computer is covered in Part III, "Finding Your Perfect Computer." For now, this chapter offers an introduction to computer memory and its associated terms, jargon, and folderol.

Say Hello to Mr. Byte

With videotape, the storage unit is a minute. You buy a videotape that records, for example, 120 minutes of stuff. The gas tank.in your car stores fuel by the gallon. The storage unit for beer is the 12-ounce can. You don't buy 72 fluid ounces of beer; you buy a six-pack. In a computer, the basic unit of storage is a *byte*.

What a byte is and how it works aren't important. What's important to know is what a byte stores:

One byte stores one character of information.

The word *byte,* for example, contains four letters, or four characters. A computer uses 4 bytes of storage to store that word. The word *closet* requires 6 bytes. The sentence above requires 45 bytes of storage, which includes all the letters, the spaces between the words, and the period at the end of the sentence.

To make a large number of bytes easy to describe, modern scientists have stolen some ancient Greek words: *kilo, mega,* and *giga,* which sound like bad guys the Power Rangers would fight but are really terms used to describe the size of something. Bytes are measured in the following terms:

- **Kilobyte:** 1,024 bytes, or about a thousand bytes

- **Megabyte:** 1,048,576 bytes, or about a million bytes

- **Gigabyte:** 1,099,511,628 bytes, or about a billion bytes

These terms are used to describe both temporary as well as permanent storage in a computer — how much room you have for the stuff you create. It's okay to round these oddball numbers to the nearest big numbers. From now on, that's what I'll do:

- **Kilobyte:** 1,000 bytes

- **Megabyte:** 1,000,000 bytes

- **Gigabyte:** 1,000,000,000 bytes

To give you a better understanding, think of a kilobyte of storage as enough room to store all the text on this page (about half a page of single-spaced typewritten text). That's 1,000 characters — a *kilobyte* of storage.

A *megabyte* is one million bytes of storage. That's enough room to store a novel or a several pictures of your cousin's family (including the dogs).

A *gigabyte* is an awesome amount of computer storage — one billion bytes, or 1,000 megabytes. Rarely does any single thing require a gigabyte of storage. Instead, you use gigabytes to store the multiple-megabyte files you and your computer collect.

You need to know about these sizes because two types of computer storage use them for measurement: the computer's memory and the computer's disk storage.

- A byte stores one character.

- One thousand bytes are in a kilobyte ("kill-uh-bite"). The abbreviation for kilobyte is K or KB.

- One million bytes are in a megabyte ("meg-uh-bite"). The abbreviation for megabyte is M or MB.

- One billion bytes are in a gigabyte ("gig-uh-bite"). The abbreviation for gigabyte is G or GB.

- That's gig-a-byte not *jig-a-byte* or *giggle-byte*.

- Beyond the gigabyte is the *terabyte,* which is one trillion bytes of storage. Outrageous? Perhaps. Consider, however, that having a computer with a 9GB hard drive today would have been considered outrageous just ten years ago, when 40MB hard drives were the rage.

- Twenty-four cans of beer are in a case, and 24 hours are in a day. Coincidence?

Memory Madness

After measuring memory in bytes, you come to the nitty-gritty of things. There are enough memory terms out there to boggle any first-time computer user. Normally no one would care. The terms used to describe memory are technical, like a lot of things in the computer, but advertisers seem to *love* the terms, so they crop up all over.

The following sections will help you sift through what's important and what's not when it comes to memory.

Behold the chip!

There must be a law somewhere that says "chip is an inefficient term for describing anything." Look at your grocery store: The "chip" section is divided into regular potato chips, flavored chips, corn chips, tortilla chips, and even anti-chips like those puffy cheese things. Computer memory is similar.

Computer memory comes in the form of chips, such as the one shown in Figure 6-1. But due to some weird scientific mumbo-jumbo, you actually need eight or nine chips to create a bank of memory.

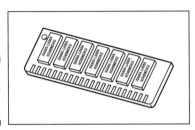

Figure 6-1:
A lonely
RAM chip.

- There are no "nacho cheese flavor" memory chips.

- Memory chips are RAM chips, though other annoying terms exist as well. See the "Some technical memory terms" section elsewhere in this chapter.

The size of the thing (capacity)

Though each memory chip is about the same size, what's really important is the chip's capacity. How many bytes of RAM are in that single chip?

RAM chips come in several sizes, from tiny one kilobyte chips to chips that can store 64MB or more all in one little package. Obviously, the more memory, the more expensive the single chip.

Which do you need? It depends on your computer and how it's set up, which is covered later in this chapter.

Fast memory and faster memory

In addition to its capacity, computer memory is gauged by its speed, similar to a microprocessor. With memory, the speed is measured in *nanoseconds* (abbreviated *ns*), or billionths of a second.

Here is one nanosecond: 0.000000001

Whew! That's fast.

You may see a RAM chip advertised as 60ns. That would mean the memory hums along at 60 nanoseconds. That's fast, but for memory it's actually kind of slow. A better speed would be 8ns.

✔ The speed describes how fast the memory can be accessed. This speed depends on your computer's configuration; adding faster RAM chips to a slow PC will not (unfortunately) perk things up.

✔ Memory speed is not seriously important when you buy the computer. The dealer will install whichever memory works best in that system. When memory speed becomes an issue is when you buy *more* memory for your computer. The speed of that additional memory should match the speed already used in your computer.

✔ Again, the faster the memory the more you pay for it. A 128MB RAM chip running at 8ns is a house payment for some people.

Goodbye, Mr. Chips!

To make handling the chips easier, memory manufacturers solder a whole bank of chips together on a single, tiny strip of fiberglass about the size of a pocket comb. That strip is called a SIMM or DIMM and it does, indeed, make up one whole bank of memory. This is very handy.

  ✔ SIMM stands for single in-line memory module.

  ✔ DIMM stands for dual in-line memory module. It's like a SIMM but starts with a D instead of an S.

As far as you're concerned, there is no difference between a SIMM or DIMM, though your computer will require one and not the other. So if you have a computer that needs a SIMM, you run to the store and buy another SIMM when it begs for more memory. Otherwise you buy a DIMM.

Like individual memory chips, SIMMs and DIMMs are described by their capacity (the amount of RAM they have) and their speed. A third measurement is the number of *pins* the SIMM or DIMM has.

SIMMs and DIMMs plug into a special slot inside the computer's case. Some slots have 72 connectors, some have 168, some have other oddball numbers. These connectors are called "pins" even though they aren't really pins. If you ever upgrade memory, you need to ensure you get the proper number of pins on a SIMM or DIMM to match your computer's needs.

  ✔ They tell me that most computers sold in the future will use DIMMs and not SIMMs. This will certainly save me some typing with future editions of this book.

  ✔ An older style of SIMM was the SIP, which actually used pins to plug into little holes inside the computer. (Today's SIMMs and DIMMS just jam into a long thin slot.)

What is "flash memory"?

Flash memory is a special type of memory chip that retains its information even when the computer is turned off. Normally, memory (RAM) requires electricity to retain its information. Turn off the power and the contents of RAM go bye-bye (which is why it's important to save information to disk, the computer's permanent storage).

Flash memory does not require electricity to retain its information. It remembers things long after the power is off. Because of this, flash memory is used for special information the computer must remember at all times.

Now it would be swell if all memory in a computer were flash memory, so you wouldn't have to worry about losing information during a power outage. Unfortunately, flash memory is very expensive and not as fast as regular memory. Someday that may be true, but not at present.

Some technical memory terms

Memory isn't simply referred to as memory. Just when the computer industry reaches the point where memory could be just "memory," they invent a new type of memory. So along comes a new acronym or technical description to distinguish the New Memory from the Old Memory. Ugh.

Honestly, the only places you'll see these terms are in memory ads. In the real world, even engineers just call it "RAM" or "memory." The rest is all scientific fluff that makes good (or bad) ad copy:

DRAM. Another term for RAM. Pronounced *dee-ram,* it stands for Dynamic Random Access Memory. It's more impressive than "RAM" I suppose, but not as impressive as SDRAM or EDO RAM. Whoa! No way!

ECC. An acronym for Error Checking and Correction, which can require extra circuits to ensure that memory is being properly written to and read from.

EDO. An acronym for Extended Data Out. Whatever that means, EDO is a special type of fast or more efficient memory. Advertisers love the term (primarily because marketing types love three-letter acronyms). Say *ee-doh-ram.*

FPM. Acronym for Fast Page Mode, often used with RAM as in FPM RAM. It's faster. Smarter. Better. And using it implies that the neighbor's dog is ugly.

Non-Parity. Memory chips that do not use parity, as described next.

Parity. Another nerdy term, this one refers to a self-check that memory chips can perform on themselves every time the memory is accessed. Do you need parity? Maybe. A computer manufacturer decides whether it wants to put parity in its PCs. Other than that information, anything else I could say about parity would put you to sleep.

PC100. Memory designed to work with very fast PCs (so called "PC100 chip" systems). This type of memory is necessary only if you have a PC with the PC100 chips or similar. (There are other PC1*xx* memory chips as well, where the *xx* is replaced by other numbers.)

SDRAM. A special form of DRAM chip, it's *Synchronous* DRAM! Basically it's better memory because of a lot of technical things no one really understands.

SRAM. An even faster type of RAM, but not as fast as EDO.

Generally speaking, these terms come and go. Some become obsolete (or worn-out). Some new ones may crop up. Sometimes a manufacturer may rename an older standard to make it sound newer in the ads. Whatever.

What about ROM?

ROM stands for Read-Only Memory. Like RAM, it's another type of memory in your computer. The microprocessor can read ROM just like RAM, but unlike RAM the contents of ROM cannot be changed.

When it comes to buying a computer, there is no need to worry about how much ROM is in a computer. All computers come with all the ROM they need.

Main Memory versus Video Memory

Memory is used in computers in two places. First, there's main memory where all the "action" takes place. Second, there's video memory, which is used to help the computer display graphics.

Both main and video memory values are often listed in computer ads. So, for example, you may see a new computer with 32MB of memory but also 8MB of video memory. That means the computer has 32MB of memory in which you can work but an additional 8MB of memory for displaying fancy graphics.

Along with this different type of memory come two utterly confusing memory terms. Often these are used in ads to describe the video memory in a computer:

SGRAM. A special type of video memory. It's just SDRAM (see the preceding section) but the G in this acronym stands for Graphics: Synchronous Graphics Random Access Memory.

VRAM. Video Random Access Memory. Another form of video memory, probably not as flashy as SGRAM because SGRAM has more letters in its acronym.

Again, this is advertisement-only information. Whenever you see VRAM or SGRAM or any other type of video-RAM-whatever, know that it's memory used by the computer for displaying graphics.

> ✔ Your computer will need both main and video memory. You cannot have one and not the other.

> ✔ Likewise, you cannot expect video and main memory to work together somehow. If the software says it requires 16MB of RAM, and you have 8MB of RAM but also 8MB of video RAM, then you're not okay. You must have 16MB of main memory for the software to work.

Banks o' Memory (RAM)

Science fiction TV shows typically feature computers with "banks" of memory. Although that term is accurate, it's a poor measurement.

The computer you buy will indeed have banks of memory. The SIMM or DIMM cards plug into these slots inside the computer. Each slot is known as a *bank*. However, the way your memory is configured in each bank may be important.

When you order your computer, try to get the manufacturer to install all your computer's memory into as few banks as possible. For example, Figure 6-2 shows a setup with four banks of memory. A 4MB SIMM card is plugged into each bank, which gives that computer a total of 16MB of RAM — barely enough to run Windows 98.

Suppose that someday you want to add another 16MB of memory to this same computer to give yourself a decent 32MB of memory. Sounds good, but because this system has only four banks and each bank is full, you have only one option: Toss out all your memory (for which you paid dearly) and replace it with 32MB of new memory. Yes, that's a waste of money.

A better situation is shown in Figure 6-3: All memory is plugged into one bank. If you want to upgrade, all you need is another SIMM or DIMM, which plugs into another, open bank. And, you still have more banks available for future upgrades.

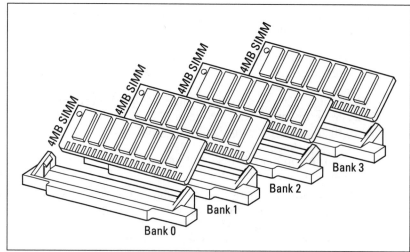

Figure 6-2:
Memory
banks in a
computer.

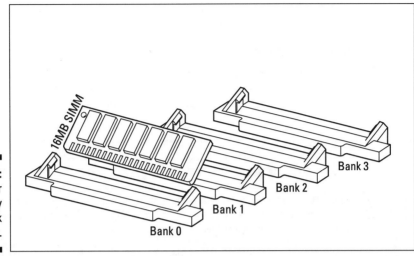

Figure 6-3:
A better
memory
bank
configuration.

✔ Try to have the dealer put as much memory as possible into a single bank.

✔ Yes, as you may have guessed, one 32MB SIMM may cost more than four 8MB SIMMs. You save money on upgrades, though.

✔ Indeed, this information is technical! For example, some computers insist that *all* memory banks have the same amount of memory in them. If you have three 16MB SIMMs in three banks and want to add a 64MB SIMM to the last bank, you can't do it. (Hey! Don't blame me! Beat up an engineer!) Also, some systems require you to install SIMMs in pairs, which requires some additional thinking when you're buying additional memory.

How Much Memory Do You Need?

How much memory will your new computer need? The answer depends on your software. The bottom line is that you need memory (or RAM) in your computer.

Memory in your computer is measured in *megabyte* units. The standard quantity for most new computers is 32MB of memory, or RAM. Some come with more memory, typically 64MB or 128MB.

Some inexpensive computers may have only 16MB of RAM — or less. Avoid them. Windows 98 barely runs in 16MB. It needs 32MB.

✔ Watch out for computers advertised with no memory or 0K or 0MB of RAM. This sales ploy makes a computer look cheaper than other models sold with memory included. All computers need memory, so you have to pay for it one way or another.

✔ Sometimes PC memory may be described as *extended* memory. That's an archaic term. All memory in a PC is just memory. If an ad says "32MB extended memory," it's the same thing as "32MB memory" or "32MB RAM."

Memory is cheap, cheap, cheap!

It's been a while since I've bought memory for a computer, so I was utterly shocked when I saw how ridiculously *cheap* computer memory really is.

The following chart shows the average cost per megabyte of computer memory for the past several years.

Memory is cheaper now because so much of it is available on a single chip. Back in 1984, it took eight or nine 4-kilobit memory chips to make one

4K bank of memory. That may have cost you $40. I remember paying $150 for a 64K bank of memory.

You can now get eight or nine 64-megabit chips to make a bank of 64MB of memory and pay only $150. (My old TRS-80 computer wouldn't know what to do with 64MB of memory, of course, but that's beside the point.) Memory is cheap!

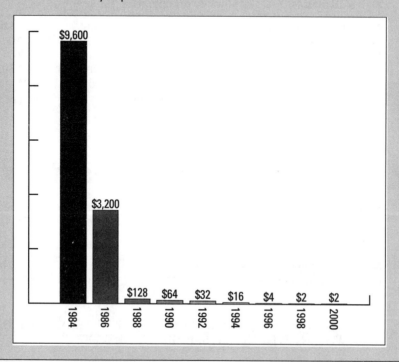

Chapter 7

Disks of Every Type (Permanent Storage)

• •

In This Chapter

▶ Understanding disk storage

▶ Knowing the different types of drives

▶ Judging a drive's speed and capacity

▶ Controlling a disk drive

▶ Choosing drives for your computer

▶ Surveying various types of drives

▶ Adding a tape drive

• •

*A*fter the microprocessor and computer memory, the next most important element in your computer is permanent storage, or the disk drives.
Most computers have several different types of disk drives, each of which is
useful for some specific task. This chapter sifts through the spinning pile of
disk information, pointing out what's necessary and offering background
information to help you read the various advertisements and try to make
sense out of them.

Why Disk Storage?

Disk storage is actually the second type of storage inside a computer. The
first type is memory, RAM. That's where the work takes place; the microprocessor busies itself there, running programs and storing all the wonderful
stuff you create.

When you're done working, you need a more permanent place to store your
stuff in the computer. That place is on a disk drive somewhere, usually the
hard drive. You direct the program you're using to "save" your stuff on the
hard drive, making a permanent copy you can use later.

- ✔ All computers need disk storage. Some computers even have several forms of disk storage: a hard drive, CD-ROM drive, and floppy drive. Each of these has specific uses, as covered later in this chapter.

- ✔ Some hand-held computers do not have physical disk drives. Instead, they contain special memory that is not erased when the power is turned off.

- ✔ Don't confuse the terms "RAM" (or "computer memory") and "disk memory." Some computer manuals and books may refer to disk storage as "disk memory." While this is technically correct, it's confusing. Disk storage and RAM are two different places in the computer. Whenever you see the term "disk memory," just think "disk storage" instead.

- ✔ For more information on microprocessors, see Chapter 5.

- ✔ Computer memory (RAM) is covered in Chapter 6.

What is a disk, and what is a drive?

There are hard disks, hard drives, and hard disk drives. What's the difference? Nothing, of course.

The disk is literally a disk. The computer writes information to the disk, where it is stored exactly like information is recorded on a cassette tape, only the disk media is flat and round.

The drive is the device that spins the disk, reading and writing information.

So a disk drive is the entire unit. Inside a typical computer, you'll find several disk drives: a hard disk drive, a CD-ROM disk drive, and a floppy disk drive. Each of those devices is the "drive," and the thing that stores the information is the "disk." See Figure 7-1.

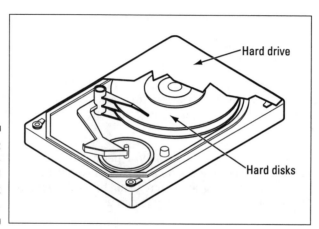

Figure 7-1:
A run-of-the-mill hard disk drive.

Hard drive

Hard disks

✔ The most common abuse of the terms "disk" and "drive" comes when referring to a hard disk drive. It can be called both the "hard disk" and the "hard drive." Since it's all contained in the same unit, both terms are correct.

✔ For other types of drives (CD-ROM, floppy, Zip), the disk is removable. Therefore, there really is a difference, for example, between a CD-ROM drive and a computer CD; the CD is the disk and the CD-ROM drive is the device that reads information from the disk.

✔ Don't mind the technical terms used so far! They're all explained later in this chapter. Just keep reading.

Types of drives

There are many interesting and unusual types of disk drives available for any computer. Most commonly, you'll find these three types of drives:

Hard drive. The standard, high-capacity, high-speed drive found in all computers, desktops, and laptops. This is the main form of disk storage.

CD-ROM. Nearly all computer software comes on CD, making a CD-ROM drive part of all standard desktop and laptop configurations. The CD-ROM, however, is a "read-only" media; you cannot "save" information to a standard CD.

Floppy. The original computer disk drive, though floppy disks are rapidly falling out of fashion. Some software still comes on floppy disk, and you can save your stuff to a floppy and mail it, but beyond that, today's large files are just too big for floppies. Still, until something better comes along, it's a required part of any PC.

The following drives are becoming more common and may someday exist on all PCs as a new standard:

DVD-ROM. Looking like a CD-ROM drive, and capable of reading computer CDs, a DVD-ROM drive is also capable of reading DVD disks and playing DVD movies. The disks store 4 to 16 times as much information as a standard CD, making them the CD-ROM drive replacement for the future.

Zip. A common supplement to the floppy disk drive is the Zip drive. Zip drives read Zip disks, which can store anywhere from 100 to 250 times the amount of information on a typical floppy disk. Someday, the Zip drive may replace the floppy drive.

LS-120. The LS-120 floppy disk or "Super Floppy" is a newer type of floppy drive that uses both normal floppy disks as well as high-capacity super floppy disks. This makes it a great alternative to a Zip drive since it can read the older floppy drives just fine.

There are even more types of drives and storage options available. Here's the incomplete list:

CD-R, CD-R/W. The same type of drive as a CD-ROM drive, but these drives allow you to save information to a special type of CD.

DVD-RAM. Like a CD-R drive, but this DVD drive lets you record your own DVD disks.

JAZ. A super version of the Zip drive, this removable disk can store 10 to 20 times more information than a typical Zip drive. That's 1,000 to 2,000 times as much information as a floppy disk.

Tape drives. These drives allow you to make a safety copy of all the information on your computer's hard drive. They read and write to special tape cassettes, allowing you to "back up" your computer's information for safekeeping.

More information about each of these drive types can be found later in this chapter.

Even more types of storage exist, though they're typically for special purposes and not sold with the standard computer setup. For example, there are various removable hard drives, magneto-optical drives, and other specific drives. Knowing whether or not you need one depends on what you do with your computer. Generally speaking, if you're in one of the specific areas of computing where those types of drives are used, you'll know about it. Otherwise, forget the weird drive types.

Capacity

The first measure of all disk drives is how much information they store. As with computer memory, the measuring rod of disk storage is the byte.

Table 7-1 lists the storage capacities of the common, popular types of disk drives.

Table 7-1	Disk Drive Storage Capacities
Drive Type	*Storage Capacity (Per Disk)*
Floppy	1.4MB
Zip	100MB to 250MB
LS-120	"Super Disk" 120MB
Tape drive	500MB on up to 8GB or higher

Drive Type	Storage Capacity (Per Disk)
CD-ROM, CD-R, CD-R/W	up to 650MB
Jaz	1GB to 2GB
Hard drive	2GB up to 20GB and even higher
DVD-ROM	up to 8GB (16GB on two sides of the disk)

The only figure you really need to pay attention to is the hard drive storage. Hard drives don't come in "standard sizes." Instead, you find hard drives that store anywhere from 2GB of information on up to a whopping 13GB and higher. You pay more for more storage or less for less. You want to ensure you get more storage than you need so that you don't run out.

- ✔ Remember that a megabyte is one million bytes and a gigabyte (GB) is one billion bytes (or 1,000MB).

- ✔ The typical hard drive sold today stores anywhere from 3GB to 8GB of information.

- ✔ How much storage capacity do you need? That depends on your software and how you use the computer. This book shows you how to calculate the exact amount, then add a bit more so that you won't run out of disk storage.

- ✔ Disk storage is relatively cheap. Buy more than you need if you can afford it.

- ✔ Even if you do run out of disk storage, most computers let you add a second hard drive internally, giving you even more storage.

Speed

The faster the disk drive, the faster you can read information from that disk drive. Faster is definitely better. And, naturally, the more expensive the disk will be. Speed doth have its price. . . .

Hard drives can have up to four measurements of their speed. Generally speaking, you can ignore the technical definitions and merely use the values for comparison:

Seek time. Measured in milliseconds (ms), the lower (faster) values are better. A good seek time is less than 10 ms.

Access time. Another measurement, similar to seek time (but technically measuring two different things). Values are in milliseconds (ms), and lower, faster values are better. Good access times are 10 ms or less.

Transfer rate. A measure of the amount of information that can be written to or read from the drive per second. The larger the value (measured in megabytes), the better. A transfer rate of 30MB/second or higher is pretty good.

RPM. A silly measurement of how fast the disk spins. This may or may not be important, but they list it in the ads.

These same values can be used for floppy disks and other removable disks, though they generally only appear when you're hard drive shopping.

Use the speed values for comparisons only! In actual, day-to-day operations, the difference between 8.8 ms access time and 9.3 ms is laughable (unless you're an engineer, of course, and you only laugh at ionization jokes).

CD-ROM drive speed

A special exception for disk drive speeds is the CD-ROM drive. It's speed is measured in terms of X. For example, you can have a 32X CD-ROM drive or a 40X CD-ROM drive.

The X is the number of times faster the drive is than the original computer CD-ROM drive. That drive, which is the same speed as a standard music CD player, was a 1X. The next generation drives could spin twice as fast and were dubbed 2X. And so on and so on.

So, for example, if you see a 32X drive advertised, you now know in your computer buying wisdom that the said CD-ROM drive is a whopping thirty-two times faster than the piddly original CD-ROM drive.

Another hard drive technical doodad: The cache

Another aspect listed in hard drive ads is the cache size.

Cache is the key here. It's pronounced *cash*. There.

The cache is a supplemental storage place on the drive, composed of a given amount of memory (special memory, not regular computer RAM). That memory is used to speed up the drive by storing often-read information in the cache memory. Reading the information from cache memory instead of the disk itself can markedly increase the hard drive's performance.

A hard drive with a cache is much better than a hard drive without one. And a hard drive with a larger cache size is better than one with a smaller cache size. (Note that cache size is often listed in kilobytes, not megabytes: 256K, 512K and so on.)

> ✔ DVD-ROM drives generally do not have X values listed. Supposedly, they're all just "fast."
>
> ✔ CD-R and CD-R/W drives typically have a low X number, such as 2X and a high X number, such as 12X. The low number is the speed at which the drive is written to; the high number is the speed at which the drive is read.

Fixed or removable?

Is your hard drive fixed? Probably. Betcha didn't even know it was broken! Ha-ha.

Oh, my sides. . . .

Seriously, a "fixed drive" is one that's mounted inside the computer case, the console. It cannot be removed, other than by taking out a screwdriver and uninstalling the thing.

The opposite of a fixed drive is a removable drive, such as a floppy drive, CD-ROM drive, and other drives where the disk actually spits out.

The mystical drive controller

The last description of a disk drive is how it connects to the rest of the computer. To do so, it needs what's called an *interface*. That's one of those $100 business words that means "to talk or exchange information." For example, "Larry cannot interface with the elevator" means Larry doesn't know how to push the buttons.

With a disk drive, the interface is how the disk drive itself communicates with the rest of the computer. The interface is merely a clutch of electronics. The disk drive uses the interface to talk with the microprocessor, BIOS, and other interesting parts of the computer.

There are several popular interface standards. I'm listing them below for your reference or curiosity. There is really no need to venture off into interface land here. Just know that your computer will come with one type of interface or another. (Refer to Chapter 10 for more interface options, if you must.)

ATA. The most common form of disk drive interface, ATA stands for Advanced Technology Attachment. It's basically no interface at all! The disk drives themselves contain the "smarts" and speak with the computer directly. Most hard drives, floppy drives, Zip, Jaz, and other drives use this interface.

Three more confusing disk drive terms

Computer jargon is endless. There's no need ever for you to memorize any computer term; as long as you have a computer dictionary handy (like the *Illustrated Computer Dictionary For Dummies*, from IDG Books Worldwide, Inc.), you'll become acquainted with any computer term. So don't be surprised when the following disk drive terms visually assault you:

Form factor. This is merely a description of the disk drive's size. Each computer console has room for different-sized drives. For example, you may have a spare half-height drive bay in your G3 Mac. You would need a half-height drive to fill that bay. That's the form factor in action. (This is obviously an issue you can refer to your dealer.)

RAID. An acronym meaning, basically, a whole stack of hard drives — like a stack of pancakes. Each hard drive mirrors information on the other drives, which means information is rarely, if ever, lost. This type of hard drive setup is used only in mission-critical applications or for servers. Individual computer buyers need not concern themselves with RAID drives (they're too spendy, for one).

Head. In addition to being the froth at the top of a sloppily poured beer, a head on a disk drive is the actual device that reads and writes information. Also called a "floating head" or "flying head."

ATAPI. A modified version of the EIDE standard, designed primarily to add CD-ROM and tape drives to the interface. ATAPI stands for Advanced Technology Attachment Packet Interface.

EIDE. An Enhanced form of the IDE standard, supplanted by ATA during the Comdex riots of 1996.

IDE. An older term for an ATA drive. IDE stands for Integrated Drive Electronics. You might find it someday as the answer in a crossword puzzle.

SCSI. Acronym for Small Computer System Interface, an interface for a variety of devices, not just disk drives. On the up side, SCSI is the most flexible interface and is able to handle more storage devices than the other standards. On the downside, SCSI devices are expensive and difficult to configure. (Definitely see Chapter 10 for more information.)

Other standards exist, including some old, moldy ones (EISA, RRL) and some new ones that have yet to catch on. My advice here is to ignore anything on the leading edge. Until these new standards start appearing in the computer ads, it's safe to avoid them. That's what I do.

Disk Driving Your Computer System

When you get your computer, you'll most likely get three disk drives in it:

- ✔ A hard drive
- ✔ A CD-ROM or DVD drive
- ✔ A floppy drive

That's one fixed disk and two removable disks, which should cover every possible disk drive need you'll ever dream up.

The following sections go into more detail about each type of disk device and describe some additional decision-making thought processes and options.

Picking a hard drive

All computers must have at least one hard drive. You can compare speed and other trivia, but the real meat on the plate is the hard drive's capacity. You want to ensure that your new computer has enough hard drive storage for all your computer software as well as all the stuff you'll create and store there.

The third part of this book tells you how to determine the amount of hard drive storage you need. Generally speaking, you'll probably need anywhere from 3GB on up to 8GB of storage. Most computers sold today typically come with a hard drive within that range, but be aware that you can order a computer with an even larger hard drive.

As an alternative to getting a larger hard drive, you can also equip your computer with two (or more) hard drives.

A second hard drive is usually an add-on made after the purchase. The first hard drive fills up, so you buy a second one — which can usually be installed inside the case right beside the first hard drive. This solves the hard-disk-storage-space dilemma, but you're better off just buying a larger capacity hard drive in the first place.

If your computer is equipped with a SCSI interface, then you can add multiple external hard drives to the system. Run out of room? Just buy another external SCSI hard drive.

✔ Your computer needs at least one hard drive.

✔ Beware! Some shifty dealers may advertise a computer without a hard drive! They do that to knock a few hundred dollars off the purchase price and make their stuff appear competitive. Don't buy anything from those people!

✔ Some smaller systems, such as game machines and hand-helds, do not require a hard drive. Instead they use special memory to store information. In the case of game systems, storage sometimes takes the form of memory cartridges which plug into the game's console.

✔ As with memory, you can always add more hard drives to your computer. The only limitation is the space inside *and* outside your computer.

✔ Ensure that you buy the proper hard drive for your computer system. Most hard drive upgrades are listed by computer make and model, but the real limitation is the hard drive's controller. Buy drives to match your computer's controllers: ATA drives for ATA controllers, and so on.

✔ Laptop hard drives are very small and very expensive. Generally, you cannot add a second hard drive to a laptop, but you can (for a high fee) replace a laptop's hard drive with a higher capacity model. My advice: Get a large hard drive in your laptop in the first place.

✔ Avoid buying any computer with less than a 3GB hard drive. Although those smaller sizes were popular a few years back, they're just not beefy enough to hold today's software.

✔ The first IBM PC was sold without a hard drive. The IBM PC/XT, introduced in 1983, came with a 10MB hard drive. Yes, that was considered oodles of storage space back then.

✔ A "controller" is the part of the hard drive that allows it to talk to the rest of the computer.

✔ Nothing is wrong with having both IDE and SCSI hard drives in a computer. The computer I'm using to write this book, in fact, has both IDE and SCSI hard drives (as well as CD-ROM drives). Call me nuts.

Your read-only, removable storage

The second-most popular disk drive in your new computer will be the read-only, removable drive. In human terms: the CD-ROM or DVD drive. Either one is a must on any new system, with the emphasis on getting a DVD drive if you possibly can.

CD-ROM and DVD drives handle read-only media. That means that you can only read from the disks; you cannot store information there like you can with a hard drive. That may sound like a gyp, but the truth is that lots of stuff you'll get for the computer is read-only. (And if you need to write information, you can always use the hard drive.)

Nearly all new computer software comes on CD-ROM disks, as do libraries of graphics files, fonts, and other reference materials. It's just handy to slip such a disk into a CD-ROM drive and have instant access to it.

Newer than CD-ROM drives are the DVD drives, where DVD stands for Digital Versatile Disc. The disk can contain gigabytes of information or, in the form of a Digital *Video* Disc, it can contain a movie.

DVD drives can read both DVD and CD-ROM disks, so having one is a bonus. They tell me that most new software will ship on DVD disks in the future, though I still think that's a few years out. DVD drives are nice, but they're not really a required item. Yet.

✔ Your computer should come with at least one CD-ROM drive.

✔ CD-ROM drives eat CD-ROM disks. Those disks look just like the CD disks you buy at the music store.

✔ You cannot write information to a CD-ROM drive. It's read-only, which is the *RO* in CD-ROM: Compact Disk, Read-Only Memory.

✔ Oh, yes, you can play musical CDs on your computer (as long as your computer has speakers so that you can hear the music). A special program is required, although it should come with your computer or the operating system.

✔ Most CD-ROM drives use the ATA (or ATAPI) interface. Some, however, use the SCSI interface.

CD-R, CD-R/W, and DVD-RAM drives

Most computers will come with a read-only CD-ROM or DVD drive. That's fine. If you're curious about creating your own CD or DVD disks, then you'll probably want a CD-R, CD-R/W, or DVD-RAM drive. Here's what all that means:

CD-R. This type of drive allows you to create your own CDs using special CD-R disks. The CDs are written to and read from just like a hard drive, but the purpose here is not to store information as much as it is to make a permanent copy. Eventually, you'll "burn" the disk, which prevents additional information from being written there but also allows the disk to be read by any other computer with a CD-ROM drive.

CD-R/W. This is a type of CD-R drive but with the added ability of being able to totally erase the disk after it's been written to. This makes the CD-R/W drive ideal for archiving or backing up a hard drive to create a safety copy of information.

DVD-RAM. Like a CD-R, this type of drive lets you create your own DVD disks.

Generally speaking, computers are not sold with these types of disks. You have to add these later, usually as external drives (though some models may be installed into the console).

For example, my PC came with a CD-ROM drive, but I added an external CD-R drive. My system now has two CD-ROM drives, so I can read CDs in either drive. The CD-R drive can also be used to create CDs, when I feel the urge.

✔ Yes, these drives are more expensive than standard CD-ROM and DVD drives.

✔ You need to buy special disks to use a CD-R, CD-R/W, or DVD-RAM drive.

✔ Special software must be used to prepare a CD-R, CD-R/W or DVD-RAM disk for writing. This software usually comes with the drive.

✔ You can use the special software to create music CDs as well.

Gotta have a floppy drive, too

The floppy is no longer a requirement for all computers. It's a nice addition, since some software still comes on floppy disks and you can still use floppy disks to transport information between computers. But necessary? Not really. In fact, the iMac doesn't come with a floppy drive at all (though it's a common peripheral people add later).

The biggest drawback to the floppy drive is that its disks store only a paltry 1.44MB of information. That's puny. In the land of the 4GB hard drive, a 1.44MB floppy drive isn't even a percentage.

Here are some floppy drive issues:

✔ You have to buy floppy disks for your floppy drive. Buy disks labeled HD or "high density" or "1.44MB."

✔ All floppy disks must be formatted before you can use them. If possible, try to buy the disks preformatted (it says so on the box). Otherwise, you have to format them yourself, which you do by using your computer's operating system.

Other, removable disks

While a floppy drive may not be entirely useful, the concept is valid: You need a small formatted, removable disk for your computer, one on which you can write information. Had the computer industry continued development of the floppy drive, it might still be a valid form of removable media. But, alas, the floppy drive was neglected. So replacements have sprouted up:

LS-120. The so-called "Super Drive" is a floppy disk replacement available on some PCs. It eats standard floppy disks as well as the "super" 120MB disks, which makes it a valuable replacement to the standard floppy drive.

Zip. The Zip disk is a 100MB to 250MB supplemental disk drive offered with many computer configurations. The disks are common and can be used to back up or transport files between computers.

Jaz. The Zip disk's big brother is the Jaz disk, capable of storing from 1GB to 2GB on a disk. This type of disk stores *more* information than a CD-R, but each disk is expensive: around $100 for a Jaz disk compared to just several dollars for a CD-R disk. Still, they make great backup and alternative storage for any computer.

Each of these disks is an excellent option for removable computer storage. If possible, try to get one with your new computer system to supplement the rather lame floppy disk standard.

> ✔ There is a difference between the Macintosh and PC variety of Zip disks. While they look alike, the disks *are* different. Make sure you buy the proper disks for whichever computer system you end up with.
>
> ✔ Many PCs come with Zip disks as an option. Get it.

Tape drives

A final type of computer storage media is the tape drive. Back in the prehistoric days of the computer, tape drives were housed in refrigerator-sized units with two reels spinning to and fro (a staple of many science fiction movies — even today!).

Computer tape drives today are smaller, usually sitting in the console or existing in a slim case outside the computer. The drives swallow tape cartridges, which on average are about the size of a deck of cards. The cartridges store anywhere from 500MB on up to gigabytes of information.

Tape drives are used primarily to backup the information on a hard drive, to create a safety copy "just in case." Special backup software is run often to make the safety copies, and several tapes are used to ensure that the information backed up is always up to date.

Tape drives are an option on all but the most expensive computers (they're usually included only on file server-level computers). People who have them and have used them in times of need swear by them. Otherwise, most beginners tend to ignore backing up.

✔ I recommend getting a tape drive for your PC. Most dealers have options where the drive can be installed at the time of purchase.

✔ Get a tape drive that eats tapes that can store as much information as your hard drive. For example, if you have a 4GB hard drive, get a tape drive that uses 4GB tapes.

✔ CD-R drives, as well as LS-120, Zip, and Jaz disks can also be used for backing up.

Chapter 8

Monitor and Graphics Stuff

● ●

In This Chapter

▶ Understanding monitors and graphics cards

▶ Gauging a monitor's size

▶ Choosing an LCD monitor

▶ Using more than one monitor

▶ Understanding the graphics adapter

▶ Taking advantage of 3-D

▶ Reading a graphics adapter description

● ●

*C*omputer monitors and graphics get far more attention than they deserve, probably because it's the monitor you see in the store. It's flashy. It's eye-catching. And such a display can be misleading since there's a lot more to a computer than its monitor.

Fortunately, monitors are pretty basic and choosing one isn't that tough. The other part of the computer graphics equation is the video adapter card, which can get a little technical. Fortunately, this chapter helps smooth out any bumps in your graphical journey.

The Graphical System

All computers have two parts to their graphical system: the monitor and the graphics adapter or controller.

The monitor is the part you see, the TV-set thing. Or in the case of game consoles, it's a real TV. But for most computers, laptops, and handheld computers, the monitor is what displays information.

The graphics adapter is the circuitry that *drives* the monitor, controlling how and where the information is displayed. See? The monitor is the dumb part, requiring another piece of hardware — the graphics adapter — to do the work.

When you buy a computer, you need both a monitor and a graphics adapter.

The Monitor Part

No personal computer is complete without a monitor. Some models, such as the iMac and all laptops and handhelds, have the monitor included. Otherwise the monitor is a required option you must select at the time of purchase.

All computer monitors sold today are color. All of them are technically the same with only a few variations. (See the sidebar, "Mysterious monitor measurements.") The only decisions you need to make about a monitor are its size and whether or not you'll go for one of the newfangled flat-screen displays.

- ✔ My best advice for judging a monitor is to look at it in the store. See whether you like the way it displays colors. Is the text crisp? Most stores have graphics or animation running on their demonstration monitors. Ask to view a document to better judge the image quality.

- ✔ Beware of computers advertised without a monitor. Because you need a monitor, you must add its cost to the computer purchase.

- ✔ You do not need to buy the same brand monitor as your computer console. If you want, you can buy the monitor separately, in which case they'll knock a few dollars off the computer purchase price. Be aware, however, that buying the same brand monitor is usually cheaper due to volume discounts offered by the manufacturer.

- ✔ What you see on the glassy part of the monitor is called the *screen,* or *display.* The term *monitor* refers to the hardware itself.

- ✔ The circuitry inside the computer that controls the monitor is referred to as the *graphics adapter.* If you want to be a real nerd, call your monitor a CRT (cathode-ray tube).

- ✔ No, you cannot use your TV set as a monitor for your computer. Although TV sets are good for watching TV, their resolution isn't good enough for watching computer information.

- ✔ Game consoles are geared for using a TV set as their monitor. This is the only exception to the above point.

- ✔ Many hand-held computers have monochrome (non-color) screens, which usually display several shades of gray. For most hand-held computers, this is just fine.

Mysterious monitor measurements

Oh, I could spend all day muttering over the various technical aspects of a computer monitor. Instead, I've jotted down some terms and descriptions that should help you if the need to know arises:

Bandwidth (frequency). The speed at which information is sent from a computer to a monitor, measured in megahertz (MHz). The higher this value, the better.

Dot pitch. The distance between each dot (or *pixel*) on the graphics screen (measured from the center of each dot). The closer the dots, the better the image. A dot pitch of 0.28 millimeters is really good, and smaller values are even better.

Interlaced/non-interlaced. The method by which a monitor paints an image on a screen. An interlaced monitor paints the image twice, which tends to cause the image to flicker. What you want is a non-interlaced monitor, which doesn't flicker (as much).

Scan rate. The rate at which a monitor's electron gun paints an image on the screen, as measured in kilohertz (kHz). The higher the scan rate value, the better.

Judge me by my size, will you?

Monitors are measured like TV sets: diagonally in inches, as shown in Figure 8-1.

A typical monitor measures about 17 inches diagonally. Cheaper models measure 15 and 14 inches diagonally. If you want to spoil yourself, consider a 19-, 20-, or 21-inch monitor. Those sizes are nice, but they also tend to cost as much as the computer itself!

✔ Beware! A monitor's diagonal measurement may *not* be the same as its viewing area. The size of the screen (viewing area) is occasionally a few inches smaller than the glass.

✔ If you want to spend a little more money, get a *flat-screen* monitor (which is not the same as an LCD monitor, which I discuss in the next section). Unlike most PC monitors, the flat screen has a flat viewing surface, which makes the image look really nice. (It looks concave if you're not used to it.)

✔ Large monitors are *very nice.* I bought one on a whim and now have *three* of them! They're spendy, and they're also *heavy.* I threw my back out lugging one up the stairs. If you get a large monitor, make sure that someone else is around to carry it so that they wreck their back and you don't wreck yours.

✔ If you're vision impaired, a 21-inch monitor is the answer to your prayers! It shows text nice and big.

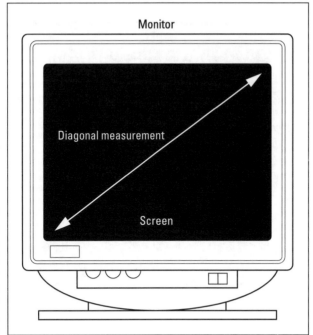

Figure 8-1:
The
diagonal
measure-
ment of a
computer
monitor.

The LCD monitor

LCD monitors are all the rage these days. These monitors are essentially the same types that appear on laptop computers, though designed for use with a desktop model. The monitors are thin, light-weight, and energy-saving. Plus they look very, very cool on your desk.

Like their glassy counterparts, LCD monitors are measured diagonally in inches. And just like regular monitors, the larger the LCD monitor the more you pay for it — lots more. Eventually the prices will drop, but for now the large (18-inches or wider) LCD monitors are horrendously expensive.

✔ LCD monitors can connect to your computer using traditional graphics adapters or using special digital adapters. Because LCD monitors are digital by nature (unlike traditional monitors which are analog), it's better to use an LCD monitor with a digital adapter.

✔ Some LCD monitors rotate 90-degrees, allowing you to view them in "portrait" or "landscape" modes.

✔ The best way to judge an LCD monitor is to view only *text* on the screen. Don't be fooled at the store by fancy graphics displays, which will always look stunning. The true test is viewing text, not graphics.

✔ Be sure to check the LCD in a variety of lighting situations. Some monitors cannot be seen in very bright lights. Some monitors cannot be seen from far right or left angles.

I'll take two, please

Both the Macintosh and PC have the ability to support more than one monitor at a time. The Mac has had the ability for years, but only PCs running Windows 98 have the ability to have two or more monitors attached.

While this feature generally remains a curiosity, having two monitors can really be a boon to productivity: Imagine viewing a Web page on one screen while working on another. (I used to write books on my old Mac SE with the outline on one screen and the word processor on the other.)

✔ If you plan to use a second monitor, consider adding it later as an upgrade. Presently I know of no computer system that comes with two monitors out of the box.

✔ Although you can plug a second USB monitor into the iMac, doing so won't let you use both monitors at once. Because of that, the iMac is an exception to the two monitor rule. Other Macs, however, can have multiple monitors installed.

✔ Each monitor requires its own graphics adapter; however, there are some dual-monitor adapters that run two monitors from a single adapter.

✔ Better than two monitors, just consider getting a single, large-screen monitor. For example, I have two 17-inch monitors on my G3 Mac, but a single 21-inch monitor would probably work a lot better.

The Graphics Adapter Part

The graphics adapter (or "card") is the part of your graphics system that lives inside the console. It controls the image displayed on the monitor's screen.

Several yardsticks measure graphics cards. Most are trivial at this stage of the game. Three worth paying attention to are: memory, 3-D graphics, and the interface (how the card communicates with the other parts of your computer).

Video RAM

Video memory is special memory (RAM) used to help your PC's graphics controller display lots of colors and high-resolution graphics. The more video memory the graphics adapter has, the better your graphics card — and the more expensive.

✔ Try to obtain a graphics card that has *at least* 4MB of video memory. A card with 16MB of memory would be just grand. More is better, of course.

✔ If possible, try to find a card that can be upgraded later — for example, a card with 8MB of video memory to which you can add even more video RAM if necessary.

✔ Video RAM is called VRAM. See Chapter 6 for more memory information.

✔ Beware of video cards with zero video memory! You need video memory, and installing it "later" shouldn't be an option. Buy your video memory when you buy the card.

The 3-D thing

Another technical description that's important to graphics hounds is the ability of the graphics card to do 3-D. That means that the graphics card contains special circuitry to speed up the creation and animation of 3-D images.

Does the 3-D stuff mean that you see everything three-dimensionally? Nope. A few graphics applications and several games insist upon the 3-D circuitry, but most software programs don't need it. (Again, it all boils down to what your software needs, which is the theme here if you haven't guessed.)

Names and acronyms

On the Mac side, graphics are graphics. No need to fuss over this type or that three-letter-acronym type. On the PC side, graphics adapters are given the acronym SVGA. Any PC graphics adapter you buy will be called SVGA or maybe XGA or even SDPDSVDGSKJGIQLGA (just kidding).

All these acronyms meant something a decade ago, when there were different graphics standards for different types of PCs. Today, however, all computers generally use the same type of graphics cards. So although the terms are meaningless now, you still see them in the ads.

SVGA stands for Super VGA. VGA stands for Video Graphics Array or something equally meaningless.

How it plugs in

There are two types of graphics adapters available, as determined by how the adapter plugs into the computer's main circuitry board: AGP and PCI. You can read more about these standards in Chapter 10. For now, here's the scoop:

- **AGP.** This is the type of graphics adapter you want, the faster of the two, which plugs into an Accelerated Graphics Port (AGP). This only works, however, if your computer has an Accelerated Graphics Port; some of them don't.

- **PCI.** If your computer lacks an AGP, then you'll plug the graphics adapter into a PCI slot inside the computer case. PCI stands for Peripheral Component Interconnect (try saying that while chewing cauliflower). It's still a worthwhile way to connect a graphics adapter to your computer, but just not as good as AGP.

And some computers have built-in graphics adapters. In those cases, you can disable the internal components and add an AGP or PCI graphics adapter. That's an easy way to upgrade your system without having to use a screwdriver or blowtorch.

Read them labels!

Sometimes, the way a PC graphics card is described in a computer ad can drive you nuts. Look at these examples:

- Monster Fusion AGP 16MB 1X with 3DFX Voodoo Banshee
- Creative Labs 3D Blaster Savage4 Card 32MB PCI
- Xpert 128 8MB PCI w/Software
- PCI 64-bit 3-D video, MPEG, 16MB VRAM

Yes, those are all real examples (well, more-or-less). All those random burps and squeaks are describing graphics cards that can plug into a PC or Macintosh computer.

In addition to the brand names and monikers (like "Voodoo"), you should be able to determine the following tidbits from these examples:

- ✔ Each of the cards comes with a specific amount of video memory: 8MB 16MB, 32MB, and so on.

- ✔ See PCI in some of them? See AGP? That's the way the card connects to your computer's innards. AGP is better, as discussed earlier in this chapter, but you need a computer that supports it.

- ✔ Monster Fusion? I'd personally like to meet the committee that approved that brand name.

- ✔ *MPEG* refers to video hardware designed to improve the performance of movies and other animation played on a computer.

- ✔ Generally speaking, use any values listed for comparison. The more advanced (and expensive) the graphics adapter, the more techy tidbits they can boast about. And, O! They will boast!

Chapter 9

Keyboard, Mouse, and Joystick

• •

• •

I enjoy eating at swanky restaurants, but I also prefer those types of restaurants that have pictures on the menus. For some reason, the descriptions themselves don't do anything for me: free-range, aioli, confit, twice-reduced, and a host of Italian and French words that, to me at least, would mean so much more if there were just simple pictures nearby. But I digress . . .

Choosing the parts to a computer should be picture-menu simple. Sometimes they are. For example, most people won't give a second thought to the keyboard or mouse included with the computer. Yet you really do have a choice. Many of the fancier dealers and manufacturers offer several brands. And you can always buy a better keyboard or mouse after the purchase. This chapter takes you on the tour, complete with pictures.

Oh, and joysticks are thrown into the mix, just 'cause they don't fit anywhere else in this book.

✔ The only time you're truly limited in your keyboard or mouse choices is with laptop or handheld computers. With those, you take what they give you.

✔ While game consoles don't have true keyboards or mice, you often do have options for the various controller pads. Alternative pads are available for nearly every game-playing paddle.

✔ No matter what type of restaurant it is, nothing irks me more than stone cold butter. What is it with those people . . . ?!

Keyboards

Keyboards allow you to "talk" to your computer. They're a necessary part of any computer system, and as such, the keyboard usually comes with the computer console right in the box. You still have a choice, though: Many computer manufacturers give you the choice of optional keyboards, and you can always buy a better, fancier keyboard after your computer purchase.

As an example of a fancier keyboard, Figure 9-1 shows the Microsoft Natural keyboard, which is designed to be easier on your wrists than standard computer keyboards. Keyboards like this are available for both PC and Macintosh computers.

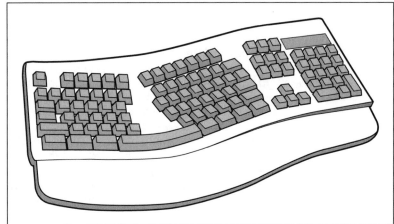

Figure 9-1: The Microsoft Natural keyboard.

✔ Macintosh and PC keyboards are different. If you're going to buy a separate keyboard from your computer, make sure it matches your computer choice.

✔ A USB keyboard will work with any Macintosh or PC that has a USB port. See Chapter 10 for more information on USB ports.

✔ The iMac uses a USB keyboard. If you buy a replacement, make sure it's a USB keyboard designed for the iMac.

✔ Handheld and palm computers have built-in keyboards or touch-pads. Generally you don't have a choice.

✔ Game consoles use game controllers (that is, joysticks) instead of keyboards.

Getting a pad

One of the best "gifts" you can give your computer is a mouse pad or wrist pad. These devices help make the computing chore easier, and I recommend them without reservation.

A mouse pad is a flat piece of foam rubber with a coated top, and either a texture, pattern, or picture appears on top. You roll the mouse around on the pad, which not only helps the mouse keep its grip but assures that you'll have some free space on your desktop on which to roll the mouse.

A wrist pad sits in front of the keyboard and provides a healthy place on which to rest your wrists. This allows you to keep your wrists comfortable and elevated, which helps to avoid some nasty physical complications.

✔ Aside from ergonomic variations, some keyboards come with special features: built-in speakers, clocks, a USB hub, calculators, and touch-pads or built-in mouse-like controllers.

✔ Before personal computers became popular, computer terminals had these incredible keyboards. They had the basic keyboard layout on a typewriter and a number of specific function keys. Some terminals had keys that actually said Insert Line, Move Block, Close File, and Get Me Chips. These days, computer keyboards are a little more conservative.

Mice and Other Nonfurry "Pointing Devices"

A mouse is an input device, like your keyboard, and is required for nearly all of today's graphical software. You can't use your computer without a mouse. For that reason, nearly every computer sold has a mouse in the box — the computer mouse kind.

✔ Just like the keyboard that comes with your computer, if you don't like your computer's mouse, you can buy yourself another one.

✔ As an example, consider the iMac's "Giant M&M" mouse (see Figure 9-2). It's not very ergonomic. Replacement iMac mice, in varying colors, are readily available to replace it.

✔ The standard PC mouse is the Microsoft mouse (Figure 9-2), though other manufacturers seem to be more creative with their mice, especially Logitech.

Specialty computer mice

The variety of computer mice is seemingly endless. You can choose from cordless mice, pen mice, tablet mice, and a whole host of other mice. See how they run? A-hem.

The most common alternative or specialty computer mouse is the trackball mouse. Often called the "upside-down mouse," a trackball has a large, easily manipulated ball on top; it does not roll around on your desktop. Artists and graphical types love this type of mouse because it offers more control over the mouse pointer on the screen than traditional, hand-held mice.

Then again, graphical artist types also love the electric pen and tablet, which is more like traditional painting than using any type of computer mouse.

✔ The current mouse craze is the IntelliMouse, from Microsoft. It has a third button, or "wheel," between the two standard buttons. As with all hardware, however, to make the best use of the IntelliMouse, you need software that works with it.

✔ There is a difference between the PC's mouse and the Macintosh's mouse, primarily that the latter has only one button. (However, computer guru Ted Nelson claims that the Mac's mouse actually has four buttons, three of which are on the keyboard.)

✔ Supposedly, future Macs will have multibutton mice. How the Mac community will react to this is anyone's guess.

✔ The plural of "computer mouse" is "computer mice," though you need only one mouse for your computer.

Figure 9-2:
An Intellimouse and an iMac mouse.

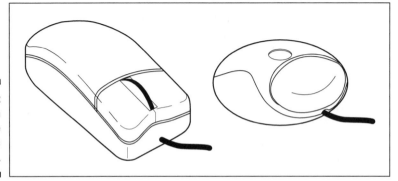

Joysticks and Game Controllers

They look at you funny these days when you call it a "joystick." That just implies too much fun for the serious-minded computer gamer. No, they're "game pads" now or "game controllers." Even the early IBM PC documentation referred to the joystick connection on the back of the computer as an "Analog-to-Digital Port." How stuffy.

The variety of joysticks available these days is almost endless. Gone are the simple so-called X-Y joysticks. Today's joysticks look like they belong in a fighter jet instead of on your desktop. There are buttons and buttons, "hat" switches, swivels, locks and all sorts of amazing doodads to flip, pull and throw (see Figure 9-3).

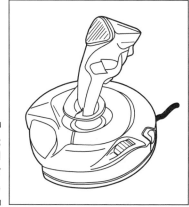

Figure 9-3: A typical (believe it or not) joystick.

Some joysticks even look like car steering wheels, complete with a set of foot pedals. For flight simulator "games" there are yokes and sticks. It's amazing.

Of course, the big question is, "Which joystick do I need?"

To pick the perfect joystick, merely look at the back of your software. Sophisticated games sport a list of recommended joysticks. Buy one of those listed. If you have more than one game that could use a joystick, choose whichever controller is compatible with (or recommended by) both games.

> ✔ Joysticks are *not* part of the traditional computer purchase. Generally you buy them later.

✔ Ensure that your computer has a joystick port or other method of attaching the joystick to the computer console (USB port, or whatever).

✔ Never just rush out and buy a joystick because it's "cool." Always confirm that your software works well with the joystick before buying.

✔ Not all computer games require a joystick. Many games, in fact, play better using the mouse or a combination of the mouse and keyboard. Quite a few game players become adept at using the keyboard by itself.

Chapter 10

Expansion Options

• •

• •

*E*very computer has flashy and non-flashy parts. The flashy stuff (graphics, microprocessors, memory, disk drives, and so on) is easy to discuss. Even an obscure concept like RAM can easily be understood. But computer expansion options? That's a tough nut to crack.

Unflashy as they are, inside your computer and on the console's rump are several connectors, slots, and methods for adding and expanding your computer system. This is trivial in that a lot of the information is technical, but it's necessary in that you want to ensure your computer is expandable. That expansion is one of the keys to any computer's success, and you'll appreciate having those options open to you when the time comes.

Connecting Stuff by Using Ports

When the Love Boat is out to sea, it's all by itself. The passengers are left to fall into and out of love, and the goofy passengers are left to provide comic entertainment with Gopher and Isaac. But when the Love Boat was in *port,* it was connected to a larger world where people could shop, mill about, see the cliff divers, and generally communicate with the real world.

In a computer, a port is another place where the computer can communicate with the real world or with other computer devices. A computer should come with a host of ports, which are different types of connectors to which a variety of wonderful and exotic devices can be attached.

Here is the list of the most common ports found on a computer:

- Printer (parallel) port
- Serial (modem) port
- Keyboard and mouse port
- ADB port
- Joystick/MIDI port
- USB port

The following sections describe each type of port, whether you need it or why you would want it.

- Not every computer needs every type of port. Just a few will do.
- In fact, in the future, computers may just come with one or two types of ports. One of them will most likely be the USB port, which is proving to be quite popular and versatile.
- Laptop and handheld computers have their own special ports. See Chapter 13 for more information on laptops.

The printer port

Shockingly enough, a printer port is the hole in the back of your computer where you plug in your printer. That's easy.

- All computers should have at least one printer port. It's part of the computer console.
- On the PC, the printer port can also be used to connect an external device in addition to a printer. You can use the printer port to add an external disk drive, CD-ROM, CD-R or CD-RW, DVD, Scanner, Zip, Jaz or any number of interesting devices.
- You can connect only one device to the printer port, in addition to the printer. If you want to connect more than one device to the printer or if you have trouble with the printer and the other device on the printer port, you need to get something called an "A-B switch." Your dealer can set you up with one, if necessary.
- The Macintosh has its own printer port and uses its own printer cables. An exception is the iMac, which must have a USB printer.

- The printer port may also be known as a parallel port, EPP/ECP port, or Centronics port. Officially it's LPT1, which is the old IBM PC designation (and still used in some remote parts of Windows).

The serial port

The serial port was the original "versatile" port on a computer. Used primarily with early computer modems, the serial port could also connect a mouse, scanner, printer, or a number of interesting devices to a computer.

Today, the serial port is generally used to connect an external modem to a computer. (See Chapter 11 for more information on modems.) It might also be used to connect two computers together for file exchange purposes. And some PCs still use the serial port to connect a computer mouse.

Beyond the simple options I mentioned, the serial port has really fallen out of favor recently. In fact, in a few years it may vanish from the computer's rear end completely, being replaced by the more efficient USB port.

- ✔ Your computer should have at least one serial port. Most PCs have two. The Mac has a serial port, which is identical to its printer port (you can hook up modems or printers to either port).

- ✔ The iMac does not have a serial port and instead uses the USB port to attach devices. (The iMac's modem is internal.)

- ✔ See the section "The USB port" elsewhere in this chapter for information on USB ports.

- ✔ Serial ports have a variety of different names used to describe them: modem port, COM1 (the old IBM PC name), AUX, Mouse port, and RS-232C port.

Mouse and keyboard ports

The mouse and keyboard ports are used to — can you guess? — connect a mouse or keyboard to your computer.

In the early days of the PC, a special keyboard port was used for the keyboard, and the mouse plugged into a serial port. Since then, PCs have grown up and now sport specialized (and identical) mouse and keyboard ports. The mouse plugs into one, the keyboard the other. And it doesn't matter which plugs into which, since they are both the same type of port.

- ✔ Beyond the keyboard and mouse, nothing else plugs into the keyboard and mouse ports on a PC.

- ✔ Older Macs used the Apple Desktop Bus (ADB) port to plug in both keyboards and mice, though that's since been replaced by the USB port. (PCs do not have the ADB port.)

The joystick/MIDI port

A *joystick port* is simply a hole into which you plug a joystick, or "game controller," for your computer.

There is a joystick port on nearly all PCs sold today; it's more-or-less standard equipment. Yup, that's where you plug in the joystick.

The joystick port also doubles as a MIDI port. You plug a special MIDI connector into the joystick port, which can be used to connect your PC to a MIDI musical instrument to help you play or compose digital music.

- ✔ Macintosh joysticks formerly plugged into the ADB port, though now all Macs support USB joysticks. Future PCs will, too.

- ✔ You can use two joysticks on a single computer by purchasing a gizmo known as a *splitter.*

- ✔ MIDI stands for Musical Instrument Digital Interface. It's a big, round, ugly hole (hey — a port!) you may have seen on any electronic musical instruments you may have lying around your house. The MIDI port is used to connect those instruments to each other and then to a computer. With the proper software, the computer can play the instruments and, lo, you have a symphony on your hands!

- ✔ The joystick port is officially known as the analog-to-digital port (or A-to-D port). The port can be used for a variety of things, most of which are of the science-fair variety: For example, I have one of those twirly wind things (an *anemometer*) that's a home-brew weatherman's kit. It sits on the roof of my office and plugs into my PC's joystick port. That way, I can tell when the wind is blowing without having to look at the trees outside.

The USB port

The most popular and versatile port you can have on a computer is the USB port. USB stands for Universal Serial Bus, and it offers a quick and easy method of adding external devices to your computer — plug-in simple, in fact.

The number of USB devices you can add to your computer is almost unlimited. The types of devices are nearly as varied: monitors, scanners, modems, game pads, keyboards, mice, Zip or Jaz drives, and the list goes on and on.

- ✔ I would insist on getting a computer with at least two USB ports.

- ✔ More USB ports can be added to any computer. A USB "hub" can be purchased to add more ports, or often some USB devices come with extra ports on them.

 ✔ Actually, there is a limit to the number of USB devices you can connect to a single computer: 127. But, hey, that's almost unlimited!

 ✔ The USB port supplants the old ADB (Apple Desktop Bus) port used on the Macintosh. Some older Macs may still sport ADB keyboards, mice, joysticks, and other input devices, but all the models sold today use USB.

 ✔ The only thing USB doesn't do well is add external disk drives. USB just isn't fast enough to do that well. Instead, a port standard known as *FireWire* does the job. See the sidebar, "The old and the new," for more information.

A Full House of Cards

The key to any computer's hardware success is expandability. The old Apple computer triumphed over it's peers in the late 1970s because the Apple II could be expanded; inside the computer's case was a row of *expansion slots.* Into those slots, users could plug *expansion cards,* which greatly increased the computer's abilities.

The first IBM PC also had expansion slots, which helped ensure its success. And though the early Macs lacked expansion slots, pressure from users eventually won Apple over, and today the G3 line sports expansion slots for power users who want them (though the iMac does not have expansion slots).

The old and the new

As one popular port fades into the sunset, another, better type of computer port rises above the horizon.

Fading away quickly is the SCSI standard. Formerly the best port for adding external storage devices (CD-R/RW, DVD, Tape backup, external hard drives), the SCSI port proved versatile but difficult to configure. It was a standard on many Macs, but required an expansion card to be added to a PC.

Rising fast is the FireWire port. It's easier to use than the SCSI port and supports a similar line of devices: external disk drives, digital cameras, plus its faster, more flexible, and easier to configure.

Presently the G3/G4 line of PowerMacs is the only standard desktop computer to come with FireWire. Supposedly, it will one day also be a standard on all computers. Until then, FireWire is a technology worth watching.

Why you might need expansion slots

Expansion slots allow you to add new options or features to those that come with a standard computer. This isn't as necessary as it was in the past; the early IBM PCs lacked such luxurious features as a video adapter, serial ports, or even extra memory. All that could be added by plugging in the proper expansion cards.

Today's computers often come with everything you need. For example, the iMac has an internal modem, network adapter, and room for more memory. Any further expansion can be added via the USB ports. But some power users may want more than that, so other computers come with expansion slots.

- Expansion slots simply increase the flexibility of your computer system.

- Some low-end, "home" computers or all-in-one systems like the iMac are designed for people who need basic computers and, therefore, probably don't need expansion slots. If you need expansion slots, however, steer clear of those systems.

- For example, to add a network card, second monitor/video adapter, satellite modem, SCSI adapter, additional ports, improved sound card, or any of a number of options, your computer will need expansion slots.

- I just upgraded my older Mac with an expansion card that contains USB ports. By adding the expansion card, I was able to give my Mac USB ports so that I can now use USB devices. The same card could have been added to a PC to give it USB expandability as well.

- Expansion cards usually ensure that you can upgrade and improve your system in the years to come.

Types of expansion slots

As with everything else, a computer can't have just one, typical expansion slot. After all, technology has vastly improved since the days of Tinker Toys.

For historical and evolutionary reasons, most computers have several different types of expansion slots inside their box. Sure, some are better than others. Still, a mixture of several types is generally preferred. Here are the popular ones:

- **PCI.** This is the most popular type of expansion slot found on both the Macintosh and PC. The PCI expansion slot connects directly to the computer's microprocessor, which makes it very fast.

✔ **AGP.** A special slot designed specifically for video adapters (see Chapter 8) is the Accelerated Graphics Port, or AGP slot. While PCI video adapters are available, if your computer has an AGP port, you're better off buying and using an AGP video adapter.

✔ **ISA.** The original slot found on the first IBM PC is still around, mostly because ISA expansion cards are still with us.

Which type of expansion slots should you have? A computer should have from three to five (or more) PCI slots. PCs (not Macs) may also have one or two ISA slots for backward compatibility (though this is optional). And having an AGP slot is nice if you want to use the latest, greatest video adapters (on the PC).

✔ Computer memory once plugged into expansion cards. Today's computers are designed, however, so that the memory chips plug directly into the computer's main circuitry.

✔ Some PCI expansion cards can even be used in either system. (I've purchased both a network card and USB expansion card that can work with either the Mac or PC.) But be aware that some PCI cards are Mac- or PC-only.

✔ SCSI is not an expansion slot itself. If you want to add a SCSI adapter to your computer, allowing you to use SCSI storage devices, then plug the SCSI expansion card into one of the computer's PCI slots.

✔ Computer scientist types refer to the expansion slots as the bus, so they use the term PCI bus rather than PCI slot. Same difference.

Chapter 11

Modems and Networking

. . . .

In This Chapter

▶ Finding a nice, fast modem

▶ Discovering various modem options

▶ Configuring your computer for a network

. . . .

*Y*our computer need not be alone in the universe. Sure, it can talk with its own peripherals. But the printer and scanner make boring companions. And, honestly, the computer gets bored talking to you through the keyboard and mouse. There has to be more out there. . . .

There are two popular ways to get your computer to talk with other computers. The first is by adding a modem, which opens up the whole world of the Internet (and all the computers on the Internet). The second is by networking your computer with other computers directly, which is more of a business thing, but it can be done if you have more than one computer at home, too.

Add a Modem

A modem is a device that lets your computer communicate with other computers using the phone line. Your computer plugs into the modem (or the modem is inside the computer); then you hook the modem up to the phone line. Within an instant (providing you have the proper software), your computer is "online" and talking with other computers. Amazing.

Of course, the real reason to get a modem in any computer is to access the Internet. When I wrote about modems in the 1980s, I had to dream up reasons why you would need a modem. Those solutions still exist, but just about anything else you can do with a modem is overshadowed by the Internet — so much so that modems are pretty much standard equipment in any new computer.

✔ If you don't plan on using the Internet or a modem, ask for a computer without one preinstalled. That will save you maybe $50 or so off the purchase price. (Modems can always be added later.)

✔ Then again, adding a modem later is always more expensive than getting one preinstalled, so the choice is up to you.

✔ By themselves, modems don't raise your phone bill. Using a modem is like using a telephone. The only difference is that your computer is doing the talking (it's more like horribly screeching) into the phone. Your phone company charges you the same whether you or your computer makes the call, and long-distance charges still apply. And, of course, you have to pay for Internet access, but that's an access fee and not a charge for using the modem.

✔ If you're going to use a modem, my advice is to have a second phone line — one dedicated to the computer — installed in your home or office.

✔ Nearly all modems sold today are also capable of sending and receiving faxes. Although the term "fax/modem" formerly described this type of modem, nearly all modems today are fax/modems, so there's no point in using the term. Special software is required to enable your computer to send and receive faxes by using the modem.

Fast modems and faster modems

You'll want the fastest modem you can afford in your new PC. The speed being measured is *bits per second,* or BPS. The higher the BPS value, the better. Even faster is the Kbps value, which is 1,000bps (K being the common computer symbol for "1,000 of something"). High Kbps values are always the best.

The current top-of-the line modems chug along at 57.6Kbps, often written as 57.6K (where the K means 1,000bps). Believe me, that's fast.

Try to avoid any modem that's slower than that. The 28.8K modems were fast a few years back, but too slow for use today.

✔ Generally speaking, your options are limited when you buy a (dealer-installed) modem with your computer. If given the option, try to get the fastest speed possible.

✔ You may also hear the term *baud rate* used to describe a modem's speed. The more accurate term is *bps;* baud rate is used to describe signal changes in Teletype equipment, which used to apply to early computer modems but is no longer the case.

Other modem options

When you buy a computer with a modem, you're generally going to get what's known as an *internal* modem. That's a modem that lives on an expansion card that somehow plugs into your computer's innards.

There are also *external* modems, which live as separate boxes outside the computer. They plug into the computer's serial or USB port and, beyond that, work just like internal modems. The advantage here is that you can add an external modem later if you like, and you can keep the modem if you ever buy a new computer. (I once used the same external modem on a Mac, PC, Apple II, and even an old TRS-80 microcomputer.)

Beyond the standard, telephone-line modems, specialty modems exist that let you communicate even faster. These modems are generally not purchased with the computer but must be added later. Here's the quick list:

- ✔ **ISDN modems.** A fast modem standard offered as an alternative to the normal phone lines. Commonly available, though not horrendously faster than a typical telephone modem.

- ✔ **xDSL modems.** The fastest local standard available, though best-suited for businesses (who can afford it). *x*DSL stands for "something" Digital Subscriber Line, where the *x* or "something" is replaced by another technical term that you don't need to worry about. This type of service is fast, but not available in most places.

- ✔ **Satellite modems.** A good, fast standard available anywhere, but you must install a special satellite dish to make it happen. Also, the speed benefit is only one way; information comes into your computer fast, but goes out through a standard modem (which is required).

- ✔ **Cable modems.** The best standard, not that expensive but not widely available.

I can recommend any of the preceding modem breeds, providing they're available in your area. For example, there isn't cable TV where I live in the remote forests of North Idaho, but I do have satellite TV. A satellite modem has served me well for a long time now.

- ✔ Typical telephone modems are known as POTS modems. POTS stands for Plain Old Telephone System. (I'm not making that up.)

- ✔ The advantage of an internal modem is that it doesn't clutter your desktop. External modems require a power cord and a cable to your PC's serial port; internal modems lack these messy items.

✔ The advantage of an external modem is that you can see its pretty lights and tell exactly what it's up to. You can turn it off by flipping its switch or set its volume by using a tiny knob. Also, you can easily move external modems from one computer to another.

✔ My wife likes her external modem because she can turn it off. This feature prevents our kids from dialing up the Internet when they're not supposed to (or until they figure out where the switch is).

✔ You buy these special types of modems *after* you buy the computer. Rarely will you find them preconfigured with a computer (though it's not unheard of).

Networking Computers

Another way to make computers talk to each other is through a network. The network is actually two or more computers connected using some type of network cable. The computers can share information, access common disk drives, and share printers.

If you decide to buy a computer and put it on a network, you must ensure that it comes with the proper network hardware.

Primarily your computer needs a NIC *(nick),* which is an insider term for Network Interface Card. That's an expansion card that either plugs into your computer or is part of the computer hardware itself, as is the case with the iMac and G3 or G4 Macintosh.

The NIC should be 10/100Base-T Ethernet compatible. There are more technical descriptions of the card, and if you already have a network, then you merely need to have the network administrator give you a spec sheet of what to get or what to avoid.

✔ Ask anyone who's ever installed a network card: It's best to have the dealer set it up when you buy the computer.

✔ I can recommend Doug Lowe's *Networking For Dummies* book as an insightful, humorous, and to-the-point work on networking your home or office. Nice job, Doug.

Chapter 12

Sound Decisions

· ·

In This Chapter

▶ Deciding on a sound system
▶ Adding external speakers
▶ Getting a microphone

· ·

*W*ith few exceptions, computers generally come with some device for making sound. They bleep. They beep. They play a tinny version of Beethoven's Fifth. Recent developments in computer sound, however, have enabled computers to make all sorts of noise, and beautiful noise at that.

This chapter covers a few of the sound decisions you may have to make when you purchase a computer. All computers come with sound, but the quality of the sound and the style of your speakers demand attention.

The Bleeping Circuitry

All computers now come with built-in sound circuitry. They are all capable of producing just about any sound from synthesized music to CD-quality sound to human-voice imitations. Many of the computer demos you see in the store actually have top-notch sound playing, but the management turns down the volume to keep the employees sane.

✔ All computers contain the basic circuitry necessary to play computer games. Rarely, if ever, is a new computer sold today incompatible with any computer game's sound requirements.

✔ Older PCs required that sound cards be added. The standard for the sound cards was modeled after the SoundBlaster brand. Even today you will see PCs advertised with SoundBlaster-compatible sound circuitry.

✔ The sound circuitry also includes a music synthesizer, which allows the computer to play music synthesizer or MIDI *(mih-dee)* files.

✔ If you plan on creating MIDI files, you'll need MIDI software plus a MIDI port on the computer. (See Chapter 10.) You don't need a MIDI port to play MIDI files; you need only a sound card that plays MIDI files (and most sound cards do).

✔ Playing a musical CD or viewing a movie on a DVD requires sound circuitry. The sound is wired from the CD or DVD through the sound card and then out your computer's speakers.

✔ Special software is required to produce a human voice on a computer. All Macintosh computers come with this software as part of the operating system; on the PC, special programs must be purchased to emulate the human voice.

Tweeting and Woofing

In addition to having sound circuitry, all computers are also sold with speakers. The number and quality of the speakers, of course, varies.

The basic computer speaker is a tiny, internal speaker right inside the computer box. This is *not* the speaker you want to hear your computer's sound from.

Some computers have stereo speakers built into the console or monitor. For example, the iMac and most Compaq Pressario models have speakers to the left and right of the console. These speakers are okay, but not the best.

Usually offered as an option for most computer purchases are external speakers, which can be plugged into the console to give you two (left and right) quality speakers through which to hear your computer.

A further option is a subwoofer, which is a bass enhancement that typically sits on the floor. The subwoofer amplifies the lower-range of the audio spectrum, which, basically, really *rocks* the floor. That makes it hard to stomp out alien invaders without waking up the neighborhood.

Finally, the ultimate in computer sound is surround sound, where you have a left, right, rear-left, rear-right, and center speaker, plus a subwoofer, for all-too-realistic sound. This works great, providing you have software that actually uses it.

✔ Different levels of external speakers are usually offered with the computer purchase. As you might expect, the more you spend, the better the quality. But, honestly, for computer sounds, you don't really have to spend a lot of money.

✔ Try to avoid battery-powered external speakers. Always make sure there is a power cord option available.

 ✔ It is possible to connect your computer to your home stereo system and use those speakers. This is practical only if the stereo is in the same room as the PC and the speakers are positioned properly. Granted, you'd have to be a real nut to try this.

 ✔ Computer speakers — including the subwoofer and 3-D sound systems — can always be purchased at a later time.

 ✔ If you really would rather not scare the neighbors with your computer sounds, you can always plug in a pair of headphones.

 ✔ I must say, hearing some computer games in stereo is impressive. As you move, the sounds around you "slide" through the speakers for a wonderful 3-D effect.

Adding a Microphone

All computer sound circuitry comes with the ability for input as well, which is provided in the form of a microphone. This allows you to record your own voice or enjoy such diversions as the Internet Phone, for example.

Whether or not a microphone is included with the computer is anyone's guess. Sometimes they come, sometimes they don't. When they do come with the computer, the microphone is usually of marginal quality or built into the monitor or console somehow — not the best possible place for a microphone.

If you're into computer recording, you can always add a nice, trusty mic later. Computers use a standard mini-din connector (teensy plug-in thing) for mic input.

Chapter 13

Special Laptop Issues

*L*aptop and notebook computers are nearly identical to their desktop brethren. They have all the same components and nearly all the same features. The big difference is, of course, that laptops are portable. Their components run from batteries, which means they must be specially designed to conserve power. Further, laptops must be lightweight, meaning their components must also save on bulk.

Buying a laptop works just like buying any computer; the same five steps outlined in Chapter 1 still apply. Beyond that, special attention must be paid to certain laptop features that differ from desktop features. This chapter outlines those issues, allowing you to select the best laptop hardware for your needs.

✔ Laptops make an ideal computer for anyone "on the go." Salespeople thrive on laptops.

✔ Laptops make an excellent second computer, allowing you to take work with you when you're away from your desktop.

✔ Laptops are ideal for students away at college, who may not have the room for a bulky desktop.

 ✔ As an old fogy who's been around the computer business for quite a while, I prefer the term "laptop" over "notebook." When you shop, you'll often see either or both terms. I use laptop since it was the first term used to describe this type of computer back in the late 1980s. (Notebooks were supposedly lighter than laptops, though that distinction is so silly I won't even bother explaining it.)

Laptop Considerations

Desktop computers won their fame by being expandable. Laptop computers won their fame by sacrificing expandability for portability; you don't buy a laptop with the notion of "upgrading it later." You buy a laptop to have a computer anywhere you are: in a plane flying across the country, in a coffee shop, or in a bungalow over the lagoon in Bora Bora.

All the technical descriptions of a desktop computer apply to laptops as well: microprocessor, RAM, disk storage, and so on. Beyond that, laptops have special considerations desktop users would never dream of. Chief among these are the following:

- Battery life
- Weight
- Pointing device
- Removable/swappable drives
- Modem/network connection

Each of these considerations is discussed in the sections that follow.

Software considerations, on the other hand, aren't really critical to owning a laptop. If the program works on a desktop system, then it also works on the laptop model. Some installation programs have options for "minimal" installations, so as not to use up all your laptop's hard drive space. And there is special laptop software that helps you use your portable system, such as a program to use the modem or configure the sound or use the CD-ROM drive — but that mostly comes with the laptop itself.

A battery of issues

A laptop can use electricity from a wall outlet or its own internal battery. The length of time that the battery can power the laptop is, obviously, important. A fancy, high-end laptop may have impressive hardware statistics, but if you can use the thing for only 20 minutes before plugging it in, you may as well lug around a desktop.

A good laptop should have batteries that power it for at least two hours. The better laptops boast that they can run for up to six hours off batteries, but that may be stretching the truth a bit. (Oftentimes the battery tests are made under ideal conditions — not the same conditions under which you'd be using the laptop.)

The best *type* of battery you can get is the Lithium ion. Second best is Nickel-metal hydride (NiMH). Both are rechargeable and can be reused without having to drain them fully.

The worst type of battery is the nickel-cadmium battery, or NiCad. These batteries are rechargeable, but they suffer from what's known as *the memory effect,* which means that if you run off battery power, you have to fully drain the battery before it's recharged, or else the battery life gets cut short.

✔ You may notice an interesting trade-off between laptop features and battery life. Items like more RAM and larger screens subtract from battery life. So if using your laptop unplugged is important to you, consider cutting back on features.

✔ Some laptops have the ability to "hot swap" batteries. That is, you use one for two hours and it goes bad. Then you can instantly replace that battery with another — without turning off the laptop. This works only if both batteries are fully charged.

✔ Beware of laptops that claim longer battery life, but yet measure that claim based on swapping batteries. You want to compare laptops based on the life of *one* battery at a time. (Second batteries are an added extra, and it takes longer to charge two batteries than it does one.)

✔ If possible, try to use your laptop as much as possible without the batteries. Most laptop owners are adept at finding power sockets in airports, hotel lobbies, and restaurants. But if you must, you can always rely on the batteries.

✔ Charge your laptop's battery the night before you leave on a trip. That way the battery will always be ready to go in the morning.

✔ Many hand-held and palm-top computers use standard batteries. Because those computers don't consume a lot of power, they can operate for hours — sometimes days — off a pair of AA or AAA batteries.

The skinny on laptop weight

A laptop should weigh under 10 pounds, ideally close to 6 pounds. But that's merely the unit itself. There is also a carrying weight that should be only a few pounds more. The idea is to pack up the laptop and everything that goes with it and be able to lug it around and *not* look like you're trying to smuggle plutonium.

✔ If weight is a serious issue for you, consider getting a hand-held or palm-top PC.

✔ The carrying weight includes everything that goes with the laptop: external disk drives, the power "brick," leather case, and so on. That stuff can add up.

   ✔ Going along with weight is the issue of size. Laptops can vary in size from
     the dimensions of a college dictionary to super-thin like a magazine.

Various pointing devices

Realizing that most laptop users will not have a handy rolling surface nearby
(unless you can negotiate the tray table away from your seatmate), laptops
generally come with built-in pointing devices, also known as computer mice.

There are several popular types of pointing devices.

   ✔ **Touchpad.** The most popular mouse replacement is the touchpad. This
     is a flat area below the keyboard that you touch or drag your finger over,
     which moves the mouse pointer on the screen. Clicking a button nearby
     the touchpad (or tapping the pad) is the same as clicking the mouse.

   ✔ **Rollerballs**. Another common mouse replacement is the rollerball or
     thumb-ball. Like a trackball mouse, the thumb-ball is rolled by using
     your thumb or index finger. Buttons on either side of the rollerball click
     the mouse.

   ✔ **Keyboard sticks.** Another common mouse alternative is the keyboard
     stick, which looks like a pencil eraser stuck between the H and J keys on
     the keyboard. The stick can be moved to manipulate the mouse pointer
     on the screen. A button near the keyboard is used to click.

Make sure you're very comfortable with whatever pointing device you
choose for your laptop. Unlike choosing a mouse for a desktop computer,
which you can readily change, you're pretty much stuck with whatever pointing device your laptop has.

Removable and swappable drives

Due to its small size, a laptop often cannot sport the many disk drives of its
desktop counterpart. To make room, certain disk drives are often made
"swappable." For example, you can remove the CD-ROM drive and replace it
with a floppy disk drive, should the need arise.

Swappable drives also serve to save weight. For example, if you're only taking
the laptop down to the local Java-Java for some away-from-the-office typing,
then why load in the CD-ROM or floppy drive? Leaving out those things saves
weight — and maybe even battery life.

Note that not every laptop has the ability to have swappable drives. This is typically a "just in case" solution. For example, a laptop may come with a floppy
drive that you can swap out with a DVD drive — which you can purchase extra.

The laptop modem and network connection

If you plan on using a modem with your laptop, try finding a laptop with a built-in modem. Ditto for a network connection. While these options can be added later (see the section on laptop ports below), it's always better to have them included with the basic laptop configuration.

Security issues

The same things that make laptops appealing to computer buyers also make them appealing to computer thieves. Laptops are easy to steal. To insure against this, get a laptop that has the ability for you to attach a security device.

✔ The security device can be as simple as inserting a locking cable through the laptop's case. You can purchase a locking cable anywhere.

✔ Forget software passwords and encryption. While that may protect your laptop's data, it's not the files on the hard drive the crooks are after — it's the unit itself! Hard drives are generally erased before the laptop is resold. You can do that whether or not your files are encrypted or password-protected.

Laptop Ports

Like desktop computers, laptops also come with ports for connecting external devices. The ports are usually of two varieties: standard ports, like a desktop computer model has, and model-specific ports for connecting special devices particular to the laptop. (An example of a model-specific port would be a special connector for attaching an external floppy drive or CD-ROM, something a desktop PC wouldn't need.)

Most often, the ports are used when the laptop is in one spot for a while, usually on a desk. For example, it's nice to have a printer port on a laptop, but although you can buy portable and battery-powered printers, you're better off waiting until you get to your desk to print rather than hogging all of row 27 on a 757.

To help you deal with ports and some of the goodies you can optionally attach, many laptops come with port replicators or docking stations. The following sections elaborate.

✔ Not every laptop has a companion port replicator or docking station.

✔ You can use either a port replicator or docking station to transform your laptop into a desktop. Replicators and docking stations allow you to easily add a full-size monitor, keyboard, and mouse to the laptop. You still use the laptop, but you can use it with full-sized, desktop computing devices.

✔ If you tend to take your work home with you, a laptop/docking station combination may be ideal. Use the laptop and docking station at work; then just lug the laptop home with you.

Port replicators

A *port replicator* is a device you attach to your laptop's rump. It plugs into a laptop-specific port or connector and may also attach using screws or thumb-tighteners. The port replicator's job is to add standard desktop computer ports to the laptop.

For example, a port replicator may add a standard keyboard port, mouse port, printer port, and video port, plus a couple of USB ports. This allows your laptop to access and use those devices without buying special adapters.

✔ It's possible (with some replicator models) to leave various desktop computer items — monitor, keyboard, mouse — plugged in to the replicator. Then you merely attach the laptop to the replicator and — ta-da! — instant desktop computer.

✔ Port replicators generally cost extra.

✔ If you tire of reconnecting printers, the network, a monitor, keyboard, and mouse every time you bring your laptop home, you need a port replicator.

Docking stations

A docking station is a sophisticated type of port replicator. Like a standard port replicator, the docking station allows your laptop to grow desktop ports and peripherals. Beyond that, the docking station may also contain a CD-ROM drive, hard drive, plus other hardware that turns your laptop into a fancy, full-on desktop computer.

✔ Docking stations do more than port replicators, so they also cost more than replicators.

✔ Docking stations are almost always extras you must buy at the time of purchase.

✔ Actually, I was just looking at the price of some docking stations and they rival the prices of some low-cost computers. Yowie!

The PCMCIA Port

Laptop computers typically don't have expansion slots. If they do, the slots are usually used for something specific, such as a modem or more memory. Laptops never have room, however, for a full PCI expansion card. For this reason, the people who make laptops developed a special expansion system standard that uses tiny, credit-card-size expansion cards. Like most computer standards, this one is an acronym: It's called PCMCIA or PC Card, for short.

PCMCIA cards allow you to add a variety of interesting things to your laptop. The most common card is a modem or network card. That's followed by mini-hard drive cards, memory cards, and security devices.

- Getting a laptop with a PCMCIA card slot is a good idea if you need expansion. However, if the laptop already comes with a modem or network option, or the laptop has a full-powered docking station, the PCMCIA slot may not be necessary.

- PCMCIA stands for Personal Computer Memory Card International Association. It's a group of developers who settled on a hardware standard for credit-card-size deals to plug into PC laptops.

- Some desktop PCs come with the capability to have a PCMCIA port, though this capability is truly useful only if you plan to share PCMCIA cards with a laptop.

- It's rumored that PCMCIA stands for People Can't Memorize Computer Industry Acronyms.

Chapter 14

Your Computer's Operating System

*A*ll computer hardware, from the slowest microprocessor to the fastest graphics system, is utterly worthless without the proper software to control it. I know, I know: Hardware is all the flash when you buy a computer. But all the hardware covered from Chapters 5 through 13 means nothing unless you have the software to take advantage of it.

The number-one piece of software in any computer is called the *operating system*. It's the first program that runs when you turn on your computer, the program other programs defer to, the head program in charge, the boss, the czar, *el queso grande,* the king o' everything. This chapter discusses your operating system options.

 ✔ Choosing an operating system is a decision you should make *before* you select computer hardware. (Hardware is covered first in this book because you need to know those terms before you can select the software.)

 ✔ Yes, there is a choice when it comes to operating systems. Much to Microsoft's chagrin, the entire world does not run on Windows. And even within Windows, there are variations and versions.

Understanding Operating Systems

An *operating system* is a program that controls your computer. It coordinates three things:

- ✓ Your computer's software
- ✓ Your computer's hardware
- ✓ You

Each of these items is important. All these items together comprise your computer system. So as the grand coordinator, the operating system is an important element, bringing it all together and keeping everything running smoothly.

- ✓ Of the three things, you (obviously) are the most important. How the operating system interacts with you is your primary concern in choosing an operating system.
- ✓ Second most important is the *software base,* the number and variety of programs available to a specific operating system.
- ✓ Finally, the operating system is written to control specific hardware.
- ✓ By itself, the operating system doesn't really *do* anything. It's not productivity software like a word processor or graphics program. It's not a game or a utility or even remotely entertaining. The operating system is merely in charge. Something has to be.

Working with you

Software is more important than hardware, and the most important piece of software is the computer's operating system. Therefore your choice of operating system must be a good one.

Forget about the hardware! Shut out the junk around the screen and merely concentrate on the information being presented by the operating system. Does it make sense? Is it easy? Does it give you the control you need? Can you figure things out? Are you familiar or comfortable with it? These are all important questions to ask, more important than "I wonder who made this nifty monitor. . . ?"

Operating systems can be either friendly or powerful. *Friendly* means the operating systems are easy to learn and use. *Powerful* means the operating system may not be friendly, but it offers you more direct control over the computer itself.

- ✓ Try out an operating system by running a program. See how it goes.
- ✓ Check out how the operating system displays information about files and folders. (Have someone in the store demonstrate this to you. Have them show you a file and a folder.)
- ✓ Make a note of which operating system appeals to you the most. Don't let any hardware prejudices unfairly influence you — not yet, at least.

✔ It's easy to become bored or frustrated with an easy/friendly operating system, even if you like that type of operating system when you first start using a computer. Therefore, if you're at all technically minded, consider a more powerful operating system instead of a friendly one.

✔ On the friendliness scale, the Macintosh operating system is about as friendly as you can get. Windows tries, but it's still not as friendly as a Mac.

✔ UNIX is the least friendly operating system. It is not only terse but also allows you to do dangerous things quite easily.

✔ As a UNIX-like operating system, Linux can be considered unfriendly. However, Linux comes with graphical *shell* programs that make it easier to use for beginners. (Though it's still not as easy as Windows or the Mac.)

✔ Friendly operating systems generally sport friendly software. The programs on a Macintosh, for example, are intuitive after you know the feel of the operating system. On the other hand, programs in UNIX are all twisted and ugly as scrap metal (and about as friendly).

Controlling the software

The second gauge of an operating system's worthiness is its *software base*. A software base is merely the number and variety of programs available to a specific operating system. The more, the better.

The trap here is a technical one. Suppose you find and love an operating system that works with you. The operating system is well designed, friendly where it's supposed to be, and powerful where you need it. But, alas, there just isn't any software available. Maybe you can find a few programs, but some of the software you really need just isn't there or isn't as nice as you'd like. In that case, forget about using that operating system.

As an example, consider the NeXT computer and its operating system, NeXTStep. The operating system was beautiful to behold, powerful, friendly, and enthralling. But the operating system lacked a lot of popular software. So despite it's elegant design and reliability, the operating system failed and gave way to inferior operating systems, like Windows. Windows had the software base.

✔ One of the operating system's jobs is to control the software. As such, software is geared to work with a particular operating system, and the software reflects many characteristics of the operating system it works under.

✔ A larger software base assures an operating system's success, even if that operating system stinks.

- ✔ Of course, more software shouldn't be the key to buying any computer. If the operating system you choose has exactly the software you need, then you're set.

- ✔ Sometimes a vast software base isn't the only way to judge an operating system. For example, most of the best graphics and design software is still available primarily for the Macintosh. Although Windows versions of such software exist, those programs are generally not as good as the Mac originals.

- ✔ If you're using proprietary software, such as an inventory system written specifically for your company, you need whichever operating system that software requires. This example is one of the rare instances in which the software base doesn't matter.

Controlling the hardware

The operating system's final task is to control the computer hardware, telling it exactly what to do with itself. So when you tell a program to print, the operating system is the one that ensures the information is properly sent to the printer.

Each operating system is written to one or more hardware standards. For example, Windows is written to the PC hardware standard. The Macintosh operating system runs only on Macintosh computers.

Some operating systems are *multiplatform,* which means they can run on a variety of hardware configurations. For example, Linux can run on a variety of computers. If you have a PC, you buy Linux for the PC, if you have some other type of computer, you buy Linux for it, and so on.

- ✔ Operating systems carry with them a software base. So, for example, you can choose Windows as your operating system because it's friendly to you and has a lot of software available.

- ✔ Operating systems are generally purchased at the time you buy the computer, which means everything is set up for you by the dealer.

- ✔ The operating system controls the microprocessor. In fact, operating systems are written for specific microprocessors.

Operating System Survey

Believe it or not, you do have a choice when it comes to selecting an operating system. Not every computer store will carry all the operating systems at once, so you may have to shop around. But options are out there and available — providing you're willing to look.

The following sections highlight the various operating systems available today. Consider this a mere survey; use your own personal observations and judgements to select an operating system just for you.

Windows 98

Windows is the most popular operating system available, sold with over 80 percent of computers. It's friendly and powerful (see Figure 14-1), with a large software base and plenty of games. Chances are that your new computer will have Windows 98 installed.

Specifically, Windows 98 is targeted toward the "consumer." What that means is that Microsoft is trying to target a more sophisticated operating system, Windows NT/2000 (see the following description), toward businesses. Both operating systems do run the same programs, more-or-less.

Windows NT/2000

Windows 2000, formerly known as Windows NT, is the all-serious version of Windows (see Figure 14-2). While it looks like Windows 98 and runs most Windows 98 software, Windows 2000 is geared toward business. It has extra security options plus special networking abilities that make it appeal to large, impersonal corporations.

- ✔ Windows 2000 is not fully compatible with all Windows 98 programs. Specifically, some games refuse to run under Windows 2000. Therefore, this should not be a consideration for home or personal use.

- ✔ Windows 2000 comes in two flavors: workstation and server. The server is designed to be a central office computer on a network. The workstation flavor can be used with or without a network.

How is the BIOS different from the operating system?

If the operating system is the main software program in charge of the computer, what's the BIOS for?

The BIOS is actually software that's written and "saved" to a ROM chip inside the computer.

Those instructions there tell the computer how to do basic things and accomplish simple tasks. But the software does not control the computer itself. Instead, the operating system takes over and uses the BIOS to help it control everything.

Windows CE

A specialized version of Windows is available for palm-top and handheld computers. Called Windows CE, it's a stripped-down version of Windows that works like Windows 98/2000 but has special portable features. (See Figure 14-3.)

Figure 14-3: Windows CE in action.

A lot of people find Windows CE to be a bit clunky, so chances are that it will undergo some form of facelift or revamping. There are, however, many desktop Windows users who love having a similar operating system on their portable computer.

I'm not sure what the CE stands for.

Mac OS

The Macintosh operating system (see Figure 14-4) is synonymous with the Macintosh hardware; buy a Mac, get an operating system. While it would be nice to purchase the Mac OS (Operating System) for the PC, you just can't. Alas.

The Mac OS is the only true alternative to Windows. Presently Mac OS has about 12 percent of the personal computer market and a substantial software base. If you're planning on using your computer for graphics, you would be remiss not to survey what's available on the Mac.

✔ The Mac OS is tightly tied to the Macintosh hardware.

✔ Be aware that in addition to being tied to a certain version of the Mac OS, Macintosh software is also geared to specific microprocessors. For today's systems, you'll want Mac software geared to the G3/G4 processor.

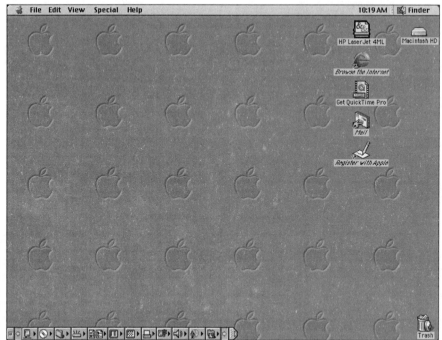

Figure 14-4:
The
Macintosh
OS looks
like this.

Linux

Linux is a free operating system that runs on just about any computer, especially PCs.

Well, Linux isn't *exactly* free. You do pay for a release of Linux, but that also includes bells and whistles and programs that make installing Linux a snap. You can even add Linux to a computer that already runs Windows and "share" both operating systems.

Linux can be cryptic at times, but providing you add a friendly *shell,* which adds a graphical user interface to the program, it can be easy to use. So unless you're a programmer or UNIX maven, look for a version of Linux with a shell program that helps you get used to the operating system. (This is the tradeoff for Linux being as powerful as it is, even more powerful than Windows NT/2000.) Figure 14-5 shows Linux being run with a shell.

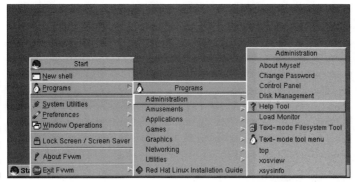

Figure 14-5:
Linux looks
like this
(with a
shell).

- Linux is similar to the UNIX operating system. If you like, you can get the UNIX operating system for your computer as well, though why bother since Linux can be had for next-to-nothing?

- Linux is sort-of available for Macintosh hardware. Still, why bother paying more for Mac hardware and *not* running Mac software? Instead, just buy an old used 386 (or better) PC and try out Linux.

- With continued modification, Linux may one day be a popular alternative to the Windows hegemony.

Palm OS

Like the Macintosh OS, the Palm OS is a proprietary operating system for the palm-type handheld computers. I mention it here because it's your only choice if you get a Palm computer. Figure 14-6 shows what it looks like.

The Palm OS is simple and elegant, not trying to do everything a desktop computer operating system does (like Windows CE has tried). There is a vast software base available, most of it free on the Internet. If only desktop operating systems could be so simple and unencumbered . . . *(wistful sigh)*.

The antique, the immortal, and the dead

There are even more operating systems available. New ones are being developed all the time, though rarely will you see a stack of software boxes in the Software-O-Rama for them. These are the curiosities. The ugly cousins. The ancestors of today's computer operating systems.

Figure 14-6:
The Palm
OS looks
like this.

DOS. Yeah, DOS is dead. IBM still makes a version of it, though, called PC-DOS. Lots of DOS programs are still out there, many of them available free (because the developers don't stand a chance of making money any other way!). A free version of DOS, called Caldera DOS, is also available from the Internet. It's quite popular with the anti-Windows crowd.

OS/2. Before Windows, OS/2 was to be the successor to DOS. Ha! Never happened. IBM still makes OS/2 available, though. But you can't get software for it, or at least nothing worth looking at. And if it has no software, then the thing really has no point to it, eh?

BeOS. The Be Operating System (the company is named "Be") is an elegant and fun operating system, though there really isn't any commercial software available. Instead, BeOS finds itself used in some proprietary devices. This knowledge doesn't really do anything for you other than earn brownie points at cocktail parties.

UNIX. The oldest operating system currently available, originally developed for minicomputers, but now available for just about every computer made. UNIX is the programmer's operating system, cold and cryptic. If you're curious about UNIX, look into Linux instead (covered above).

I could probably rattle off about a dozen other operating systems that have come and gone over the years. Each one had its time and place, but now they're on the dustbin of history. (If you ever get into computer archeology, consider looking up the following antique operating systems: ProDOS, TRS-DOS, LDOS, DR DOS, QDOS, OS/9, Xenix, GEOS, and the list goes on.)

Chapter 15

Everything You Wanted to Know about Software (But Were Afraid to Ask)

• •

In This Chapter

▶ Understanding software

▶ Word-processing programs

▶ Desktop publishing

▶ Spreadsheet software

▶ Database applications

▶ Graphics programs

▶ All about bundled software

▶ Communications and the Internet

▶ Games and learning software

▶ Utility programs

▶ Writing your own programs

▶ Free and almost free software

• •

*Y*our computer needs software like an orchestra needs a conductor, like a car needs a driver, like an actor needs a script — you get the idea. Whatever it is that a computer does, it does it because of software. And you can choose from a great deal of software out there.

The information in this chapter properly describes the more popular categories of software and what each one does. Odds are good that you'll pick one or more of the following types of software, depending on your needs, likes, and whims.

Word Processors

The most popular type of application on any computer is the word processor, as shown in Figure 15-1. As an office tool, the computer first replaced the typewriter. Word processors have come a long way, of course, from being just a better typewriter. Modern word processors can correct grammar and spelling as you type, plus they allow you to include pictures and format your text in various and sundry ways.

At one time, several "levels" of word processor existed: one for beginners, one for writers, one for lawyers, and so on. However, most of the major programs have combined all these tools from the different levels; you pay for them whether you need them or not. That situation makes word processors full featured yet expensive.

✔ Most computer operating systems come with a basic word processor or text editor.

✔ The most popular word processor is Microsoft Word. It's one big program to chew, so make sure that you buy a copy of *Word 2000 For Windows For Dummies,* written by yours truly (and published by IDG Books Worldwide, Inc.) or whichever book is appropriate for the version you use.

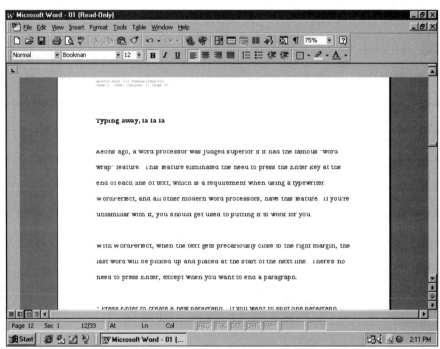

Figure 15-1:
A word
processor.

- ✔ Both PC and Mac versions of Word are available.

- ✔ The second most popular word processor is WordPerfect. As with Word, there are versions of WordPerfect for both the Mac and PC.

- ✔ On the Macintosh, AppleWorks contains a word processor that many Mac users find more than adequate.

- ✔ The original, arcane word processor for all personal computers was called WordStar.

- ✔ If you're into writing plays or movies, some special word-processing software has been developed especially for you. This type of software is advertised in the back of both movie and computer magazines.

Desktop Publishing

An offshoot of word processing is *desktop publishing,* in which you combine words and pictures and create a "layout" of your finished page — for example, to create a pamphlet, a church bulletin, or even a novel (see Figure 15-2).

Many word processors incorporate desktop publishing features as part of their design. You can mix different type styles on the screen so that you can see in advance exactly what will be printed. This style of word processor is called *WYSIWYG* ("wizzy wig"), which stands for What You See Is What You Get. You can even add graphics to your text to spice things up.

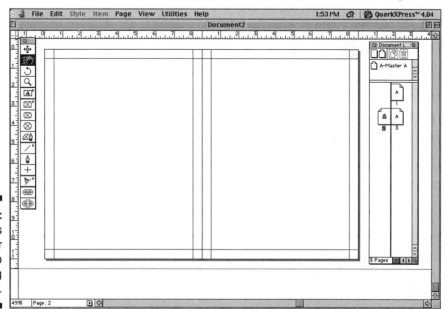

Figure 15-2:
QuarkXPress
is a popular
desktop
publishing
package.

For desktop publishing in particular, you usually need separate word-processing and graphics software. Make sure that the desktop publishing package is compatible with your word-processing and graphics software.

- ✔ Desktop publishing is abbreviated DTP.

- ✔ The most popular desktop publishing programs are QuarkXPress and PageMaker. Unfortunately, they're also the most expensive and difficult to learn. ("Professional" software usually is.)

- ✔ More common (and easier-to-learn) DTP programs include Microsoft Publisher, Print Shop, and Adobe's InDesign.

- ✔ Although some word processors approach desktop publishing in their sophistication, buying a separate desktop publishing application is always a better idea (the right tool for the right job, and all that).

Spreadsheets

The second thing the computer replaced in the office was the adding machine, or calculator. To work with numbers, you use spreadsheet software. It enables you to plug numbers into a grid, with each "cell" in the grid calculated by using values from other cells. Using a spreadsheet, you can manipulate, examine, and change numeric values and their relationships to other values, but it's really not that boring.

Used primarily for business applications, spreadsheets enable you to design an electronic balance sheet or general ledger for your company. You can also manipulate various figures and instantly see how other figures are affected. You can see, for example, how it's possible to embezzle funds without anyone noticing!

- ✔ Spreadsheets are not just for numbers. They can produce graphs, charts, and organizational charts; and spreadsheets work with any type of lists (see Figure 15-3). If your information appears in any type of grid, working with it in a spreadsheet is a breeze.

- ✔ The most popular spreadsheet program for the PC is Microsoft Excel, and Excel is also available on the Mac.

- ✔ AppleWorks is another popular spreadsheet program for the Macintosh.

- ✔ The most popular program used to be Lotus 1-2-3 (Lotus was the name of the company, and 1-2-3 was the name of the program). It's still around, though Microsoft Excel is more common.

- ✔ The original, prototype spreadsheet was called VisiCalc. It stood for *visi*ble *calc*ulator. You may find a copy in a computer museum near you.

Home-budgeting software

Although spreadsheets are fine for home use, what you probably need is some type of home budgeting software. These programs can do more than just balance your checkbook or print your checks (with the proper check-like paper). They can track investments and loans and even make forecasts.

Several popular home-budgeting and checking packages are available, and you can quickly figure out how to use any of them. The most popular are Quicken (both Mac and PC) and Microsoft Money (PC only).

Be careful when you're ordering computer-printed checks for your home-budgeting software: You don't have to order them from the company that makes the software. Inquire at your bank to see whether it offers computer-printed checks. They're often cheaper than the ones the software company offers.

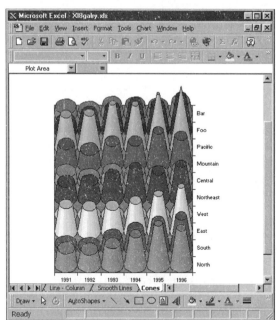

Figure 15-3: A spread-sheet in action.

Databases

A *database* program is used to manipulate information, such as a listing of your record collection or a tally of unruly employees. The database software stores the information and then helps you sort it, sift it, print it, retrieve it, or mangle it in any number of interesting ways.

You may not believe it, but more database programs are out there than anything else — even word processors. The major packages are more like programming languages: They let you create your own database and write a teeny program that somehow controls it. These programs are for diehards.

If you're looking for a home database or you want something easier than the programming language database, consider a customized database program. For example, you may find an address program for keeping track of your friends and contacts that can also print mailing labels.

Another popular example is personal organizer software, which includes an address list, appointment calendar, and other goodies. These programs vary from simple phone lists to advanced tickler systems that keep details about customers or vendors or overseas secret agents.

- ✔ Tons of popular databases are out there, although Microsoft Access is the most common — not because it's the best, but because Access is included with the popular Microsoft Office program.

- ✔ The original database program for personal computers was called Vulcan — after Mr. Spock, from *Star Trek!* It was later renamed dBASE (short for database), which was for years the most popular PC database program.

Graphics

Graphics software falls into two categories: drawing and painting programs. These programs enable you to create and manipulate a graphical image on the screen. Each one uses a different technique to create the image.

Drawing programs (also known as *CAD,* or *computer-assisted design* programs) are much more precise than painting programs. CAD deals with "objects" rather than dots on the screen.

Painting programs are more recreational and not as accurate as CAD. They enable you to paint more realistic images, as shown in Figure 15-4. Drawing programs, on the other hand, are more technical in nature, just as a blueprint is more technical than a painting of the eventual structure.

- ✔ If you're an engineer or architect, you probably will spend some serious bucks for a decent graphics system. The advantage of these systems is that changing a design is easy because the thing is stored in a computer.

- ✔ Almost every aspect of graphic arts is now done by using a computer. Most of the best stuff is available on the Macintosh, with some applications also available on Windows.

✔ The most popular CAD program is AutoCAD. It's very, *very* expensive and requires special computer hardware to make it work.

✔ A popular drawing program is CorelDraw for Windows. For the Mac crowd, it's Adobe Illustrator.

✔ A popular painting program is called Painter. It comes in a paint can rather than in a box! I've seen some artists do absolutely amazing things with it.

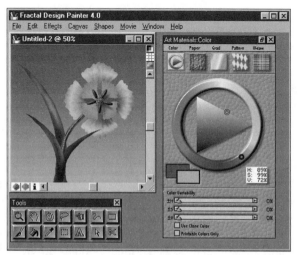

Figure 15-4:
A painting
program.

Bundled Software Packages

Chances are that you'll probably need a buncha software when you first start out computing. This fact surprised me when I first bought a computer, in 1982. I took it home and turned it on only to find that it didn't really do anything, so I drove back to the store and bought some software. I hope that you don't make the same mistake.

Because software developers know that you will buy a stack of stuff to get started, they've created special bundled software packages. These packages come in several different types and flavors, each designed to get you started with just what you need.

At home with the office

A popular tactic of major software vendors is to distribute the "office" integrated package of software. For example, Microsoft Office and WordPerfect Office (which includes WordPerfect) are two popular packages you can find.

These office packages include a real word processor, database, and spreadsheet. They aren't cheapie versions either; the companies just combine all their top-selling stuff and sell it for a lower price in a bundle.

Buying your software bundled in an office package has many advantages, and low cost is the most obvious. Buying one office package is often cheaper than buying everything a piece at a time. Even if you use only two of the applications in the office package, you come out ahead.

The disadvantage to integrated software is that some of it isn't integrated. For example, the package may consist of two or three unrelated programs that can't share information between them.

Another major disadvantage lies in upgrading the software. After six months to a year, most software developers produce a newer, better version of their programs. The cost of upgrading each one, especially when you have an "office," can be outrageous. Refer to Chapter 21 for more information about upgrading and how to deal with it.

- ✔ For the PC, Microsoft Office is the most popular office program, followed by WordPerfect Office.

- ✔ Microsoft Works is a popular alternative to Microsoft Office for the PC. It contains many useful programs, many of which are easier to use and learn than the full-on Microsoft Office products.

- ✔ For the Macintosh, AppleWorks is the most popular program, followed by Microsoft Office. Many iMacs come with AppleWorks as part of the computer purchase.

Bundled software

Another type of bundled software is stuff that comes with the computer "for free," especially with laptops. I haven't bought a laptop in the past six years that didn't come with megabytes of crap I really didn't want or need. Some of the stuff is useful, of course, but what's the point of it's being "for free" if you have to uninstall it?

If possible, remember to ask which types of programs come bundled with a computer when you buy it. In a common practice among many of the major computer makers, they offer a variety of "for free" packages, from business to home to entertainment.

In addition to seeing what's available, ask whether you can easily remove any of the add-ons. For example, does the program that lets you use your modem to hail a taxi from any phone booth in Manhattan come with an "uninstall" program? (I have no idea why anyone would ever need that type of program anyway.)

✔ Obviously, bundled software isn't a bonus if you don't plan to use it.

✔ If you don't need any bundled software, see whether the dealer can knock some money off the purchase price. (A discount rarely happens, because a dealer generally pays up front for the bundled stuff.)

Communications and Internet Software

Communications software enables your computer to take advantage of a modem and the phone system to talk with other computers. It does so in two ways: through the Internet or by directly phoning up another computer with a modem.

Doing the Internet

The Internet can be informative, fun, and a tremendous waste of time. Take your pick. The computer industry is now all a-spaz about the Internet. Personally, I could take it or leave it. Why not see for yourself, though? To do that, you need software to access the Internet.

To use the Internet on a basic level, you need two pieces of software:

✔ A Web browser

✔ An e-mail program

Both the Mac OS and Windows come with a Web browser and an e-mail program, so you never really have to buy anything (though options are available if you care to find something more suited to your needs).

In addition to the basics, you might also need a news reader, chat client, telnet, FTP, and other random programs, each of which serves a specific function for accessing some remote corner of the Internet. The good news is that all this stuff either comes with your computer or you can find it available freely on the Web.

✔ Your computer needs a modem in order to connect to the Internet (refer to Chapter 11).

✔ To connect to the Internet, you need a dialer program — the software that connects your computer (using a modem) to the Internet. Windows comes with one, as does the Mac operating system.

- ✔ For the PC, I recommend using Internet Explorer as it's so closely integrated with Windows that there really is no other option. (Thanks, Bill!) On the Mac, you can use either Internet Explorer or Netscape, both of which come with many Macintosh configurations right out of the box.

- ✔ There's much to do on the Internet, and it can be overwhelming. My advice is to find a good book about the subject if you want to dive in. (Get the book *after* you buy your computer.)

Doing AOL

Another popular way to access the Internet is America Online (AOL). A sign-up kit for AOL is shipped with just about every computer.

The advantage of AOL is that it's all over the place. Throw a cat into a crowd of people and you'll probably hit two or three AOL users. It seems just about everyone is on AOL. So why not join them?

On the downside, AOL's access to the Internet is indirect. You must first dial into AOL's computers, which then connect you to the Internet — and sometimes cannot connect you because they're busy. (And AOL is "busy" a lot.)

- ✔ If you sign up for AOL, go through the free trial and discover how much of AOL you use. Then, if you don't use it much, consider changing your billing plan so that you're only paying for the parts of AOL you use.

- ✔ AOL has some nifty features unavailable to regular Internet users, such as the Buddy List feature and AOL Instant Messenger software.

- ✔ On the other hand, accessing the Internet directly through an ISP is often cheaper and more reliable than AOL. It's up to you.

- ✔ Refer to Chapter 25 for more information on finding an ISP.

Recreation and Education

Though few admit it, computers can be used to play games. Oh, and don't forget education — although with a computer, a thin line exists between education and entertainment; both are rather fun.

Games

This whole personal computer craze really started with the home arcade games of the early 1980s. Although the arcade games are going strong, it's hard to compare those machines that only play games with a computer that plays games *and* does other things, like process words and browse the Internet.

Many different types of computer games are available: arcade-style, shoot-'em-ups; classics, such as Chess, Go, and Othello; adventure games; "little man" games à la Pac Man; and simulation games: flight simulators, war simulators, and business simulators. The creativity well never runs dry with computer games.

Education

If computers are magnets, then kids are tiny balls of steel. They love computers. They're bold. And there's a reason for that. Nope, it's not that kids today are smarter than we were. It's that kids have no fear. In fact, I recommend that you get your kids their own computer. Data loss means little to them.

Some great educational programs are out there, from stuff to teach toddlers their colors and numbers to encyclopedias and SAT exam simulators. Thankfully, much of what's out there is really good. Although some bad programs are out there, just ask around at a PTO meeting, and you'll quickly find out what's good and what stinks.

- ✔ Generally speaking, all the Microsoft reference titles tend to be very good.
- ✔ For small kids, I can recommend programs in the Jumpstart series. Also, my kids love the *Sesame Street* and *Dr. Seuss* programs. They're also nuts about the Nanosaur game that comes with the iMac.

Utility Programs

A special category of software is the *utility* program. These programs differ from applications in that they aren't used for productivity. A utility program doesn't do your work on the computer; it works on the computer itself. A utility program typically does one of three things: improve performance, diagnose a problem (see Figure 15-5), or repair something.

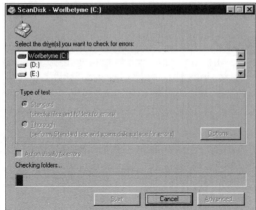

Figure 15-5:
The
ScanDisk
utility
checks your
hard drive.

Utilities come in bundles of several dozen programs. For example, one program may recover files you deleted, another may rescue a damaged hard drive, and another may optimize the way your PC uses memory. Other utility-like programs include calculators, appointment books, and little word processors (called *text editors*).

- Utilities are also referred to as *tools*.

- Your computer's operating system comes with a host of utilities for doing various computer chores.

- About the oldest and most venerated set of utility programs is the Norton Utilities.

- One of the best utilities to own is a virus scanner. This type of program ensures that your computer is not infected with a nasty program (a *virus*) that can really foul things up. The most popular antivirus program is made by McAfee.

- If you ever find yourself saying, "I wish I had just one little program that could. . . ." or "I keep repeating these same steps over and over. Can't the computer do that for me?" — you need a utility. Chances are that something is available which does that specific job. If not, you can write your own computer program, as covered in the next section.

Programming

Programming languages enable you to write and run your own computer software. Check out the instructions in Figure 15-6. Many programming languages are available, some easy to get a grasp on and some hard. You don't have to be good at math to understand a programming language. Just having a healthy curiosity about computers helps.

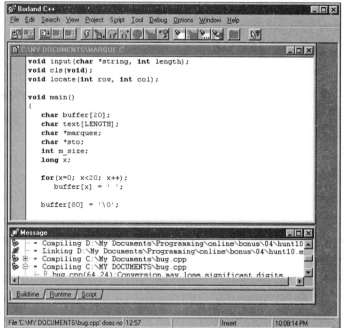

```
void input(char *string, int length);
void cls(void);
void locate(int row, int col);

void main()
{
    char buffer[20];
    char text[LENGTH];
    char *marquee;
    char *sto;
    int m_size;
    long x;

    for(x=0; x<20; x++);
        buffer[x] = ' ';

    buffer[80] = '\0';
```

```
Message
- Compiling D:\My Documents\Programming\online\bonus\04\hunt10
- Linking D:\My Documents\Programming\online\bonus\04\hunt10.e
- Compiling C:\My Documents\bug.cpp
- Compiling C:\MY DOCUMENTS\bug.cpp
  bug cpp(64 24) Conversion may lose significant digits
```

Figure 15-6:
A C pro-
gramming
language
package.

Nowadays, no one using a computer has to know how to program the thing. In the olden days, that's all you could do with one. Fortunately, however, enough people who do program the things have created all the other types of programs covered in this chapter. Still, if you're curious or you just want to have ultimate control over the thing, you can program.

✔ Don't be fooled: It takes a long time to write a program, even a simple one. Still, you can do it. No one will stop you. It's one of the more charming things about a computer.

✔ To program, you must know a programming language, which is a dialogue you use to tell a computer to do certain things.

✔ The most popular programming language is C++. Unfortunately, it's not the easiest to start using.

✔ Two popular versions of the C/C++ language are available, one from Borland and the other from Microsoft. I prefer the Borland stuff.

✔ The easiest programming language to use is BASIC. The most popular version is Microsoft Visual Basic. In a way, it lets you create a Windows program as easily as cut-and-paste.

✔ Other languages are available, each with its own army of followers and individual charms and detractions.

Software for Nothing and Almost Free

Believe it or not, not all software costs money. A good number of programs, in fact, are available for free or almost free. Some software may come "free" with your computer; some may be available from nice people who write software and give it away because they're eccentric geniuses and expect their rewards in the hereafter.

Please keep in mind that, though software is available for nothing or next to nothing, not all software is free. Don't accept any software that you can buy from a store as a freebie from a well-meaning friend. This practice constitutes theft. Only if the software states that it's free (or it's a "demo") can you legally use it without paying.

✔ You can find these free and almost free software programs all over the place. Computer stores sometimes have bins full of disks of free stuff (though you pay for the disk it's copied on).

✔ The most popular place to pick up free software? The Internet.

✔ These freebie programs are often a source of computer viruses. It's not that all free stuff is tainted; however, a few unscrupulous individuals pass off supposedly free software that is in fact plagued with a virus. The best way to be sure is to get your free stuff from a reputable source or buy a virus-scanning utility.

Public domain software

Software that costs nothing is known as *public-domain* software. These software packages are written by little men in small rooms who stay up all night and think philanthropic thoughts. They program their brains out and then give away the software. Not all the programs are junk, either; some really nice applications occasionally rise up from the swamp.

✔ Public-domain software says so, either in the program or in the documentation. Never assume that something is public domain just because someone else tells you that it is.

✔ Do not sell public-domain software or buy it from anyone. It's free!

Freeware

Freeware is the term used for software that has no cost and is not in the public domain. The primary difference is ownership. Because public-domain software has no owner, anyone could, theoretically, modify it and resell it. With freeware, the author gives the stuff away but may, at some later point, decide to sell it instead.

- ✔ An example of freeware is Linux. The program is given away freely. (What you pay for is a Linux distribution, not Linux itself — a weird concept a lawyer might be able to explain to you.)
- ✔ Quite a hefty amount of Palm OS software is freeware, including the addicting Hearts game.

Shareware

A popular form of free software is referred to as *shareware*. It's distributed for free, just like public-domain software and freeware. The exception is that if you use and enjoy the program, the author requests that you contribute a donation.

- ✔ I've used many shareware programs and pay for those I continue to use.
- ✔ The fee for buying shareware is really cheap, often $10 or less.
- ✔ Unlike real software, which you cannot give away, shareware authors encourage you to give their programs away.

Demo software

Another category of free software is the *demo* program. These programs are special versions of major applications you can try before you buy. Sometimes, they're the real thing and lack only a few features. Other times, the demo software "self-destructs" after a few weeks (the demo is over).

Chapter 16

Shopping for Software

. . . .

In This Chapter

▶ Test-driving software

▶ Looking for help

▶ Checking for developer support

▶ Reading the software box

▶ Filling in the software worksheet

. . . .

*S*ee computer. See computer go. Go, computer go! And how does the computer go? Software!

The second step in buying a computer — any computer — is to shop for software. After all, it's the *software* that does the work for you. Even though a computer's technical specs may look great on paper, or the advertising promises the latest and greatest hardware, that means nothing without the software to drive it. Gotta have that software! This chapter tells you how to find stuff that works with you and gets your job done.

How to Buy Software

Before heading off to the Mr. Software store, you should know what it is that you're about to do. I don't want you to walk around and pick up various software boxes because they're pretty or look impressively hefty. No, you need a plan of attack. Here 'tis:

✔ Take a test-drive

✔ Check for support

✔ Obtain product information

✔ Fill in this book's software worksheet

Before you buy anything, you have to take a test-drive — that is, use the software before you buy it. Then you see what kind of support a developer provides for its software. After that, look on the side of the software box, and jot down that information on your software worksheets — the worksheets that help you pick out the hardware to run your software.

The sections that follow outline each of the steps in your software plan of attack.

- ✔ Don't buy anything just yet! You're shopping, not buying.

- ✔ A fad among software developers in the late 1980s involved making software boxes *very large*. For a time, the large boxes were full of manuals and disks and stuff you needed. Then, they started putting the manual *on* the disk electronically — but kept the box the same size! They sold a lot of air in those days. . . .

- ✔ Another trivial point: All software boxes are a certain size because that's the size that looks good on the shelf at the software store. The box isn't designed to hold the disks and manuals!

- ✔ I have a theory that developers make their software packages large so as to literally push the competition off the shelves!

- ✔ More pointless trivia: For a while, the product name on the software box appeared one-third of the way from the top. The reason was that the shelves at Egghead Software were tilted in such a way that you couldn't see the top third of the box. (Even today, the name appears on the lower-half of the software box.)

Taking a test-drive

Buying software is a matter of taste. Like discovering new food, you should sit down at a computer and try out any software you plan to buy. Any store that sells software should let you do so. All you have to do is ask, "Can I try out the Mobius Spreadsheet?" As a buyer, you're entitled to take a test-drive.

What should you look for? Look for things you like. If the program is a word processor, how easy is it for you to start typing? Do the various things on the screen look obvious to you? Is it cryptic? Does it feel slow or awkward? Make a note of these things, and, if the word processor isn't to your liking, try another. You should apply this technique to all the software you test-drive.

- ✔ Most decent computer stores have machines set up on which you can test-drive the software. Some of the large office-type stores may not let you do that, however.

- ✔ Don't feel guilty about asking to test-drive! If the stores have computers available for it, then they should let you. Otherwise, go somewhere else.

✔ Please, please don't have a salesperson demo the software; they're often too familiar with it to do you any good. It's up to you to fiddle with it.

✔ When you find something you like, fill out a software worksheet for it (see the sample worksheet at the end of this chapter).

Other sources for test-driving

Not everyone lives near the dream Software-o-Rama that carries everything and lets you test-drive *and* has truly knowledgeable and trustworthy employees. If you're not so lucky, you can consider some other test-driving sources:

Your guru: Having a computer-knowledgeable friend can be a boost to picking out some good software. Let your friend show you some of his or her favorite software packages. That's how I got started, a dozen or so years ago; I basically used everything my "computer guru" was using on his computer. Although it wasn't what I ended up with, it was a good start.

Computer groups: Most areas have coffee groups that meet to discuss computers and hear guest speakers. These groups are listed in the newspaper or local computer circulars. Stop by and visit one to find out what people use and what their opinions are.

Magazines: Computer magazines offer reviews of major software brands all the time. You may have to pick up a few to get an idea of what you need or order back issues.

Buy what's popular: Another tactic some people use is to look at what's popular. If you live out in the boonies (like I do), call up a mail-order place and ask what sells best (for example, "What's the best-selling database for a philatelist like me?"). Then have the person you're talking to read the requirements from the side of the box for you. That person may also be able to fax you information, if you have access to a fax machine.

Check the Internet. If you're already blessed with a computer, you can surf the net, visiting both software stores and the manufacturer's own home page for information.

Use school or the office: An easy way to instantly decide which software is best for you is to go with what you know. If you use WordPerfect at work, why not buy it for home? Likewise, find out what kind of software you child uses in school and buy that to use at home.

Please make sure that you don't "borrow" software from work or school. Though it seems an easy and effortless thing to do, it's really theft. Always buy every software package you use or own unless it states right up front that it's free or in the public domain.

How Helpful Is It?

Most software developers have given up on "user-friendly." Thank goodness. Whenever a developer tries to make something user-friendly, it usually winds up being inane or boring. Rather than look for software that's friendly, you should examine the various ways the developer has to offer you help.

You should find two kinds of help in any software package you plan to buy: help in the form of online help (while the program is running) and help from the software developer in the form of phone support.

- ✔ User-friendly software never works, because the programmer and development staff are way too intimate with the product to understand the needs of someone new. It all makes sense to them, after all!

- ✔ Whenever the computer industry attempts to make something user-friendly, it usually winds up making something dopey or stupid.

- ✔ If you can't get help using your software, you probably bought the wrong thing in the first place (which is what this chapter tries to prevent).

- ✔ Because many places don't let you return computer software after you open it, make sure that you're buying the right thing in the first place.

Types of help you find in software

Programs that are nice enough to offer help come in two varieties: online help and contextual help.

Online help. Wherever you are in the program, you can press a special key and see a list of commands or a copy of the manual. This technique is good for looking up topics or seeing how things are done. (Online help is different from help on the Internet; see below.)

Contextual help. It's the same kind of help as online help, except that the helpful information you see pertains to whatever you're doing in the program. If you're about to print, for example, the helpful information is about printing. If you're about to save something to a disk, the helpful information is about saving.

Tutorial help. When you pay a bit more for a program, it usually comes with a manual for reference and a tutorial for learning. This is always a good thing. The tutorial trains you in the program step-by-step. Even if it's poorly written, you'll find that doing the exercises is the best way to become familiar with the program. (Consider getting a good book on the product if the tutorial really reeks.)

Ah! The stinking manual!

Nothing is more delightful than poking fun at the traditional computer manual. They were bad! They were confusing! They were next to useless!

I'm happy to tell you that computer manuals are better now than they've ever been. Why? Because they're no longer included with the software! That's right — to save weight and production costs, few developers bother with manuals anymore. That's good and bad news.

The good news is that you no longer have to fiddle with a manual. The bad news is that the same manual you no longer have to fiddle with is now on the same disk the product came with. If you can't get the product to work, however, you can't access the manual on disk. It must be a mixed blessing.

Fortunately, whether the manual is put on paper or on a disk, you have a decent alternative: Buy a good computer book instead.

Internet help. Help can also be obtained from the Internet. The company may have an e-mail address you can use or offer support on a Web page (look for the "FAQ," Frequently Asked Questions). Online forums in the newsgroups can also be found to get help from regular schmos who use the program.

Don't forget support!

Some software manufacturers offer telephone support for when you really get stuck. With phone support, you can call up the company and directly ask questions about the software. Strange but true. In fact, one of the reasons WordPerfect shot to the top of the charts in the late 1980s was because of its toll-free phone support.

Not all software phone support is created equal. It comes in what I call the four flavors: vanilla, chocolate, carob, and fudge. These are my flavors, by the way — not an industry standard (well, maybe in the ice cream industry).

Vanilla: With this type of phone support, you pay not only for the phone call but also for the support. When the software developer answers the phone, you're usually greeted with, "Hi! What's your credit card number?" These software houses charge you per call (often per minute) just so that you can ask questions about their product. For mission-critical packages such as Server software, however, this price may be agreeable.

Chocolate: With this type of support, which is better than the vanilla type, you pay only for the phone call. After you get connected, you simply wait on hold until someone happens by to answer your question. The *answer* is free; it's just that most of these places tend to involve long-distance calls.

Carob: This type of support is like chocolate, but not as good. It starts out like chocolate: You get free support but must pay for the phone call. After 90 days (or so), you pay for everything — the phone call *and* the support. (I call it carob because it's like chocolate, but not really as good.)

Fudge: Fudge phone support is the best. With this kind of support, you get an 800 number to call — a free phone call for free support. The only drawback is that these numbers are busy — all the time.

Tangential to this type of support is support on the Internet. For the cost of an e-mail message (next to nothing), you can write to the company and complain away. I can't properly rate this support, though. In some cases, the questions were answered immediately and properly. In other cases, the questions were outright ignored. Until this evens out, rate software on its phone support as described above.

- ✔ Take note of the kind of support offered by the developer of the software you've chosen. If the type of support isn't listed on the box, ask a salesperson what type of support is available.

- ✔ The computer industry is geared toward selling hundreds of software packages at a time to major corporations and big business. Its support polices are designed mostly to please those big customers. People like you and me (and small businesses), who are intrepid enough to buy our own computer, are often left out in the cold.

- ✔ I find it interesting that WordPerfect started its slide from dominance just about the same time the suits cut back on the free support. You think the computer industry would learn from this, but no.

After You Find What You Want . . .

When you feel that you've found a software package that will get your work done much easier, don't buy it! Instead, make a note of it. Fill out a form similar to the one shown at the end of this chapter. Describe the software you've found to get the job done.

- ✔ Fill in forms for *all* the software you're interested in, even stuff you might plan on buying later. Just go nuts! The reasons for this will become obvious in the next chapter.

- ✔ After you've found your software, wait. Buying time isn't here yet. Your next step is to find the hardware to match the software you've selected. For now, keep your software worksheets handy.

✔ Write down information about *all* the software packages you're interested in. If you can't decide between two packages, fill out a worksheet for both. You can decide which one you want to buy later, when you buy a computer.

Stuff you find on the software box

Software comes in a box. Inside the box are the disks, the infamous manual (or the manual may be on the disk), and other goodies, such as registration cards, keyboard templates, bumper stickers, buttons, and more sheets of paper than you ever find in a Publisher's Clearing House giveaway.

On the side of the box are the software program's "nutritional requirements." You should find a list of the equipment the software requires. You typically find one or more of these informational tidbits:

✔ Which computer or operating system is required. If it's an operating system, then a version number may be listed.

✔ Which microprocessor is required.

✔ How much memory (RAM) it needs.

✔ How much hard drive space it needs.

✔ Which type of graphics is required (graphics memory, 3-D support, resolution, and so on).

✔ Whether it has any special hardware requirements (mouse or joystick, for example).

✔ Whether any sound equipment or multimedia support is offered.

✔ Other, preferred hardware.

✔ Which kind of support is offered.

You may see even more information about even more confusing issues. Don't let that boggle you now! (If you need to, review Part II of this book to reacquaint yourself with computer hardware.)

✔ Information on the side of the software package tells you which type of computer runs the software best. If you eventually buy computer hardware that matches or exceeds those requirements, you're doing just great.

✔ Never buy any software without first reading its box! I'm serious. Even a pro (well, myself!) should read the box before buying. I've had to return a few software packages because they were for the wrong computer or incompatible with my equipment. Reading the box would have saved me — uh, I mean "those people" — some time.

Things to look out for in software descriptions

Before getting all excited, you should bear in mind a few warnings when you're reading the information on the side of a software box.

If the word *recommended* is used, beware! The box may say, for example, that it requires 3MB (megabytes) of RAM and that 10MB are recommended. This recommendation usually means that you *need* 10MB, or else the product won't perform to expectations.

Beware of the "upgrade" version. Sometimes software is sold as an *upgrade*, which means that its manufacturer assumes that you have the old or original version already on your computer. If you don't, the upgrade may not install properly, and you'll be out of luck and money. (Because upgrade versions are generally cheaper, don't think that you've found a bargain or are saving money by getting one when you don't have the original version already.)

Filling in the form: Example 1

Figure 16-1 shows the information on the side of a software box, just like you find in a store. It's from a program called Adobe Acrobat, which is a file-sharing utility.

Figure 16-1:
Software requirements on the side of the box.

System Requirements

- Power Macintosh

- Apple System Software version 7.5.3 or later

- 6MB of RAM
  (12MB recommended)

- 60MB of available hard disk space

- CD-ROM drive

Assume that the product costs $270. Also, after asking a salesperson, suppose that you find out that the manufacturer offers chocolate support. In addition to that information, here is a distillation of what the software tells you about itself:

- ✔ You need a Power Macintosh, which is really any Macintosh with a G3 or G4 microprocessor.

- ✔ You need Apple System Software (Mac OS) version 7.5.3 or a later version.

- ✔ You need 12MB of RAM. I know, 6MB is claimed, but 12MB is recommended, so you go with that value.

- ✔ You need 60MB of available hard disk space, which is quite a chunk, actually.

- ✔ The computer needs a CD-ROM drive. Obviously, the software comes on a CD.

You would fill in the software worksheet according to the information specified in this list. If you don't know how to fill in one of the items, leave it blank (or ask a salesperson for more information). Figure 16-2 shows how you would fill out the worksheet.

- ✔ Adobe Acrobat is a publishing utility, which lets you save any document to a special format that can be read by any computer.

- ✔ Generally, if some information isn't listed, it's probably not crucial to the operation of the software. Don't worry about it.

- ✔ Note that this product, Adobe Acrobat, is a Macintosh product, running on the Mac OS ("System Software"). There is, doubtless, a PC version available as well. If you're undecided between PC and Mac, take down information for *both* versions — including price.

Filling in the form: Example 2

Microsoft is anything but brief. Its description for the requirement to run Microsoft Office 2000 isn't exactly an example of brevity, as shown in Figure 16-3. What's there can be deciphered, though. Assume that this package costs $600 and that Microsoft is famous for its carob level of support:

- ✔ You need a Pentium running at 75MHz or higher, though a 166MHz Pentium is recommended.

- ✔ You need either Windows 95 (or later) or the Windows NT Workstation Version 4.0.

✔ How much RAM is enough? Gads, it's hard to tell! It says 16MB for Windows 95/98 *plus* 4MB each for the programs you run (8MB in some cases, 16MB in one case). Adding all that up on the box gives you:

$(8MB \times 3) + 16MB + (4MB \times 5) =$

$24MB + 16MB + 20MB =$

60MB + 16MB for Windows, which equals 76MB RAM total. Whew!

(For Windows NT it's 92MB of RAM total.)

✔ Disk space? Three values are listed for various "disks" (which are the CD-ROM disks included with the package). When in doubt, add them up: 252MB plus 174MB plus 100MB plus another 100MB is 626MB of hard disk space. That's the value you want (even if you don't plan on using everything). Sneaky wording, huh? Microsoft is sensitive about their products hogging up too much disk space.

✔ You need a CD-ROM drive.

✔ You need Super VGA or better graphics. Most PCs are sold with this, so you should be okay. (You cannot run Windows without that level of graphics.)

✔ A mouse is also required, which is required for Windows so it's not really worth mentioning.

Software Worksheet

Category: Office   Word processing   Spreadsheet
Recreation   Database   Graphics
(Utility)   Communications   Internet
Education   Programming   Personal finance
Multimedia   Reference   Productivity

Product name: **Adobe Acrobat**

Developer: **Adobe**

Price: **$270**

Type of support: Vanilla   (Chocolate)   Carob   Fudge

Operating system: Windows 98   Windows NT   Version: **7.5.3**
Windows 95   (Mac)   OS/2
Windows 3.1   DOS   Other: _____

Microprocessor: 486/better   Pentium MMXG3/G4   Pentium: _____
Speed:_____ MHz

Memory needed: ____**12**____ Megabytes

Hard disk storage: ____**60**____ Megabytes

CD-ROM: (Yes)   No   ?

Graphics: SVGA   No special requirements   Other: **Color monitor**
Graphics memory: _____ Megabytes

Sound: SoundBlaster   AdLib   (None)   Other: _____

Special printer: (Nope)   Recommended:_____

Special peripherals: Scanner   Modem   Microphone
MIDI   Joystick   Special mouse: _____

Other stuff: _____

Figure 16-2:
A filled-out
software
worksheet.

To use Microsoft Office 2000 Premium you need:

- PC with Pentium 75 MHz or higher processor; Pentium 166 or higher required by Microsoft PhotoDraw
- Microsoft Windows 95 or later operating system, or Microsoft Windows NT® Workstation operating system version 4.0 or later
- For Windows 95 or Windows 98:
  –16MB of RAM for the operating system, plus an additional 4MB of RAM for each application running simultaneously (8MB for Outlook, Access, or FrontPage; 16MB for PhotoDraw).
- For Windows NT Workstation version 4.0 or later:
  – 32MB of RAM for the operating system, plus an additional 4MB of RAM for each application running simultaneously (8MB for Outlook, Access, or FrontPage; 16MB for PhotoDraw).
- Available hard-disk space (Numbers indicate typical installation; your hard-disk usage will vary depending on configuration. Choices made during custom installation may require more or less hard-disk space):
  – 252MB for Disc 1 (Word, Excel, Outlook, PowerPoint, Access, FrontPage)
  – 174MB for Disc 2 (Publisher, Small Business Tolls)
  –100MB for Disc 3 (PhotoDraw); for optimal performance, we recommend an additional 100MB of free hard-disk space for user graphics and temporary image caches
- CD-ROM drive
- VGA or higher-resolution monitor; Super VGA recommended
- Microsoft mouse, Microsoft IntelliMouse, or compatible pointing device

Figure 16-3:
Software requirements (really!).

Figure 16-4 shows how the software worksheet could be filled in for Microsoft Office 2000.

Software Worksheet

Category: (Office) Word processing Spreadsheet
Recreation Database Graphics
Utility Communications Internet
Education Programming Personal finance
Multimedia Reference Productivity

Product name: Microsoft Office 2000

Developer: Microsoft

Price: $600

Type of support: Vanilla Chocolate (Carob) Fudge

Operating system: (Windows 98) (Windows NT) Version: 4.0
(Windows 95) Mac OS/2
Windows 3.1 DOS Other: _____

Microprocessor: 486/better Pentium MMX Pentium_____
Speed: 166 MHz G3/G4:

Memory needed: ___32___ Megabytes

Hard disk storage: _250-626_ Megabytes

CD-ROM: (Yes) No

Graphics: (SVGA) No special requirements Other: 256 colors
Graphics memory: _____ Megabytes

Sound: SoundBlaster AdLib (None) Other: _____

Special printer: (Nope) Recommended:_____

Special peripherals: Scanner Modem Microphone
MIDI Joystick (Special mouse: IntelliMouse)

Other stuff: _____

Figure 16-4:
A software
worksheet
for Office
2000.

✔ The RAM total for Microsoft Office, as calculated above according to the box, is a *maximum* figure. Yet that's the value you want. The idea is to calculate the *maximum* amount of RAM required by the program in a worst-cast scenario.

✔ As a user of Microsoft Office 2000, I can assure you that it all works just fine on a PC with 64MB of RAM total. (Of course, if I were to try to run *all* the programs at once — the worst-cast scenario — I might have problems.)

At last: The software worksheet

Figure 16-5 shows the software worksheet before it has been filled out. You should use a sheet like this one when you software shop. You can even customize it, adding special items you find along the way. The idea is to document as much information as you can from a software box.

Fill out the sheets as you software shop. Look for stuff you like, stuff you need now and stuff you're thinking about for later. Then get ready to move on to the next step in the buying process.

Software Worksheet

Category: Office   Word processing   Spreadsheet
Recreation   Database   Graphics
Utility   Communications   Internet
Education   Programming   Personal finance
Multimedia   Reference   Productivity

Product name: _____

Developer: _____

Price: _____

Type of support: Vanilla   Chocolate   Carob   Fudge

Operating system: Windows 98   Windows NT   Version: _____
Windows 95   Mac   OS/2
Windows 3.1   DOS   Other: _____

Microprocessor: 486/better   Pentium MMX   Pentium_____

Speed:_____ MHz   G3/G4:

Memory needed: _____ Megabytes

Hard disk storage: _____ Megabytes

CD-ROM: Yes   No

Graphics: SVGA   No special requirements   Other: _____

Graphics memory: _____ Megabytes

Sound: SoundBlaster   AdLib   None   Other: _____

Special printer: Nope   Recommended:_____

Special peripherals: Scanner   Modem   Microphone
MIDI   Joystick   Special mouse: _____

Other stuff: _____

Part III
Finding Your Perfect Computer

The 5th Wave   By Rich Tennant

It happens at every Windows show – group air-mousing.

In this part . . .

*I*f buying groceries were as complex as buying a computer, we'd all starve. Food is easy to buy in a store, probably because you enjoy eating. I'll even bet that the first caveperson to eat an avocado wasn't thinking about whether it was a fruit or vegetable, or how much fat was in it or which vitamins it supplied or what other kinds of food would go well with it. Nope, he was thinking, "Big pit."

This part of the book continues with the five-step process of buying a computer. The next several chapters continue with Steps 2–5: the task of hunting for software, finding hardware, searching for service and support and finally buying the computer. The idea here is to remove the complexity and make computer buying as easy as grocery shopping.

Oh, and an avocado is a fruit. So is a tomato. (But for political reasons, the United States Government legally declared that a tomato is a vegetable. Go figure.)

Chapter 17

Matching Hardware to Your Software

*O*nly after discovering which software you need do you even think about looking for computer hardware. And even then, you're not buying anything — you're still just shopping. The idea is to match up the hardware requirements of the software (which does the work) to the hardware. That way you're assured that your software will do the job and that you won't be returning to the store for an upgrade before the computer is two weeks old.

This chapter covers the *...For Dummies* computer-buying hardware worksheet. Filling that in is the third step toward buying a computer.

> ✔ Buying the computer is still two steps away, so don't get ahead of yourself!
>
> ✔ Please continue to avoid brand names and part numbers at this stage.
>
> ✔ If you have not yet worked through Chapter 16, consider reviewing it to learn the information-gathering stage for your future computer's software.

The For Dummies Hardware Worksheet

Your software will get the job done for you, but only if you find the hardware horsepower to make the software happy. Welcome to the second-biggest mistake people make when they're buying a computer: not getting enough hardware. Fortunately, that mistake won't happen to you.

Figure 17-1 shows the hardware worksheet. When you fill out this worksheet properly, it tells you exactly which type of computer you need. It doesn't tell you a brand name, and it doesn't recommend a store. That stuff comes later.

Hardware Worksheet

Operating system:	Windows 98 Windows NT/2000
	OS/2 Mac Other: _____
Microprocessor:	Pentium: _____ G3/G4 Speed: _____ MHz
Memory:	_____ Megabytes
Hard drive storage:	_____ Gigabytes
SCSI:	Yes No
Floppy drive(s):	Drive A 3½-inch 1.44MB LS-120
	5¼-inch 1.2MB
Removable:	Zip drive Jaz drive MO drive
Tape backup:	Capacity: _____ DAT
CD-ROM:	Speed: ____ X Tray Cartridge CD-R CD-RW DVD
Graphics:	SVGA Other: _____
	Graphics memory: _____ Megabytes
Monitor:	Diagonal: _____ inches Dot pitch: _____ mm
	Multiscanning LCD
Modem:	Internal External
	Speed: _____ bits per second
Mouse:	Standard mouse Trackball Other: _____
	"Wheel" mouse
Sound:	SoundBlaster AdLib Other: _____
	External speakers Subwoofer
Ports:	Serial: COM1 COM2 COM3 COM4
	Parallel: LPT1 LPT2
	USB FireWire
	Joystick MIDI
Other options:	_____

Figure 17-1:
The For
Dummies
hardware
worksheet.

With the worksheet filled out and in your hand, you'll be able to visit any computer store in the known universe and find the computer that's perfect for you.

Filling in the worksheet (step-by-step)

Use a piece of paper to create your own copy of the Hardware Worksheet. As you go through each of the following sections, write down the information you've gathered from your various software worksheets.

If you are still up in the air between a Macintosh or PC, then create two hardware worksheets. (The same applies for any two types of computer system, though the decisions aren't as varied for game consoles or portable computers.)

It might also help to keep a calculator handy.

Choose an operating system

Look over all your software worksheets, and locate the most advanced operating system listed. That's the operating system you need on your new computer. Granted, there are a few things to note:

✔ All Macintosh computers come with the latest version of the Mac OS (or "Apple System Software"). If you're leaning toward a Macintosh, then just circle Macintosh on that form.

✔ If any application is for Windows 95/98 only (*not* Windows NT/2000), then that limits your selection to Windows 98. The reason here is that some software *will not* run on Windows NT/2000. If so, then you don't want that operating system.

✔ If all your software is Windows NT/2000 compatible, then consider that operating system instead of "regular" Windows.

Write down your operating system selection.

Pick a microprocessor

You want the latest and fastest microprocessor you can afford. For the sake of filling out this worksheet, however, write down the latest microprocessor your software specified.

For example, you may get these results:

- ✔ 486 or better
- ✔ Pentium
- ✔ Pentium with MMX
- ✔ Pentium II

The latest, greatest system in that bunch is a Pentium II. (All Pentium II and later systems come with MMX built-in.)

For the processor speed, write down the fastest rating specified by any software package. For example, if some game program says that it needs at least a 90 MHz Pentium, write down that value.

- ✔ Yes, yes: You'll probably get something much faster and maybe fancier than the minimum requirements you're writing on the hardware worksheet. Be patient.
- ✔ All Macintosh G4 computers are compatible with G3 and all Power Macintosh software.

Calculate your memory needs

Memory is a *maximum* value; it's not totaled. To find out how much memory your computer should have, just look for the *highest* value specified on your software worksheets.

Suppose that the memory requirements from various software packages are 12MB, 8MB, 24MB, and 16MB. You pick the highest value, which is 24MB. That's the *minimum* amount of memory your computer should have.

Memory is happiest when it's configured in a multiple of 16, however. So after you know the minimum amount of memory you need, you should round up to the nearest value listed here:

    16MB
    32MB
    48MB
    64MB
    96 MB
    128MB

In this example, the next higher value to 24MB is 32MB.

Again, as with the microprocessor, if you can afford it, you'll probably get even more memory. The value you calculate here merely tells you a good *minimum* amount of memory you should have. Calculate that value and enter it on your hardware worksheet.

- ✔ The amount of memory the software needs should be *less* than the total amount of memory in your computer. You never want to cut this value short.

- ✔ If a memory size is recommended, always go with it. The minimum memory size is put there by marketing types who want the package to have the widest appeal. The engineers who design the software specify the "recommended" value.

Calculate your hard drive storage

Unlike computer memory, hard disk storage is a cumulative thing. It adds up. And you will, eventually, run out of hard drive storage. The idea is to put that day off as far in the future as possible.

Add together the hard disk storage requirements from all your software worksheets. If the package doesn't list the storage requirements, use the value 10MB. Total 'em all up.

Suppose that you have the following storage requirements (the two for 10MB are from two packages that didn't list hard drive storage requirements):

    131MB

    10MB

    10MB

    26MB

    65MB

    210MB

The total of those values is 452MB.

After you add the values, double the result. In this example, the amount is 904MB. If you're using a database or graphics program, double the number again. The result is approximately the *minimum* amount of disk space you need in order to use your computer.

Now round up the value to the nearest gigabyte. In most cases, it's probably only 1GB. That's fine because most hard drives are 2GB at minimum. You have room to spare — which is the point of this exercise.

- ✔ Of all applications, the ones whose documents hog the most disk space are graphics programs. A typical graphics file can use anywhere from a few kilobytes of disk storage to several megabytes.

- ✔ Computer animation files also tend to be huge.

- ✔ Databases also take up a huge amount of disk space. Maybe not at first, but after a few years any database should grow to be several times larger than you originally thought.

- ✔ Disk storage is different from memory storage. A program uses memory only when it runs. Every program, however, as well as the files and documents the program creates, has to be stored on the hard disk.

Do you need SCSI?

If you plan to use a number of SCSI peripherals (tape backup units, external hard drives, external removable drives, extra CD-ROM and CD-R drives, scanners, and the whole lot), you should get SCSI. Mark that down on the worksheet, and remember to tell your dealer that you want a SCSI hard drive.

- ✔ If you don't need SCSI, you'll be happy with whatever the dealer gives you for a hard drive interface. Ain't no big deal.

- ✔ If your computer comes with the FireWire standard, then you won't at all, ever, nope not never, need SCSI.

More storage decisions

Chances are that your software will not require any specific type of disk drive, such as a CD-R or Zip or Jaz disk. If it does, jot down that information. Otherwise, you probably can get by with whatever comes with the computer.

- ✔ I can recommend a Zip or Jaz drive if you're working on graphics and need some way to move those graphics files to another location. These types of removable disks are also wonderful for taking work home from the office.

- ✔ Don't lament the iMac's lack of a floppy disk drive. You can always add a USB floppy drive later if you discover that you *really* need one. Ditto for any other floppy drive-less computer.

- ✔ If the dealer offers a tape backup drive, take it! The capacity of your tape backup drive should be equal to or greater than the capacity of your hard drive; for example, a 4GB backup tape for a 3.1GB hard drive.

✔ Write down the fastest CD-ROM rating listed on your software work-sheets. If one program requires a 12X CD-ROM, for example, write down that value. Otherwise, you can leave this item blank; whatever the dealer gives you should be fast enough.

✔ If you can, try to specify the "tray" type of CD-ROM, where a tray slides out and you lay the disk into the tray. Personally, I find that method of sticking CDs into the drive easier than using the cartridge, in which case you must insert the CD into a plastic case and then insert the case into the CD-ROM drive. If this issue doesn't matter to you now, leave it blank on the worksheet.

Other hardware stuff

After your memory and storage requirements, the rest of a computer system tends to fall into place without many heavy decisions on your part. Here's a rundown of almost everything left in your computer system:

Graphics: Write down any specific graphics requirements your software lists; for example, "256 color display" or "4MB video memory recommended." You must make sure that whatever graphics adapter you buy is capable of those feats, at least at minimum.

Monitor: A monitor is a personal-preference item. For me, a 17-inch monitor is a great size, though my wife loves her 19-inch monster (and all computer users drool over the 21-inch size). Bigger monitors are more expensive.

Make sure that you get a multiscanning, noninterlaced monitor. If you can't afford it, that's okay. I recommend it, though. Also make sure that the dot pitch is at least .28 mm or *smaller*.

If you're going with an LCD monitor, get a digital graphics adapter.

Modem: Gotta have it if you plan on using the Internet. Get at least a 56Kbps modem.

Mouse: You can have many fancy mice, so make sure that you visit a computer store to see what's available. The dealer will probably give you a choice. Remember to get a fancy mouse, such as the "wheel" mouse, only if your software knows what to do with it.

Sound: Most sound cards sold with computers are generally compatible with all the games out there. Only if your software requests a specific sound card should you write it down on the worksheet.

Be sure that your computer comes with external speakers. For extra money, you can get the subwoofer option, which beefs up your computer's sound. All this equipment is extra and not truly required. If your money is tight, you should spend it elsewhere.

Ports: PCs should have at least two COM (serial) ports and one LPT1 (printer) port. Any extra ports you get depend on your needs.

All computers, Mac and PC, should have at least two USB ports. Having a FireWire in addition to USB is even better.

The joystick port generally is provided on any PC with sound, though you should always inquire about it. Macintoshes need to use USB joysticks.

Other options: Specify any other items your PC may need: a scanner, backup power supply, graphics tablet, or whatever else your software programs may specify.

Part II has more specific information about the hardware mentioned in this list.

A Sample for You to Review

Figure 17-2 shows how a sample worksheet could be filled in. Your sheet should look something like this when you're through reviewing your software requirements. (Or you might have two sheets, one for a future Mac and another for a future PC.)

✔ The first thing to notice is that not every item is required.

✔ Remember that you're configuring a minimal computer. The model you probably get will have more stuff in it.

Hardware Worksheet

Operating system: Windows 98 ~~Windows NT/2000~~
OS/2 (Mac) Other: _____

Microprocessor: Pentium: _____ (G3/G4) Speed: __400__ MHz

Memory: __128__ Megabytes

Hard drive storage: __8__ Gigabytes

SCSI: Yes (No)

Floppy drive(s): Drive A (3½-inch) 1.44MB LS-120
5¼-inch 1.2MB

Removable: (Zip drive) Jaz drive MO drive

Tape backup: Capacity: _____ DAT

CD-ROM: Speed: ___ X Tray Cartridge CD-R CD-RW (DVD)

Graphics: (SVGA) Other: _____
Graphics memory: __16__ Megabytes

Monitor: Diagonal: __19__ inches Dot pitch: _____ mm
Multiscanning LCD

Modem: (Internal) External
Speed: __56K__ bits per second

Mouse: Standard mouse (Trackball) Other: _____
"Wheel" mouse

Sound: (SoundBlaster) AdLib Other: _____
External speakers Subwoofer

Ports: Serial: (COM1) (COM2) COM3 COM4
Parallel: LPT1 LPT2
(USB) (FireWire)
(Joystick) MIDI

Other options: _____

Figure 17-2: A sample filled-in hardware worksheet.

Chapter 18

Surveying the Shopping Landscape

In This Chapter

▶ Reading a computer ad
▶ Avoiding advertising tricks
▶ A shopping Q&A
▶ Visiting your local computer store
▶ Visiting a megastore
▶ Ordering mail-order computers

*F*inding a place to buy a computer is easy. They sell computers every-where. A computer is like a toaster, really. "Two slurpies, a lotto ticket, and one of those Pentiums, please." Of course, you don't want to walk into just anywhere to buy your computer.

Lots and lots of places sell computers. Some are dedicated computer stores, some are mom-and-pop places, some do mail order, some sell directly from the factory, and some places even sell washers and dryers right next to the iMacs. This chapter describes each place and gives you an idea of what to expect when you walk in.

Where do you start? Probably by picking up the paper and reading the com-puter ads. Heck, you've probably been doing that already. Now find out what it all really means.

Reading a Computer Ad

The first step in buying that computer is to look at computer ads. Although this process can be boring, it's definitely not as boring as browsing in a warehouse-size computer store. After all, you're going to show up knowing exactly what you need; you don't have to be sold anything. Computer stores aren't really set up for that kind of customer (just look around the next time you visit one).

Finding computer advertisements

You can find computer ads in computer magazines, your local newspaper, and freebie computer fliers.

First, look in your newspaper, in the sports section on Saturday (don't ask me why). That's usually where you find some computer-related ads from some local stores. You may also want to check the business section throughout the week. Some newspapers even have computer-specific inserts. (As soon as newspaper editors realize that a computer-literate buying public is out there, more will come.)

Second, visit a magazine rack and look for computer magazines. It doesn't matter how technical they are. Just grab some thick magazines to help you with your research. The library is a great place for this kind of research.

Finally, several cities across the land have supplemental computer "magazines" published locally. These freebie publications are crammed full of ads from local vendors. If you can plug your nose long enough to get by their editorial articles, you may find some local dealers with some prices — plus service and support — that meet your needs.

Dissecting an ad

Figure 18-1 shows a computer ad I mocked up myself this morning. It lists various "systems" along with their hardware contents and prices.

First, realize that the systems displayed in ads are set up primarily for price comparison with competitors. You can assemble any PC you want with any microprocessor, amount of memory, hard drive size — whatever your needs are. Don't be put off by a place because it may not have your personal computer right there in the ad.

Second, notice that the ads use lots of abbreviations. Although I'm sure that some fondness for computer jargon is responsible, space restrictions are the most likely reason that the ads say *RAM* rather than *memory* and *MB* or *M* rather than *megabytes*. You may even see *HDD* used in place of *hard disk drive*. *VRAM* means *video RAM* or *video memory*. You often find customized products, such as the "clackity" keyboard or maybe some special type of mouse.

One important abbreviation you often see is $CALL. It means that the advertiser wants you to phone up to see what price it offers. You can interpret $CALL in several ways: The price is too ridiculously cheap to advertise (which happens), the price changes frequently (that happens, too), or someone there just wants to talk to someone on the phone (not often).

Jerry's Computer Village

Bargains!   Deals!   Internet!

Model 100   Model 200   Model 300

Model 100	Model 200	Model 300
400MHz AMD K6 MMX * 32MB SDRAM std, 64MB max * 3.9GB ATA hard drive * 20X CD-ROM drive * 56K bps modem * Q-pro speakers * 64-bit PCI 3-D graphics	500MHz Pentium III * 512KB level 2 cache * 64MB EDO RAM std. * 8GB HDD * 24X CD-ROM * 56K bps * internal modem * Lumina 64-bit 2M VRAM * 3-D sound system	600MHz Pentium III processor * 512KB Level 2 cache * 128MB SyncDRAM * 13GB SCSI hard drive * 56Kbps internal modem * 16MB SVGA 3-D graphics * DVD-ROM drive.
$499.00	**$1199.00**	**$1799.00**

Options

MONITORS		PRINTERS		SOFTWARE
15" (13.8" viewable)	$250.00	Voov Color Ink, 1200 x 600 dpi * 4 ppm. $230.00		Every system sold comes with Windows 98 and one of the following packages:
17" (16" viewable)	$500.00	Strombo Photo Ink, 720 x 360 dpi * 8 ppm. $380.00		* Home office, includes Microsoft Office & Quicken
19" (18" viewable)	$600.00	PagePro Laser, 600 x 600 dpi * 20 ppm. $1000.00		* Gamer Pack, includes DOOM & Tomb Raider & similar stuff
21" (20" viewable)	$900.00	Color Laser, 1200 dpi * 10 ppm black / 3 ppm color $CALL		* Graphics Pack, includes Adobe Illustrator & Photoshop
15" LCD	$900.00			
17" LCD	$1600.00			
18" LCD	$2800.00			

Jerry's PC Village
1940 Debbie Drive
Temecula, CA 92592

909-555-1899
Open Monday ~ Friday, 9:00 am 'till 8:30 pm
Saturday from 9:00 am to 6:00 pm
Closed Sundays!

Call for our outrageous selection of other quality PC stuff!
We've got modems! We've got scanners! Name it, we've got it!
Tons of software! Bins o' shareware! Magazines & Books!

When you need a new PC, it takes a Village!

Figure 18-1:
A typical computer ad.

Third, some items are missing from the computers' descriptions. Most importantly, *where is the monitor?* Those prices may look cheap, but all PCs need a monitor. Also, should you assume that the computer has a serial port and printer port? What about a USB port? I would ask.

Fourth — a good thing — the phone number *and* address are listed. Although just about any place lists its phone number (and its fax number and maybe its Internet address), you know that a dealer is legit if it has an address. (Some fly-by-night operations never give addresses.)

Finally, don't forget service and support! The ad may not say anything about what's offered, so be sure to phone or visit the store before you make a decision.

   ✔ Name brand manufacturers (Dell, Compaq, Micron, and so on) also have ads similar to Figure 18-1. Even though your system may not be listed, remember that you can mix and match.

   ✔ Macintosh and PC advertising just don't mix. Rare is the place where you can buy both systems (I know that some CompUSA stores stock both). If you can't find information on Macintosh computers, buy a Macintosh-specific magazine, like *MacWorld*.

Looking at a buying grid

Your PC can be configured any way you want. True, some of the preconfigured models, such as the ones Jerry's Computer Village offers (refer to Figure 18-1), are cheaper. Why? Because they're preconfigured! A customized PC will cost you a little more.

Manufacturers that offer different configurations commonly supply a price grid; a sample is shown in Figure 18-2. After you find your microprocessor, memory requirements, hard drive, and CD-ROM or DVD, you get a good idea of what you'll pay.

   ✔ Buying grids usually accompany standard configurations, telling you about the graphics card, ports, floppy drive, and whatnot.

   ✔ Some manufacturers may even "part out" the entire PC piece by piece, letting you know how much each item costs if you want to "roll your own" PC.

   ✔ Notice what's missing from the grid — monitor, mouse, graphics.

   ✔ Use the grids only for a price comparison (what I personally need is rarely shown in the grid).

Model	Processor	RAM	HDD	CD-ROM	Our Price
C/400	Celeron 400	32M	3.1G	24X	$650.00
C/400x	Celeron 400	64M	6.2G	24X	$799.00
C/450	Celeron 450	32M	3.1G	24X	$700.00
C/450x	Celeron 450	64M	6.2G	DVD	$899.00
P/333	Pentium II 333	32M	3.1G	24X	$750.00
P/333x	Pentium II 333	64M	6.2G	24X	$850.00
P/333d	Pentium II 333	64M	6.2G	DVD	$925.00
P/400	Pentium II 400	32M	3.1G	24X	$900.00
P/400x	Pentium II 400	64M	3.1G	24X	$975.00
P/450d	Pentium II 450	64M	6.2G	DVD	$1,050.00
P/450x	Pentium II 450	128M	6.2G	DVD	$1,100.00
P3/400	Pentium III 400	64M	4.1G	DVD	$1,075.00
P3/450	Pentium III 450	64M	6.2G	DVD	$1,175.00
P3/500	Pentium III 500	128M	10.4G	DVD	$1,500.00
P3/550	Pentium III 550	128M	10.4G	DVD	$1,650.00

Figure 18-2:
A price grid.

Recognizing common tricks used to make an advertised price look really cheap

Because the competition is fierce, computer dealers go to great lengths to make their systems look cheaper than the other guys'. Here are some common tricks you may want to look for or inquire about when you find a ridiculous price:

- ✔ Not including any memory in the computer. Look for 0K RAM or 0MB RAM in the ads, or see whether the memory value is missing altogether.

- ✔ Not including the price of the keyboard.

- ✔ Not including the price of the monitor or video adapter card (the most common trick).

- ✔ Not including the price of the microprocessor (although this practice sounds ridiculous, it happens).

- ✔ Not including the price of the operating system. Technically, this item should be "thrown in," but the dealer may be saving a few bucks by not including it.

- ✔ Including manufacturer's rebate coupons, which lower the price only *after* you turn them in.

- ✔ Omitting support or service!

✔ Showing an unrelated illustration, usually a picture of a computer that may or may not look like what's being advertised. For example, watch out for "Model 400 shown" or "Optional monitor shown" written in tiny print below the illustration.

The myth of the free (or almost-free) computer

The final trick you'll find lurking out there is the free, $0, or $100 computer. You probably have some questions about this, for example:

Q: Are they out of their minds?

A: No. In fact, they're being very clever. Nothing is free, remember. You do pay something. If the price is zero, then you still have to cough up money. What you pay supposedly is rebated to you should you sign up for Internet service or return manufacturer's coupons.

Q: Why is the price so low?

A: The price isn't low at all. What you're doing is signing up for long-term Internet service and not really buying a computer. You pay $20 a month for two or three years and that's $480 to $720 over time. It's worth it for the Internet company to buy the computer for you if they guarantee that you'll be a customer that long.

Q: Is it worth it?

A: That depends. If you plan on signing up for Internet service *and* that same service offered with the "free" computer is what you need, then it's worth it. If not, then you're stuck with paying for the Internet service whether or not you keep the PC — for the next several years, possibly.

Q: But what if the computer is just what I need?

A: Then great. However, many computer industry pundits are claiming that Internet service itself will be *free* in a few years. (It's already free in the UK.) If that happens, then you're stuck with a low-end computer paying for Internet service others are getting free.

My advice? If — and that's a big if — the computer is exactly what you need according to this book *and* you have the proper service and support for it, then consider the "free" or cheap computer as an option. However, also keep in mind that I'm not recommending them to any of my friends, not even as a joke.

Some Q&A Before You Rush Out to Buy

In keeping with the theme of the previous section, there are probably even more buying questions you have right now. The following are general questions and answers (the previous section is specific to the free computer phenomena). Hopefully, the one question you want to ask is among the following:

Should I get a quote?

Most stores offer a "meet or beat" way to price a computer. They claim to meet or beat any advertised price on similar or the same equipment. If you like to shop this way, get several quotes from different sources before you buy.

When you're comparing prices, don't forget to factor in a few dollars for service and support. How much? Anywhere from $50 to $300, depending on the kind of support that's added. A lack of support will cost you from $50 to $300 to maybe much, much more if you're not careful.

 ✔ Although some hole-in-the-wall place always wants your business when you buy something, will it want to see you again when you have a question or need help?

 ✔ Why add so much for service and support? That's probably how much it will cost you when you *don't* get it: Add up gas, phone calls, the cost of a tutor or community college course — you get the idea.

 ✔ Chapter 19 discusses how to easily comparison shop on the Internet.

Can I haggle?

The days of haggling over buying a computer are long gone. It used to be that computers were marked up so much that only a complete nebbish would pay the list price. You could typically count on a 20 to 50 percent discount in swankier stores.

Now the competition between stores is too great to allow for any haggling. The price you see advertised is usually what it sells for. Computers still have a manufacturer's suggested retail price (MSRP), and you may see that ridiculous value listed above the store's "discount." Whatever. Don't expect to get any more breaks than that.

Should I get a discount off the manufacturer's suggested retail price?

Yes. Especially on software. The "street price" of all computer whatnots is always less than the manufacturer's price — a weird holdover from the days of haggling.

Isn't there any way to get a deal on a computer?

About the only way left to get a lower price on a new computer is to buy two or more at a time. This technique works just about anywhere and with anything: Buy two or more cars, and the car dealer will cut you some slack. Be forewarned, however, that some computer stores don't start to cut deals until the 10th or 100th computer you buy!

 You probably don't need two or more computers for your first computer purchase. Does that leave you out? Nope! Just find an associate or willing relative who is also on the verge of buying. Sometimes you can receive substantial discounts for purchasing two computers at the same time, often without losing valued service and support.

Is it better to buy from a noncommissioned salesperson?

I've been buying computers for more than 17 years and have yet to find a commissioned salesperson. Because most stores are either discount or locally owned, there is no commission to be made. I would guess that only the manufacturer's direct sales reps who sell to major accounts get commissions, although I doubt that even that's the case anymore.

If commissioned salespeople bug you, you can always consider going elsewhere.

"What about buying a used computer?"

A used computer is a bad idea for a first-time buyer. Why? Because you're cutting off your service and support. You get no guarantees or warranties with used equipment. For a second purchase, sure, but not when you're just starting out.

What about refurbished stuff?

I've purchased a few refurbished computers, but only because they came with a manufacturer's warranty. The equipment was older, but because it served the purpose I had in mind, it was fine for me. And it was cheap!

You didn't say anything about the swap meet

The reason I don't mention swap meets — even computer swap meets — is that no service and support are available. True, if you find a local dealer that is simply making its presence known at the swap meet, that's okay — as long as the dealer has local service and classes or some kind of support.

Swap meets are havens for fly-by-night outfits and jerks who sell stolen or substandard crap from the back of pickup trucks. I don't mean that everyone there is shifty; some reputable dealers do show up. If you do business with a jerk, though, don't expect him to be there the next weekend.

Where to Buy

Looking over the ads gives you an idea of what's out there. Eventually, however, you have to pick a few places to phone or visit and get a more lasting impression. You don't want to shop by price alone. A store's reputation is based on service and support, which you can't determine over the phone.

When it comes time to narrow your choices, you can buy your computer from several types of places:

- A local computer store
- National chains
- A megastore
- Mail order

Any of these is fine by me for buying a first-time computer. Even mail-order places offer service and support, though the support takes place over the phone rather than in a classroom.

One additional place to buy a computer is the Internet. Obviously, you need a computer to use the Internet so if you don't yet have one, that choice won't do you any good right now. Still, Chapter 19 covers the topic of online buying if you already have Internet access.

Your locally owned and operated computer store

If you're one to support your local economy, a locally owned store is probably your first choice for buying a computer. These places may look tacky. Although they may have stuff on Costco tables and boxes stacked in back, they may also have fair prices and owners who offer more personal support than their Big Brother competitors.

The most serious issue about a local store is how long it has been in business. Any store that has been around for three years or more probably has an excellent reputation (or at least a reputation you can verify). Give new places a chance, but consider hanging out in the lobby or checking the service counter to see whether it has any disgruntled customers. You may also ask for a list of satisfied customers to confirm its reputation.

- ✔ I often go to local stores to pick up something quick: a keyboard, modem, or some piece of software that they have in stock.

- ✔ Some smaller stores may have to order your computer or assemble it. Although this process takes time, you're getting a custom computer. Larger stores tend to sell more things off the rack.

- ✔ Another type of local store is a university bookstore, but don't think that it's cheaper! It used to be that some computer manufacturers offered decent discounts to students who bought computers at the school bookstore. That may not be the case anymore. Never assume that the school bookstore is cheaper than a local store.

National chains

National computer stores aren't what they used to be. Those upscale, haughty computer stores of the late 1980s suffered when smart shoppers realized that local and discount stores carried the same stuff and that the national stores charged a premium and offered little in return.

National computer chains have been replaced by computer megastores (see the next section). However, some national stores that are not necessarily computer stores do carry computers: Sears, Radio Shack, K-Mart, Costco, Sam's Club, and other places sell computers — even Macintoshes — right next to stereos and videotape.

The big benefit of buying a computer at a national chain is that they're every-where. Unlike with local dealers, you never have to worry about finding a Radio Shack or Sears, because they're all over the place.

The big drawback to national chains is that they're not geared specifically toward helping people buy computers. Although some places are exceptions, it's hard to expect sincere support from the guy who sells you a computer, a hair dryer, and a country-and-western compact disc. They don't have a class-room to teach you about AppleWorks or Windows, and don't expect to get far when you phone up to ask a question about formatting a disk.

The megastore

Megastores are those super computer stores, some bigger than a grocery store, that have everything and anything to do with a computer. You can browse, check out new hardware, ask questions, take classes, and spend money until you have to take out a third mortgage.

Megastores are quickly replacing the mom-and-pop local dealers and national chains as the place to go for computers. Megastores offer substantial dis-counts and usually have on-site service and support, and everything is in stock.

One downfall of these stores is that their sales staff turns over quickly. Just as I start a relationship with someone, he's off to another job. This quibble is a minor one as long as the new clerk is just as knowledgeable as the guy he's replacing.

Before you commit to one of these megastores, be sure to check on its war-ranties and return policies, and double-check on its service and support. Also find out *who* fixes the stuff. Is it fixed there, or does the store just ship broken stuff to some factory in another state?

Mail-order brand names

Welcome to the millenium, where you can have just about anything mailed to your house — including a computer! You typically order from a catalog or magazine article, someone quotes you a price, and a few days or weeks later, your computer shows up, ready to go.

(Okay, the computer shows up in a box, and you have to set it up. Don't worry — this book shows you how! See chapter 22.)

What about building your own computer?

Do you want to build your own computer from scratch? It certainly is possible for the PC (Macs are made only by Apple). Many places sell the pieces' parts, and everything plugs in or is screwed in to one thing or another. Buy a book about making your own PC, use a knowledgeable friend's help, or do it on your own. It's possible. Unfortunately, it's not a task I recommend for anyone starting out.

The main problem with rolling your own PC is that you get no service or support. Even if you're gutsy enough to try, you have no one to turn to when something doesn't work right. Individual parts may be covered by a warranty, but not the complete unit.

Some may argue that building your own computer is cheaper, which may or may not be true. However, I would seriously factor into the bottom line the support you're not getting. Never build your first computer. Your second or third, okay — but not the first.

Mail-order computers offer the same things as your local dealer or megastore. The only difference is that it's sent to your home or office rather than to a loading dock. The price is often cheaper because you aren't charged an in-store markup, and often you can dodge your state's sales tax (though I'm not recommending that you do so).

Many people are concerned about mail-order computers showing up dead or damaged. Before you order, make sure that you get a no-questions-asked return policy and that the manufacturer pays (or reimburses you) for shipping. Most places have these types of polices, and, even so, rarely does equipment arrive damaged.

About the only downside to mail-order computers is that their support takes place over the phone. Most places offer an 800 number you can call at just about any time to ask a question. If you're more comfortable with in-person support, however, consider a local dealer or megastore.

One other perk to look for is free on-site service. This service is especially important if you live or work in the boonies, as I do. Make sure that this service is offered even after the warranty period expires, and double-check that your city and state are included in the on-site service deal.

Mail-order pieces' parts

There is a difference between a mail-order brand-name computer and what I call "mail-order pieces' parts." That is, no one should buy a mail-order pieces' parts computer as a first computer. Instead, if you take the mail-order route, buy a brand name you know: Apple, Compaq, Dell, Gateway, IBM, Micron, and a host of others I don't have time to list.

The main way you can recognize a pieces' parts mail-order outfit is that it sells pieces' parts in addition to complete computer systems. Right along with its main Pentium systems, you see a list of hard drives, memory, video cards, modems, printers, and other stock, ready to roll. Sure, those prices look good, but if the outfit doesn't offer the kind of service and support you need, why bother?

Chapter 19

Tips for Online Shopping

● ●

In This Chapter

▶ Buying a computer on the Web

▶ Using a catalog store

▶ Building your own PC on a Web site

▶ Computer buying tips

▶ Using a shopping agent

▶ Tracking your order

● ●

*I*t took the World Wide Web to make the Internet popular. With the Web, accessing information is as easy as reading a magazine. But it took shopping to make the Internet the current rage that it is! The computer with its modem, an online retailer, and your Visa card can make for a popular and expensive combination.

If you have access to the Internet, you can use it as a resource for computer shopping. Every major computer manufacturer and nearly all the national catalogs plus many local stores have an Internet presence. The advantages and disadvantages of this new approach are what's covered in this chapter, along with other related information for anyone willing to computer shop on the Web.

Buying on the World Wide Web

Can you buy a computer on the Web? Certainly! Every computer I've bought in the last two years has been purchased through the Web. The last time I phoned in a computer order from a catalog was in 1997. (The last time I bought a computer in a store was in 1988!) But that's me. What about you?

If you're new to buying a computer, I don't recommend getting your first computer from the Internet. Why? Because you're undercutting the kind of service and support that would be available to you otherwise. It's hard enough to find those things when you're shopping locally; imagine trying to find them on the Internet!

For people who are already bathed in the computer experience, buying online has some real advantages. As an example, if you know *exactly* what you want, it's easy to find it online as opposed to searching through a catalog or wasting time on the phone or in a computer warehouse.

- ✔ Service and support *is* available from the Internet. Chapter 20 covers this issue.

- ✔ Buying on the Internet is often cheaper because you're not paying for overhead.

- ✔ An exception to my first-time rule for buying on the Internet is when you've chosen a Macintosh or iMac. Because there aren't that many stores that carry the Mac, if you decide to buy one, then buying on the Web (or through a catalog) is often the only way you have to get one. (A Sears store near you may carry the iMac.)

- ✔ If you already have a computer, then it's easy to buy peripherals or upgrades on the Internet. However, I recommend this only when you *know* what you want.

- ✔ Buying online isn't foolproof. I've never had trouble with any computer company, but other online retailers have turned out to be rotten apples. As usual, if you have a recommendation from a friend or reliable source, go with it.

Finding a place to buy

Every major computer manufacturer, most catalogs, and even local dealers have a presence on the Web. Therefore finding them on the Internet is as easy as knowing their name.

Generally speaking, there are two types of stores you'll find on the Internet. One is the catalog store, which is essentially an electronic version of the same type of catalog you may receive as junk mail from time to time. The second is the store that lets you configure your computer the way you want, which is more the traditional walk-in computer store model.

An example of a catalog store is `Zones.com`, which sells hardware for both the PC and Macintosh platforms, as well as handhelds and palm computers. Figure 19-1 shows the opening page for the PC Zone.

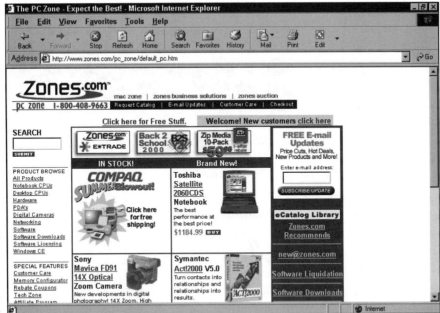

Figure 19-1:
A Web page
shopping
catalog.

A Web page catalog usually opens with a list of bargains or popular deals. Somewhere on the page you should find a list of categories to browse or a place where you can search for specific hardware. In Figure 19-1, the Search box is just above the category list on the left side of the page.

Clicking the Desktop CPUs link in the Product Browse list displays various deals and items currently available from Zones.com (or whichever online retailer you're browsing). Products may be listed by manufacturer, type of microprocessor, or price.

Note that nearly all the products listed are sold as is. With a catalog type Web page, you cannot reconfigure items, and the choice of options is limited to what the manufacturer provides. This means the price is cheaper than if you have special requests, but your choices are limited.

Another way to shop (a way more in tune with how this book is set up) is to build your own computer. That usually happens only with manufacturer's Web pages and their online stores. A good example of this is Micron's Web page, as shown in Figure 19-2.

The manufacturer begins with a basic system setup. Then you use the Web page, as shown in Figure 19-2, to select various options. (The Micron site lets you select *everything;* only a small portion of the site can be seen in Figure 19-2).

Figure 19-2:
Building
your own
computer at
Micron.

Some Web pages may list the cost/savings for each item. For example, adding another 64MB of memory may cost you $220, but selecting a smaller monitor may save you $100.

As you work the steps on the Web page, the cost of the computer configuration is calculated. You then select an operating system, software options, and then shipping options.

If you make an error, such as selecting an incompatible piece of hardware, the Web page lets you know.

Even if you're not buying right now, the Web page can really help you get an idea of what each option costs and how much it will save you if you change a configuration.

Remember to use your hardware worksheet from Chapter 17 to help you get the best possible computer to match your software. Buying more hardware than you need (if you can afford it) is great!

- ✔ Zones.com can be visited at `www.zones.com`

- ✔ Micron's home page is `www.micronpc.com`

- ✔ A complete list of online computer retailers can be found on Yahoo! if you visit:

  `http://shopping.yahoo.com/computers/`

- ✔ I am not paid by nor do I own stock in either Zones.com or Micron. I do buy from them regularly and have had relatively good luck.

- ✔ Dell Computer, Gateway, and others also have configuration options similar to the one illustrated in this section.

- ✔ Make sure that the vendor has a phone number and street address. You don't want to get stuck online and have to fumble with e-mail to get satisfaction. It's just doesn't work.

- ✔ You can buy, buy, buy online all you like! Items you select are placed into a special virtual shopping cart where they wait until you're ready to check out. You don't need to buy one thing at a time.

Placing your order

Eventually you'll reach a place on the Web page where you have to place the order. It's either the checkout button or the shopping cart button or some other obvious means to tell the Web page that you're done shopping and are ready to buy.

When you're ready to check out, review the items in your order. Figure 19-3 shows such an order. You can confirm items and quantities or remove items from the list. Use the "update" button if you change quantities or remove items.

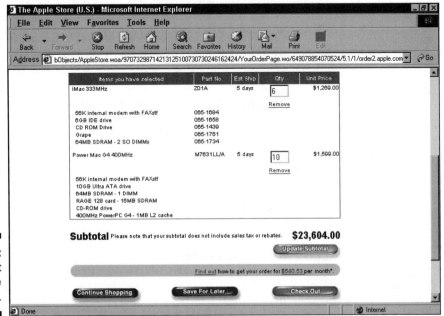

Figure 19-3:
Check-out
time at the
Apple store.

When you're ready to buy, click the Check-out button or a Continue button. The next few Web pages contain forms you must fill out.

Many Web pages will want you to "log in" at this point, which is merely a handy way to recognize a returning customer. If you haven't been to the Web page before, you should create a new account. Having an account means you don't have to reenter information each time you buy something.

You need to list your billing and shipping address. Eventually you'll have to cough up a credit card number and expiration date. Gotta pay for it, you know.

After filling in everything and clicking the proper buttons, you'll eventually see an order confirmation page. *Print this page.* The page contains your order number, the items you ordered, plus the final damage to your credit card. If you cannot print the page, then carefully copy down the order number. Do this for future reference.

Many online retailers will send an e-mail confirmation of your order. Print that out as well.

Now you just sit and wait for the computer to arrive. You did opt for the express delivery option, right?

- If you're afraid to order online, then look for an option that lets you print or e-mail the order form. You can then phone in the order using an order ID number or simply quote off the catalog numbers over the phone.

- There is nothing wrong with ordering online. As long as you heed my advice in this book, you should have a pleasant experience and be able to quickly handle any problems that may crop up.

- There has never been a reported case of credit card fraud involving an online retailer. Never! Buying online is as safe, if not safer, than ordering from a catalog or buying something in a store.

- Always pay with a credit card when you buy online. Though there has never been any reported fraud, I would be very leery of a company wanting your bank account or social security number to buy a computer. This is absolutely not required.

- Avoid places that require your credit card number *before* you've selected anything to buy.

- When you create an account for an online retailer, use a common user name/ID for yourself but a unique password. Do not use your credit card number as a password.

- Always have your order shipped by a shipping company, not by the post office. Shipping companies (like UPS, Federal Express, and Airborne) keep track of each parcel they ship. Tracking the orders is covered at the end of this chapter.

✔ To be honest with you, there are two times I've had trouble buying things on the Internet. The first was a company (now out of business) that charged my credit card *before* shipping my order. The second was a company that didn't list any phone number, so when my order never arrived I had only e-mail to communicate with them — which didn't work. As long as you follow my advice in this chapter, you should never have problems similar to these when you shop online.

Comparison shopping

Buying a computer is not about getting the lowest price. But if you've discovered that the computer you want is a common model — like a Pressario or an iMac — then you can take advantage of the Web to search for the lowest possible price. One such Web page is mySimon.com.

The mySimon site doesn't sell anything. It collects items and prices from various online retailers and shows you what comes up. Figure 19-4 shows various items selected: computer manufacturer, processor, speed, and price. Figure 19-5 shows the result mySimon found from scouring various online retailers.

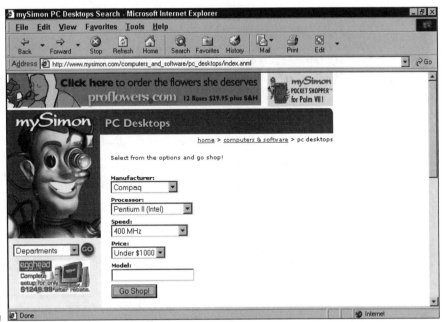

Figure 19-4: Searching for a specific computer.

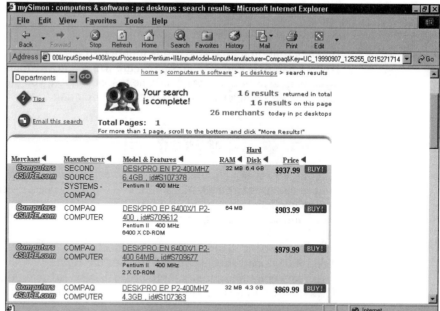

Figure 19-5:
mySimon
finds some
matching
hardware.

Obviously, this is not my preferred method for shopping. Only (and it's a big only) if your hardware worksheets have shown that you can have a generic type of prepackaged computer will this help you find the best price. Otherwise, you might need to stick with a build-your-own method similar to the one offered by the Micron site, which is shown earlier in this chapter.

✔ mySimon can be found at www.mysimon.com.

✔ Technically, mySimon is known as a *shopping agent*.

✔ Other shopping agents include:

    Roboshopper: www.roboshopper.com

    Cadabra: www.cadabra.com

Sleazy tricks used by online retailers

Not every online retailer is a jerk. Many of them offer quality stuff at low prices and ship it cheap. Some places cut corners to save money or to look better than their competition. The following list warns of some well-known tactics used by the less-reputable online dealers.

✔ **Bait-and-switch.** A very cheap computer or component is advertised but — oh, no! — it's suddenly out-of-stock or backordered when you check into it. An alternative is offered instead for a much higher price.

✔ **Repackaged goods are sold without any warning.** While nothing's wrong with returns or refurbished equipment, you should have the option of buying them or new stuff if you like. Refurbished goods should clearly be marked as such.

✔ **Handling charges or exorbitant shipping charges.** The cheapest price may not be the least you'll spend! Some sleazy dealers add "handling" charges to your purchase, which really jacks up the price. Watch for phone retailers who begin by asking at what site you found your price. They may have higher shipping and handling prices to make up the shortfall. Be sure you understand all the charges that you're going to pay before you buy.

✔ **Credit cards are charged at the time of order, rather than upon shipping.** If this is the case, you do not have to pay. Inform your credit card company and they will be happy to hold the charge for you. Tell them you want to place the charge "in dispute." Instructions for doing this are on the back of your credit card bill. You do not have to pay for something you didn't receive or for receiving something you didn't order. This is known as fraud, and it is illegal.

✔ **Your stuff is shipped elsewhere, and you're told it's your fault.** It's not your fault. It's their fault. They must correct it or you don't have to pay. (See the previous point on placing a charge in dispute.) I'm certain there are even more tricks, but keep in mind that many of these can also be done by mail-order catalogs and local dealers, too.

Alas, there is no central location where you can hear good or bad information about online retailers. As usual, the best way to find out who is good and who's not is to ask around. People freely offer advice — but go with people you know or trust. Online shopping forums may contain shills that push their own stuff and put down the competition. *Caveat emptor.*

Tracking Your Order

The benefit of signing up with a Web retailer is not only that you don't have to reenter shipping information every time, but you can revisit the site to check the progress of your order.

Using your order number, you can visit the Web page again and enter the number to see how it's doing. You'll find that most catalog stores have everything in stock and ship overnight. Otherwise, you can review your order and see its status. Is it "in production" or "backordered" or whatever. (Backorders do happen, so be patient.)

Keeping up-to-date

Web pages and places come and go. New places to shop and new services appear all the time. And some old places rust over and disappear. To help keep you up-to-date with Web shopping, I've created a companion Web page for this book:

```
http://www.wambooli.com/Buying_
A_Computer/
```

That's the location of this book's support page on the Web. Currently, the page offers a list of links for places on the Internet where you can go to buy a computer, comparison shop, and track shipments. Since it's a Web page, I can keep it up-to-date. So if you notice that a Web page link has expired in this book, refer to the above Web page for current information.

When the order ships, you can track it on its merry way to your home or office. This is why I recommend you have your order shipped by an overnight courier or Express Mail from the post office. Using the tracking number (which is usually found on the order sheet or on the Web page), you can visit the courier's Web page to see exactly where your parcels are and when they're most likely due.

With the tracking number you can visit one of the following Web sites to track your order as it's shipped across the country:

- ✔ **Airborne Express:** www.airborne.com/trace/
- ✔ **DHL:** http://dhl.com/track/track.html
- ✔ **Federal Express:** www.fedex.com/
- ✔ **UPS:** www.ups.com/tracking/tracking.html
- ✔ **USPS Express Mail:** www.usps.gov/cttgate/

Receiving your order works just like ordering from a catalog. When the computer arrives, refer to Chapter 22 for setup information.

Chapter 20

Searching for Service and Support

· ·

· ·

A common mistake new computer buyers make is spending all their time worrying about the brand name of a computer or the size of its monitor. But you can't overlook one extremely important factor: the service and support you need after you set up your computer.

Step four in the buying process is to shop for service and support, which is covered in this chapter. If you know anyone who has had a bad computer-buying experience, that person probably forgot this step. After reading this chapter, you won't be the one making that mistake.

How to Find Service and Support

In this section, I make some enemies: Large warehouse stores and department stores are the worst places to buy a computer. Sure, the price may be nice, but after you buy your computer, you're on your own, and that's a mighty lonely place to be if you have a computer question with nowhere to go to get help. It's almost sad, really. My eyes are welling up now, just thinking about it (sniff, sniff).

The moral to this pathetic story is that shopping for service and computer support is just as important as shopping for the computer itself — more so if you're buying your first computer and don't want to feel lost.

To help you, use the list of questions in the next section to grill your prospective computer salesperson. If the salesperson answers most of the questions to your satisfaction, you've found your service and support. If not, you buy somewhere else.

✔ Price is not the most important part of buying a computer. You need service and support more than you need a deal.

✔ Not all warehouse or department stores have awful-to-no service and support. It helps to ask, though, so that you don't become one of the legions who discover a lack of it later.

Service Questions

Service means "Where does my computer get fixed?" and also "Who pays for it?" Consider asking the following questions.

How long is your warranty?

A typical computer warranty is only about half a page long, but that's not important. What is important is the length of *time* the warranty covers your computer.

All major computer manufacturers offer some type of warranty, from a few months to several years. Does the dealer support that warranty and offer additional coverage? Consider it a plus.

✔ Computer warranties may seem rather short: 90 days? But, really, that's enough to cover it. Electronic things, like computers, will break early in their life cycle if anything is wrong. Otherwise, after 90 days of smooth operation, your computer should be good for at least 4 or 5 years.

✔ Be sure to check if the warranty is a replacement or repair warranty. Replacement is better; very few things on a computer can be repaired in a cost-effective way.

✔ After 4 or 5 years the hard drive tends to die and the computer's internal battery needs replacing.

Do you fix the computers at your shop?

If the place that sells your computer fixes them too, great. If your dealer has to send your computer to Japan to have it fixed, buy it somewhere else.

Note that many dealers do not fix the computers they sell. Instead you must contact the manufacturer directly. They won't even accept bad equipment and rarely will they ship it for you. This is not a plus.

Extended-service policies? Don't bother

I don't recommend that anyone purchase an extended-service policy for a computer. The reason is simple: Computers are electronics. If it's going to break, it will break during the first few weeks of use. If your computer can survive that long, then it will be around for its full lifetime, which should be anywhere from 4 to 5 years — longer if you take good care of your equipment.

The first things to break on any computer are its moving parts: the disk drives, hard drive, power supply, and CD-ROM drive. When those things go, the odds are high that you can buy a replacement part that's cheaper, that works better, and that is much faster than the original. In addition, the replacement part probably costs less than any extended-service policy a dealer will try to sell you.

For years, I've followed this rule of never buying an extended-service policy and have never had any problems. When I do, the something that breaks is usually covered by the warranty. In fact, the only time I ever buy any type of extended-service policy is for my car because I trust my personal mechanic more than I trust any car dealer's service department (but that's another story).

Can you fix my computer at my home/office?

Because I live in a remote part of northern Idaho, I always insist that any computer I buy comes with an on-site service policy. When one of my computers broke awhile back, a representative from the company came to my home and fixed it right there on my kitchen table. (And, the service rep had a great view of the lake while fixing my computer.)

- ✔ On-site service is a bonus, well worth it if you have to pay extra for it — especially if you live way out of town, like in Idaho.

- ✔ Don't pay for more than a year of on-site service. See the sidebar entitled "Extended-service policies? Don't bother" for the scoop on why.

Support Questions

Support is help after the sale. It's not help in fixing the computer; it's help for you as a computer user.

For your software, you use the developer's phone support — or buy a good book. For some hardware, you may have to call the hardware manufacturer directly; for what you buy from your dealer, however, you should be able to call them. (Some super nice dealers even help you with your software questions.)

A sample support question to ask

If you're unsure about whether a dealer truly allows you to ask questions after the sale, call up before you buy and ask this question:

I am installing a game, and it says that I need to "swap disks." What does that mean?

The answer to this question is something along the lines of "Take one diskette out of the disk drive and put the next diskette into the disk drive." It works just like changing cassettes in your car radio. If the dealer makes it sound easy on the phone, you've found good support. If the person sounds annoyed by the question or tells you to call the game developer, buy your computer somewhere else.

Can I phone someone to ask questions?

This question is very important. Will the dealer have someone available to help you? Many super-discount places lack the proper support staff to deal with your after-sale troubles. Nothing is more frustrating than to plunk down Big Bucks for a computer and have the dealer ignore you when you come back for help 24 hours later.

> ✔ *Hint:* Any place that also sells TV sets and Levis next to its computers probably won't give you much after-sale service and support.

> ✔ Your salesperson may not be the person you end up calling for support. Salespeople sell. Support people answer questions. (Although sometimes your salesperson may help, don't count on it.)

> ✔ Test the dealer! See the nearby sidebar, "A sample support question to ask," just to make sure that the sales rep is being honest about phone support.

Do you offer classes?

All the better computer dealers have a classroom with a real live, human teacher right there, ready to help you do something bizarre, such as run Windows. A major plus. Some dealers have classes in conjunction with local universities or high schools. Great.

> ✔ Expect to pay perhaps a little more for the support, handholding, and general warm-fuzzy feeling you want. The price you pay is more than offset by removing after-sale anxiety.

✔ Obviously, buying from a catalog or on the Internet means you won't have any classroom handy. That's right! A good reason to consider paying a bit more for local service and support.

✔ I first went out to buy a computer with $1,500 in my pocket. I waited and waited in the showroom and eventually grabbed a salesman by the arm and said, "What can you tell me about this Apple II computer?" He said, "Why don't you just go out and buy a book on it?" Needless to say, I bought my first computer elsewhere.

Support Issues for Buying on the Internet

Buying on the Internet is just like mail-order when it comes to getting support. Depending on what you bought and where, you could end up with an 800 number, on-site service, or the lonely echoes of your palpitating heart. But with buying online, you have to *dig* to find out which type of support is available and how the service works. Here are my suggestions:

✔ Always buy from places offering toll-free tech support. Many on-line dealers have a support line for everything they sell. Some have you call the manufacturer, which can be a letdown.

✔ Ensure that the dealer supports what they sell and that they don't redirect you elsewhere. This is a "fine print" issue. Always read all the conditions when you buy. Sometimes you have to click a special link to discover what the conditions are. Beware!

✔ If possible, try to sign up for on-site service.

✔ Scour that Web page! Look for support issues like a FAQ (Frequently Asked Questions) list, troubleshooting guide, comment location, feedback, or even maybe a chat room. Oftentimes common problems and their solutions can be found on a vendor's Web page.

✔ E-mail support works, but it's spotty. When I ordered a computer online and the monitor was bad, I e-mailed the vendor. They replied quickly and sent me a new monitor along with a shipping tag. I put the old monitor in the new monitor's box and shipped it back. It cost me nothing and I never spoke with a person. To me, that was amazing.

✔ On the flip-side of e-mail support, there is the runaround issue. You can e-mail Microsoft all you want about their software bundled with your new computer, but Microsoft will tell you it's up to the dealer to give you support. The dealer will claim it's Microsoft's job. And so it goes.

✔ If buying on the Internet worries you in any way, then don't!

Chapter 21

Buying the Computer

· ·

In This Chapter

▶ A quick review of the buying process

▶ Spending your "extra" money

▶ Taking the plunge and making the purchase

▶ Remembering some last-minute buying tips

· ·

*F*ind someone whose fingernails have been chewed to the nubs, and he has probably been looking for a computer. Simply mention "buying a computer" to anyone, especially someone who is now looking, and he'll probably faint, maybe even die.

The book arms you with all the knowledge you need to know what a computer does. You've been braced, studied, quizzed, and oriented. Time to buy. A whole chapter for that? Yup. Buying is the big move that many people put off. This chapter is devoted entirely to motivating you to go for it.

A Review of the Five Steps

Buying a computer is cinchy, providing you follow the five steps as outlined in Chapter 1. As a review, here they are:

1. **Identify your computer needs.**

   This is easy. What do you want the computer to do? Answer that question and everything else falls into place.

2. **Find the software to meet those needs.**

   This is where you software shop, which is covered in Chapter 16. The software boxes themselves describe the hardware required to run the software. (Remember, it's the software that's more important). Filling out your software worksheets marks the end of this step.

3. **Find the hardware to run your software.**

   Part II of this book reviews all the hardware and software issues for you. Matching up all your software worksheets to the hardware worksheet is covered in Chapter 17.

4. **Locate a place you can do business with — some outfit with both the service and support you need.**

   The most neglected step. If you ever have any problems buying a computer, or know of anyone who relates a horror story, their problem was omitting this important step.

5. **Buy the computer.**

   Do it!

Why is this last step so hard? Because buying a computer frightens many people. Hopefully those people will turn to this chapter first; then read the previous chapters to bone-up on what's important. After that, this last step should be a snap.

What to Spend "Extra" Money On

Buying anything above and beyond what you have written down on your worksheets depends on how much you can afford. So the real question is "Where should I spend my money first?"

Without a doubt, spend any "extra" money you may have on the following items, in this order:

- **Microprocessor:** First and foremost, buy yourself the fastest microprocessor you can afford. This is a must. If your software craves only a simple Pentium II, then go for a Pentium III. If you can afford the fastest Pentium III, spend your money there. You won't regret it.

- **Hard drive:** Second, buy a higher-capacity hard drive. If you've followed the hard drive size calculation from Chapter 17 and can afford a larger hard drive, buy it.

- **Memory:** Third, get more memory. If your software can get by with 32MB, then 64MB is even better. If you can afford it, get 128MB with 256MB around the corner.

- **Monitor:** True, a 17-inch monitor is plenty big enough, but 19 inches impresses. And those 21-inch monitors — if you have the money — are wonderful.

The idea is to spend more money on the things that are the hardest to upgrade later. Everything on a computer can be swapped out for something faster and better, although some things are more easily swapped than others.

The most difficult upgrade is the microprocessor, so that gets first priority. Then comes the hard drive and the memory. Most computers can sport a second hard drive, and memory is easy to upgrade. Doing so first, however, saves you the trouble later (especially if you have the money now). Finally, monitors can be replaced at any time.

When Do I Get My Computer?

It's possible to go to buy a computer and walk out of the store with it that day. Most home and personal systems can be found this way. The iMac, for example, comes in its own friendly box, as do numerous low-end and home PCs. There's everything you need! But if you've ordered a special configuration, it may take longer.

Most of the time, plan on waiting anywhere from a couple of hours to several days for your computer, depending on how busy the dealer is and whether the dealer tests on your computer before giving it to you. (Read more about that in Chapter 22.)

Mail-order computers may arrive right away, or they may take anywhere from a week to three weeks to arrive. The amount of time depends on how busy the dealer is and whether the parts you need are in stock. Always ask! Never assume that the Federal Express driver is sitting there with his engine idling waiting to unload your new computer.

✔ Computer sales are seasonal, like most things. End-of-the year, back-to-school, and Christmas are the busiest times to order and the longest times to wait for custom systems.

✔ High demand means you'll have to wait.

✔ Custom computers take time to build as well. I've waited up to three weeks before one of my systems was waiting for pickup on the dock. (I was able to track it's progress on the Web — which was very interesting to watch.)

Don't Ever Put a "Deposit" on a Computer!

When someone asks you for a deposit up front for your computer, run like the wind! Up-front deposits are one surefire way to find a shady computer dealer. You should never put down a deposit on a computer. The best way to be sure is to always pay by credit card.

Not everyone is out to rip you off. Most of the classic computer-store scams, however, involve a "rob Peter to pay Paul" scheme. Writing a check for your computer at this type of place usually means that you lose your money.

Paying with a credit card is the best option because you can always cancel your order. Most dealers don't charge your card until the computer ships or you pick it up. If you don't receive it and the charge shows up on your bill, call the dealer and ask what's up. If their answers or attitude don't sit well with you, immediately phone your credit card company and place the charge "in dispute." The credit card company will tell you what to do from there.

Don't fret over having to put a deposit down to hold a special on-order item. For example, you may need some special piece of equipment that's not in stock. If so, a 5 to 20 percent deposit is okay to hold it. Again, use the dealer's reputation as the deciding factor and pay by credit card.

Hey, Bud! You're Ready to Buy

It's time to take the plunge. Jump in with both feet, and get that computer. As always, you need to take into consideration and remember some things when you're buying your dream computer:

- ✔ Ask your dealer about *burn-in,* a period of time before you buy a computer when the dealer puts it through its paces, just to ensure that everything is working properly.

- ✔ Don't forget software! You need software to make your computer hardware go. Software is expensive; you'll eventually spend as much on software as you spend on your computer.

- ✔ There are other items you may want to get your computer: a printer, scanner, digital camera, or other "toys." These are covered in Chapters 23 and 24, but for now just worry about the computer. You'll have enough to deal with when you get it!

- ✔ If your dealer offers classes, now would be a good time to sign up for one. Give yourself a week or so alone with your computer before you show up (with your yellow pad full of questions).

A few last-minute buying tips

Never worry about technology making your computer obsolete. For example, there may be a rumor out now that Apple is coming up with a new, more powerful line of iMacs. . . . So what! Buy your iMac now and start using it now. The difference between today and tomorrow's computer is so slight it's not worth mentioning. (Now today's computer verses next year's computer is another thing, but you won't be waiting that long.)

Computer ads are riddled with cryptograms and small words that may earn you big points in Scrabble but confuse the heck out of any first-time computer buyer. Check any unfamiliar terms with *The Illustrated Computer Dictionary For Dummies,* 3rd Edition, which my wife and I wrote (and IDG Books Worldwide, Inc., published). Also look in that book's index to find a more detailed definition or explanation.

Never pay for a computer with a check; use a credit card.

Try not to buy your computer on a Saturday. This advice has nothing to do with the zodiac. It's just that Saturday tends to be the busiest day for buying a computer. Also, most computer stores close on Sunday, so if you get stuck, you have no one to call.

Allow yourself time to get to know your computer. Don't expect to rush home and instantly be brilliant with it. These things take time.

The final step is to . . .

Go for it! When you're finally ready to buy, take a deep breath and buy your computer!

Part IV
Living With Your Computer

The 5th Wave   By Rich Tennant

"YES, I THINK IT'S AN ERROR MESSAGE."

In this part . . .

Wouldn't it be great if expedient and cheery young people in white lab coats set up your new computer for you, making everything just so? It's close to that. Many of today's systems come nearly ready to go with only a few things for you to assemble. Other systems take more time, but the issue here is that the buying process doesn't really stop after you've signed the receipt. No, there's more to do and this book is here to help you do it.

This part of the book is devoted to after-sale euphoria — or depression. There's no sense in being left in a lurch with boxes, unpacking, assembling and trying to work with things. So this part of the book takes you through the stages of computer assembly and getting it up and running. Then I'll cover other things you need or might want for the computer, along with some good advice on how to maintain your computer for years to come.

Chapter 22

Helpful Hints on Computer Setup

· ·

· ·

*N*othing can be more satisfying than opening up something new. Computer marketing types even have a name for it: the out-of-box experience. It almost sounds religious.

"Yes, Doctor, I had an out-of-box experience. For a moment, I saw our old bread machine. And then the water heater that blew up last year. It told me that I had to go back . . . go back to assemble my computer."

Sheesh.

If you haven't yet put your computer together, this chapter offers some helpful hints and strategies. If your computer is fully assembled and up and running, skim to the section "Breaking It In: The Burn-In Test," later in this chapter, for some helpful hints for putting your computer's wee li'l rubber feet to the fire.

Check the Shipment

First things first. When you get the computer, review the packing slip. Compare it with your order. Ensure that everything you're due has come.

If you ordered from a catalog or the Internet, review the boxes before signing the delivery sheet. The friendly delivery service guy will even help you out if you notice a damaged box. Most services will return the box immediately if it appears damaged. Just remember *not* to sign for damaged material!

> ✔ Count the boxes! An iMac comes in one box, but most other computers come in two, one for the monitor and another for the console. If you've ordered a printer, scanner, or other peripherals (like mondo speakers), then they'll probably come in extra boxes as well.

> ✔ Sometimes packing lists come separately, or you may have an invoice. Either way, make sure that you have all the boxes you need.

Setting Up the Computer

Unless the nice person you bought your computer from sets it up right there on your desk, you have to do it yourself. It's much easier than it was in the early days. The first Apple computer (which cost $666 in 1977, by the way) came as a bag of diodes and electronic parts. You had to solder the whole thing together from scratch!

Today, assembling a computer is easy, often easier than assembling a stereo or hooking up a VCR (but not by much). You won't even need a screwdriver.

Open the boxes

Setting up a computer starts with opening big boxes — typically, two to three.

If one box screams "Open me first!" open it first. It probably contains instructions. Otherwise, open the console box and look for the setup instructions.

After you find the instructions, locate the sheet that lists all the parts that came with your computer. Try to find all the parts to make sure that you have everything. Nothing is more distressing than discovering on Saturday that you're missing a part and having to wait until late in the day on Monday to use your computer.

Box-opening etiquette

Be careful when you're opening any box. The "grab and rip" approach can be dangerous because those massive ugly staples used to close the box can fling off and give you an unwanted body piercing. (It's fashionable in parts of Silicon Valley to have a large staple through the eyebrow.)

The same holds true with using a box knife; use a small blade because you don't want to slice through or into anything electronic — or fleshy, for that matter.

If you bought any expansion options — extra memory or a network card, for example — the dealer will have installed them. You don't have to plug them in on your own.

Also, don't panic if you can't find some small computer part (like the keyboard) when you're unpacking your computer. These beasts come in lots of boxes and in boxes within boxes. Look everywhere before calling your dealer and accusing him of omitting something.

✔ Some boxes have opening instructions. I kid you not! My huge monitor had to be opened on top and then turned upside down so that I could lift the box off of the monitor. Remember that gravity is your friend.

✔ There is no easy way to ensure that the stuff installed inside the computer is really what you paid for. Generally speaking, however, news of improperly installed hardware or "switcheroos" travels quickly. Your computer guru can quickly tell you if your computer's console contains all the guts you've paid for.

✔ Always keep the phone numbers of your dealer and computer manufacturer handy. (Space is provided on the Cheat Sheet in the front of this book.) Also, look out for special support numbers; some manufacturers offer a 24-hour, toll-free support number. Write them numbers down!

What can I toss out?

Nothing, yet. You can unpack most of the material in the boxes now if you like, setting each item aside. There will probably be several stacks:

✔ The monitor, with its cables

✔ The console

✔ The power cable

- ✔ The mouse
- ✔ The keyboard
- ✔ A stack of disks
- ✔ A stack of "free" offers and other paperwork
- ✔ Reference material

Just keep everything in its stack for now. You'll need each item as you build the computer. And just about everything you'll want to keep. Some of the "free" offers can get tossed, but don't throw anything out yet until you *know* what it is.

Should I keep the boxes?

Computers are shipped with a great deal of packing material, plastic bags, twist ties, rubber bands, nylons, and Hershey bars. For now, keep *everything*.

There are two reasons to keep the boxes and packing materials: to return a bum computer to the dealer and for when you move.

If the computer dies on you, you'll need something in which to ship it back. Believe me, it's worth it to keep the original boxes. Some dealers claim that by not shipping the computer in its original box it voids your warranty. That's not good.

If you move a lot, you should keep the boxes. Many moving companies won't insure your computers unless they're in the original packing material with the original foam peanuts and Hershey bars.

- ✔ Also, be on the lookout for boxes within boxes! Don't toss out any box until you've examined it thoroughly for anything you may need.
- ✔ The Hershey bars thing is a joke loosely related to a speech given in the film *Dr. Strangelove*. (A Hershey bar is a chocolate candy bar; this is for my friends in the UK, where they're called Mars bars.)
- ✔ The boxes do make for clutter. After a year, I throw my boxes out. A year is usually well past the time a computer or monitor will turn sour, so then it's okay. (Back when I moved a lot, though, I kept all my boxes forever.)

Do I have to read the manuals?

Nope. I recommend looking over all the manuals, though, just to see what you have. You may get a humorous tutorial or guide for assembling your computer. Keep all the manuals together in one spot so that you can read them later — if you dare!

✔ Most computers don't come with any real manuals anymore. If any information is to be found, it's displayed by the computer itself. (This won't help you much when the power goes out, though.)

✔ I have a special shelf in my office where I keep all my computer disks and manuals. Each computer has its own area on the shelf and, I admit, it looks junky. But at least I know where all the material is located.

Putting It Together

Now that you know where the computer goes and you have everything situated for optimal computer usage, go ahead and put it together. How? Although each computer is different, you put everything together in some standard ways.

The whole operation takes about half an hour, more if you have additional items such as printers or scanners to install.

✔ Be patient. Take care. Give yourself plenty of room and time.

✔ Keep pets and small children at a distance when you set up your computer. If you keep a cold beverage handy, put it in a safe place (like in another time zone) where spilling it won't be a problem.

✔ You may need a flashlight to see behind your computer after it's set up.

Where will Mr. Computer live?

Find a home for your computer. Clear off your desk- or tabletop, allowing enough room for the computer and keyboard. Remember that your computer will have an octopus of cables and peripherals around it. Make room for all that stuff, too.

The computer must live somewhere near a power outlet, preferably an independent circuit with a grounded plug.

If it's a 20 amp circuit, all the better, though most computers and laser printers can function fine from standard 15 amp circuits. (And if this amp stuff confuses you, never mind.)

✔ Computers need room to breathe. Don't put your computer in a closet, box, recessed vault, grotto, or other cave-like place with poor ventilation.

✔ Don't put your computer by a sunny window because that heats up the computer and gives it anxiety.

- ✔ If you can sit on the table, then the table can support the computer. Don't put Mr. Computer on a wobbly table or anything you wouldn't sit on yourself (like the cat).

- ✔ The obvious place to set the computer is on a well-supported computer desk.

- ✔ An "independent circuit" is one that's not shared by other devices in your home or office. For example, if you plug your computer into the same circuit as the refrigerator or air conditioner, then it may blow a fuse when either of those devices is turned on.

- ✔ If you have a desktop computer, you can set the monitor on top of the console. If you have a mini-tower, set the monitor to the side. The mini-tower can even go on the floor, if you like.

- ✔ Try to position the computer so that no lights shine directly into the monitor. Your eyes can get really frazzled from the glare of the lights or the sun. My eye doctor tells me that monitor glare is, in fact, the biggest cause of eye fatigue from using a computer.

Preparing to plug things in

Just about everything on a computer has a plug that plugs into the wall socket. Your monitor, computer box, printer, and anything else that's peripheral (such as a modem) has to plug into a wall socket. Find that wall socket now!

Before plugging anything else in, make sure that the computer is turned off! You don't want to plug something into the computer when it's turned on, or else you may damage its electronic components. Double-check to make sure that you have everything switched off. (For switches with a I and an O, the I means On.)

- ✔ I recommend buying one of those *power strips* that lets you plug four, six, or more items into one receptacle.

- ✔ An even better deal is to get a *surge suppressor* or a *UPS* (short for Uninterruptible Power Supply). A surge suppressor protects your computer against power surges, and a UPS gives you time to save your work when the power goes down. Check out the sidebar entitled "Ode to plugging things into the wall" for more information.

Setting up the console

The first thing you'll most likely set up is the *console,* which is the box that everything else plugs into. This is the least mobile of the units you unpack, so setting it up first gives you a good starting base.

Remove the console from its plastic bag, if you haven't already done so.

Don't slide the console against the back of the desk just yet. In fact, twist the console around 90 degrees so that it's facing right or left. You need access to the back of the console.

Plug the power cable into the console and then — ensuring that the console is turned off — plug the power cable into the wall. If you hear the console switch on after you plug it in, no problem: Just turn it off.

There may be a map or large sheet of paper that came with your computer. That sheet tells you how and where to plug various things in. Refer to that sheet as you work through the following sections.

Attaching the mouse and keyboard

Plug the mouse and keyboard into the console.

On a PC, the mouse and keyboard each have their own tiny hole into which they plug. They plug in only one way (you have to line up the pins with the holes). You have to push hard to plug them in wrong, so don't force things.

String the mouse cable out on your desk to ensure that it's not tangled or looped.

Set the keyboard and mouse out of the way so that you can attach other devices.

For the Mac, the keyboard plugs into the console and then the mouse plugs into the keyboard.

Attaching other devices

If your computer has special external speakers, plug them in now. Locate the speaker holes on the computer. Plug the speakers in.

If there are left and right speaker holes, great! Otherwise, you'll need to plug in one speaker and then plug the second speaker's cord into the back of the first speaker. If there is a woofer unit, then everything probably plugs into it first.

If the speakers need electrical power, ensure that the speakers are off and then plug them into the power strip.

Ode to plugging things into the wall

Nearly everything that comes with a computer should be plugged into the wall or some similar wall-socket-like device. Ideally, the console and monitor should be plugged into a UPS or Uninterruptable Power Supply — a power source capable of running the computer during brief power outages.

Other devices should be plugged into a power strip or surge protector.

Printers can also be plugged into a power strip. A laser printer, however, should be plugged directly into the wall. (Printers do not need to be plugged into a UPS; just wait until the power comes on again to print.)

Here are some other power/electrical issues and rules:

✔ Never use an extension cord to meet your power needs. People trip over extension cords and routinely unplug them.

✔ Don't use any power splitters or those octopus-like things that turn one socket into three.

✔ Computers need grounded sockets, which must have three prongs in them.

✔ If the UPS has extra sockets, plug in your desk clock or an external modem.

✔ Secondary monitors (you can have more than one; see Chapter 8) need not be plugged into the UPS.

✔ Not every UPS has full UPS sockets. For example, some UPS devices may have two full UPS sockets and two surge-protected sockets that are not backed up by battery.

Setting up the monitor

If your monitor is separate from the console, then set the monitor beside the console. This is not its final resting place, merely a way to set it down while you work.

Plug the monitor into the console.

Ensure that the monitor is turned off and then plug it into a power receptacle. If you have a UPS, plug the monitor into the UPS.

Plugging in other stuff

Finally, anything else you bought also has to be plugged into the computer box. For example, an *external* modem (one that lives outside your computer), has a cable that connects the modem to your computer. The modem also has a cable that connects to a phone jack in the wall, plus a place for you to plug your desktop phone into the modem. (Yes, this process is complex, but if it weren't, it wouldn't be a computer!)

If you already have a printer, plug its printer cable into its back. Then plug the other end of the cable into the back of the console.

Plug in anything else as well.

Finishing up

Plug all the power cords into the wall socket. Ensure that everything is switched off and then plug it all in.

Reorient the console so that it's facing forward and the ugly cables are 'round back. (Do this gently so you don't unplug anything.)

If you have a desktop computer, you can set the monitor on top of the computer now.

Set up everything just the way you want.

✔ Do not set a 19-inch or larger monitor on top of a desktop PC unit. The heavy monitor may crush the console, which is designed to support lighter-weight monitors only.

✔ If there isn't enough cable to put the keyboard and monitor to one side of the console, you can buy extension cables at your favorite computer store.

✔ Some monitors come with a tilt-and-swivel base, which enables you to move the monitor to various orientations, albeit stiffly. This type of base is also an option you can buy for the monitor if it's not already built in.

✔ As with the console, the monitor needs to breathe. Don't set anything on top of the monitor or cover its wee tiny air vents in any way.

Turning the Thing On

To use your computer, turn everything on!

What to turn on first?

Almost everything connected to a computer has an on-off switch. So the question is obviously, "Which thing do I turn on first." An equally valid question is, "What do I turn off last?" Decisions, decisions. . . .

The answer? Seriously, turn on the console *last*. Turning everything on at once is okay, but if you have a choice, make the console the last thing you turn on. That way it will "see" and recognize all the devices plugged into it.

Turning it off

For both the Mac and PC, you must properly shut down the computer. This involves choosing a Shutdown menu item. Where it can be found depends on which version of Windows or the Apple System Software you're using.

If the computer shuts down by itself, great. The console will turn itself off and you can turn off everything else by flipping its switch. If the console doesn't switch off automatically, flip its switch (or punch its button) as well.

Breaking It In: The Burn-In Test

One way to ensure that your new equipment is up to snuff is to put it through a special test — the *burn-in test*. The object of this test is to break in your new computer during its warranty period. If something is amiss, you want to know about it before the warranty expires.

When you take your new computer home, follow these two instructions:

- ✔ Keep your computer turned on 24 hours a day for two weeks.
- ✔ Once a day, turn the machine off, wait a minute, and then turn it back on.

Because of the way electronic components are designed, faulty chips usually go bad within their first 48 hours of use. By testing your computer this way, you're certain to find any faults immediately. Turning the power supply off and on each day helps to ensure that it's tough enough to stand the load.

After the two-week test, you can obey whatever on-off habits you've deemed proper for your computer. At that point, in fact, it will probably behave itself for years!

What's Next?

With the computer all set up and ready to roll, you're probably tempted to turn it on. But, wait. You should look for a few things before you steamroller ahead:

✔ Find any manuals that came with your computer. Look for the ones that contain directions and troubleshooting help. Keep these manuals handy.

✔ Always retain the manuals that came with your computer plus any software manuals. Keep any disks and their software manuals together.

✔ You can throw away most of the little scraps of paper now. Don't throw away anything that has a phone number on it until you've written the number down elsewhere.

✔ Mail in your registration or warranty card. Make a note of the computer's serial number, and file it away as well. In an office situation, you should keep track of all your equipment's serial numbers.

Dealing with software

You may have purchased some software with your computer. If so, great. However, leave all those boxes alone for now. One mistake many beginners make is overwhelming themselves with computer software. Although it's okay to buy lots of software (and if you haven't, you'll probably buy more later), it's counterproductive to use it all right away.

✔ Your computer's operating system is the most important piece of software you have. Find out about it first.

✔ See Chapter 14 for more information about operating systems.

✔ If you have anything you must do — a priority project, for example — set the software you need aside from the rest of the stuff. For example, if learning how to use Quicken, Word, or QuarkXPress is your top priority, set aside the software and get ready to learn and use it first. Everything else can wait.

✔ Remember that no job can be done immediately. No matter how annoying your boss is, you must learn to use software before you can be productive with it. Give yourself at least two weeks before you squeeze something brilliant from a computer.

Dealing with other hardware

You may have purchased other hardware goodies, each waiting for hookup and installation. Put them on hold for now. Trying to learn too much can boggle you. Handle the basics first, install extra hardware later.

✔ Hardware is added to a computer either internally or externally.

✔ Installing internal hardware requires some type of computer nerd. True, you can do it yourself. Many books and magazine articles go into the details, if you want to bother with installing internal hardware. My advice is to force someone else to do it.

   ✔ External hardware requires a power cable and some type of cable to connect it with the computer. A few devices don't use a power cable (they run off your brain waves). Also, you need special software to run the external hardware; a scanner requires scanning software, and a modem requires communications software.

Understanding Your System

Give yourself time to read about your system, time to play, and time to relax and have fun with your computer. Believe it or not, the best way to understand how to use a computer system is to play around with it. Poke around. Test things. Try weird options, and see what they do. As long as you're not rushed to start your serious work, you have time to easily grow with the system. After the workload comes, you'll feel good about the system, and, lo, that expected and much-rumored frustration won't be there.

   ✔ After you've used your software for about a month, go back and reread the manual; you'll be surprised at how much clearer it seems. It actually makes sense! (People who write manuals are overly familiar with the product and forget what it's like to be a novice.)

   ✔ By reading the manual a second time, you pick up a few more tips and some shortcuts. This trick is just another one the experts use to become experts.

   ✔ As a kind word of advice, give yourself two weeks to find out about your software before you start doing any serious work with it.

   ✔ The more time you have to play with and figure out how to use your software, the more productive you become.

   ✔ Give yourself three weeks (if you have it) to become used to your new computer system. Then, when you're ready to get to work, you'll know some tricks and you should proceed smoothly. Heck, you'll be a computer wizard by then!

Chapter 23

Time to Get a Printer

● ●

In This Chapter

▶ Understanding the various types of printers

▶ Buying a printer

▶ Buying extra items for the printer

▶ Setting up your printer

● ●

*Y*our new computer will need a printer. It's a necessary part of the purchase — like software. You can buy the computer and the printer together, or you can come back for it later. Either way, every computer needs a printer eventually.

This chapter covers the printer purchase. Fortunately, if you already have your computer and its software, picking a printer will be a snap. As with the computer, it's software that controls your printer. Your software can instantly help you narrow the printer choices and options.

Different Printers for Different Printing

Forget brand names. When it comes to printers, there are two basic models you can choose from:

✔ Laser printers

✔ Ink jet printers

Both types of printers get the job done. Both can do color. Beyond that, they differ in speed, quality, and cost.

✔ Generally speaking, you'll probably get an ink jet printer. They're fast, quiet, and relatively inexpensive — and they do color.

✔ Laser printers are a must if you're in business. They're fast, quiet, and produce a better-quality image than ink jet printers (but not by much).

- ✓ If you want color, go with an ink jet printer. Nearly all ink jet printers sold today do color. Some laser printers do color, although their price is quite steep and they're slow.

- ✓ Other types of printers exist. The most common of them is the all-in-one printer/copier/scanner/fax, such as the Hewlett-Packard OfficeJet.

- ✓ Impact printers are required if you're printing on multipart forms. This used to be the most popular type of computer printer (the "dot matrix" printers of days gone by). Now it's usually a special order item.

Printer speed

A printer's speed is measured in pages per minute, or ppm. The higher the value, the better. Some laser printers can manage 20 ppm, under optimal conditions, of course (usually repeatedly printing the same page of simple text). The more complex the graphics, the slower the printer goes.

Most ink jet printers manage between 4 and 8 ppm. Color laser printers are very slow, typically dribbling out 4 ppm or fewer. Remember that what you see in the ads is an optimal value. The page-per-minute values you experience will doubtless be less.

The print quality

Print quality is judged by how well the printer produces an image on paper, which depends on how many tiny dots the printer can squeeze on a square inch of paper. The more dots, the higher the printer's resolution and the better the image.

Early laser printers could print 300 dots horizontally by 300 dots vertically. Today's models can easily manage 600 x 600 dots in a square inch. Some models can manage 1,200 dots per inch (dpi), which is the same resolution as a professional typesetting machine.

Ink jet printers have similar dots-per-inch values. Higher resolution is available, but you pay more for it. Also, the print quality on an ink jet printer depends greatly on the paper quality. Special ink-jet-printer paper is available and produces a much better image (the paper literally absorbs the image).

How much?

Printers range in price from $150 for a cheap model I wouldn't wish on anyone to $2,000 for high-quality color printers. You'll probably pay anywhere from $250 to $600 or more for your printer, depending on what you get.

A typical laser printer ranges in price from $500 up to several thousand dollars for the color laser printers.

Ink jet printers start out at a couple hundred dollars and climb up to more than $500 for the high-output color models.

There are several things that affect a printer's price. The top two are quality and speed. But between the various models, you'll find subtle differences based on the following factors:

- ✔ **Memory.** Some printers come with about a megabyte of their own RAM, more or less. The more memory you add to a printer, the faster it goes — especially for graphics. In fact, if you plan to print lots of graphics, pay the extra money and load your printer up with RAM.

- ✔ **Fonts.** You pay more for printers that know how to use lots of fonts. This capability really isn't important; the operating system sends the printer any font you see on the screen. The fonts the printer knows about (called, remarkably, *printer fonts*) print faster and generally look better than other fonts. The more fonts your printer has, the more money it costs.

- ✔ **Brains.** Some printers are actually computers, ones that are specifically designed to print on paper (not foul up your phone bill). Cheaper printers? They're cheap because they don't have brains.

  For example, you may notice that one color ink printer costs $800 and another model — just as technically good — costs $250. The difference? The $800 model has a brain. The $250 model uses your computer as its brain, which means that it takes that model longer to print *and* your computer slows down while the printer is printing.

- ✔ **PostScript.** A special type of laser printer is the PostScript printer. Essentially another type of computer, this one is dedicated to producing high-quality images. The PostScript printer does all the thinking on its own. Your software merely says "Do this," and the printer does the rest, freeing up the computer to do other things.

  PostScript printers originally appeared for the Macintosh computer. Although you can get one for your PC as well, you have two pills to swallow. The first is that PostScript printers are expensive. All them thar PostScript brains cost money. The second pill to swallow is that PostScript printers work best with software that produces PostScript output, primarily graphics applications, though you can look on the side of any software box to see whether it's PostScript happy.

- ✔ **Other stuff:** Oh, and other factors determine a printer's price: whether it has an optional serial port, networking options, and other details too technical to bore you with here.

- ✔ For some reason, the USB version of a printer costs more than the printer port version of the same printer.

Remember that all Macintoshes now use USB printers. If you need one, you can purchase special Mac printer port/USB cable adapters. However, it's best to buy the printer that goes with your computer.

Printers can also be wide or narrow. I paid a little more and got a wide ink printer so that I can do posters for our local theater.

Laser Printers Go "Fwoom Pkt Shhh!"

Laser printers are similar to the desktop copying machine, and they work on the same principles. The difference is that a laser printer receives its information from the computer instead of using a reflected image, which is how the copy machine does it. A laser beam is used to draw the image.

Laser printers have really come down in price over the past decade. Today's models are cheap and reliable and don't use all the watts required of the earlier models.

To print the image, the laser printer uses a toner cartridge. These can be expensive! If you have a choice between two laser printers of similar quality, check the cost of the toner cartridge. You may think you're saving money on a printer now, but if it costs you $150 a year (or more often) to replace the toner cartridge, are you really saving money?

Ink Printers Go "Thwip, Sft-Sft-Sft, Clunk!"

Up front, what you fear: Ink printers work by spewing ink all over paper, similar to the way a three-year-old spits water on his little brother in the bathtub.

Now, the truth: An *ink jet printer* works by lobbing a tiny ball of ink precisely at the paper, forming a teensy-tiny dot on the page. The ink dries instantly, and the resulting piece of paper does not smudge. In many cases, the paper looks *exactly* like it came from a spendy laser printer.

Another truth: Ink can be any color. Most of the newer, swankier ink jet printers actually lob four different colors of ink at the page: black, cyan (red), yellow, and magenta (blue). These colors combine to make outstanding — almost photographic — output.

Truly, an ink jet printer is ideal for most situations. Although it's not as fast or spiffy as a laser printer, its output is impressive — especially when you print on top-quality printer paper. Ink jet printers are also the least expensive way to print color, which is perfect for the home or small business.

Why are ink jet printers so expensive? Because the ink cartridges themselves are outrageously expensive! Not only that, the cartridges run dry when you print a lot, forcing you to constantly pay for newer cartridges! It's an endless cycle!

- ✔ Odds are pretty good that you'll get an ink printer for your first computer purchase. It's a good way to go.

- ✔ If you can afford it, get a four-color ink jet printer. That's one black ink source, plus a three-color ink source (cyan, yellow, and magenta).

- ✔ Because little mechanical movement is involved, ink jet printers are quiet. Sometimes the brand name implies something about the printer's silence: Quietwriter, Whisperwriter, and Gaspingforairwriter, for example.

- ✔ Ink jet printers keep their ink in a reservoir rather than on a ribbon. Some brands have a number of reservoirs, each with a different color. When you buy the printer, make sure to buy some spare ink cartridges.

- ✔ Try to get an ink printer that has separate ink cartridges, one for color (or one that has separate colors) and the other for black ink.

- ✔ That special photographic paper is expensive. I just bought a box of eight sheets for $15. (Call me dumb, but it's what I do for a living.) The output on that paper, however, is almost the same as an 8-x-10 photograph.

Buying the Printer

Buying a printer can be done at the time you buy the computer or later after you've toyed with the computer a while. There is no rule that says every computer must have a printer. And you don't have to print everything you do on the computer.

- ✔ Your computer manufacturer's brand-name printer is not required for your brand-name computer. Just about any computer can have any printer attached. It doesn't matter.

✔ Printers can be added to a computer at any time.

✔ Your computer has the ability to control more than one printer at a time. You can add many printers via the USB cable. On a PC without USB, you must add additional printer ports to connect more than one printer.

What does your software say?

To find out which printer will work best for you, check your software.

Not every software has specific printer suggestions. Some software merely says on the box, "Any PC or Windows compatible printer." But some types of software, especially graphics programs, will say, "Any compatible printer or PostScript printer." In that case, you should look into getting a PostScript printer for the best possible (and fastest) output.

Printer shopping

You don't have to buy the printer at the same place you bought the computer. It's nice, for example, if you had a pleasant buying experience and would like to honor them with repeat business. But if their price is too high or they don't sell what you want, feel free to go elsewhere.

✔ If you're set on a specific make and model of printer, consider using the Internet to shop — after all, you have a computer now! Use a shopping agent like mySimon (as described in Chapter 19) to help you find the cheapest printer.

✔ The same rules for buying a computer — or buying any extra hardware — apply for buying a printer.

Printers do not come with cables!

Before diving in to the fast and exciting world of printer types, it's important to note one little-known axiom of the computer-buying world: Printers do not come with cables. Gasp!

Unlike a stereo or VCR, which comes with all the required cables, a computer printer doesn't come with everything you need to hook it up to your computer. The reason is simple: Not all printers are hooked up to the same type of computer.

- ✔ The printer cable can't be more than 20 feet long, which is kind of common sense because the best place for your printer should be within arm's reach — or did you know that? Well, now you do.

- ✔ A USB printer cable should be 3 meters (9 feet) or less in length.

- ✔ Note that there are "A" and "B" connectors for a USB cable. Ensure you get the proper one for your printer to plug into your computer.

- ✔ Most of today's computers are sold with a "smart" printer port. If your printer takes advantage of the smart printer port, ensure that you buy a smart printer cable. Some cheaper printer cables lack the smart feature (which is merely a few extra lines of data).

Printers don't come with paper, either!

It almost goes without saying that your printer needs paper. Laser printers eat regular copy-machine paper, or you can pay more to get special high-quality paper.

Ink jet printers can print on any paper as well, though do yourself a favor and get special ink printer paper. It costs more, but the quality is worth it. Also, specialty papers are available for creating photographic-quality output, as well as iron-on T-shirt transfers, transparencies, and other fancy time-wasters.

Don't bother with fanfold paper (the kind with the sheets connected to each other) unless you have a printer that has a proper paper feeder. Some ink printers have them, nearly all impact printers have them, but laser printers do not.

- ✔ Always buy the proper paper for your printer. Look in the documentation that came with your printer. Sometimes printer manufacturers recommend the kind of paper that is best for your printer.

- ✔ Stock up on paper! Nothing is worse than running out of paper and not having any backup. Go to a discount paper warehouse place, if one is near you, and buy a whole box.

Buy some extra ink

As long as you're at it, buy your printer a second toner cartridge or backup ink supply. That way, should you run out quicker than you expected, you'll have the replacement handy.

Setting Up the Printer

Setting up a printer is a snap. The hard part comes later, when you must force your software to recognize and control the printer. (You'll need to refer to how your operating system does that, which you can find in a book about your operating system.) You set up the printer similarly to the way you set up everything else. Take it out of the box, unpack it, and then set it where you want it. Put the printer near the computer — the nearer, the better — although it doesn't need to be too close.

✔ Keeping the printer at arm's length can come in handy.

✔ Be sure to look inside the printer box for manuals, font cartridges, and other stuff the printer needs.

Printer pieces' parts

Printers come in many pieces. You have the printer itself, the ribbon or toner cartridge, and the thing that holds the paper. An instruction sheet that comes with the printer explains what goes where. Find that sheet and heed its instructions.

Basic printer setup requires yanking a few shipping items from the printer's insides, installing the ribbon and toner cartridge, setting up the paper-feeding mechanism or paper tray, adding any font cards, and plugging in the cables.

✔ Si la feuille du mode d'emploi a l'air français, c'est peut-être parce que c'est écrit en français. La plupart des modes d'emploi ont des directives en plusieurs langues. Il faut chercher la version en anglais.

✔ If the instruction sheet reads like it's written in French, it probably is. Most instruction sheets list instructions in several languages. Look for the English version.

✔ Some printers may require a detailed internal setup, which means that you yank out several plastic doohickeys, peel tape, and apply salve to the printer's aching foot pads. Those parts hold the printer's insides inside during shipment. You don't need to keep them; freely toss them out (even if you plan on moving the printer later).

✔ If you purchased extra memory for your printer, install it before you turn the printer on. Or, better still, have your dealer install it for you.

✔ If you have a font cartridge, it goes into the special font slot hidden somewhere on the printer. An instruction sheet should tell you where it goes. Make sure that the printer is turned off when you plug in the font cartridge.

Connecting the printer cables

Printers have two required cables: the power cable, which plugs into a wall socket, and the printer cable, which plugs into the computer. (Congress passed a law ten years ago requiring that every computing device have, at minimum, two cables.)

- The majority of printers plug into the computer's printer port. Aren't you glad that makes sense?

- Some PCs use a serial printer that plugs into the PC's serial port.

- If your printer has both printer port and serial port options, use the printer port one. You'll thank me later.

- The PC standard of tomorrow is the Macintosh standard of today: All Mac printers plug into the USB port.

Chapter 24

Moving to Your New Computer

● ●

● ●

*O*ftentimes your new computer purchase is really a replacement computer purchase. For example, you were computing in the stone age with an original IBM PC or maybe you're upgrading your old 486 to a brand-spanking new Pentium III powerhouse. For myself, I upgrade my office computers after four years. It's a thrill!

While the new computer may delight you, what do you do with all your *stuff* on your old computer. Does it just sit there? Or can you move it over to the new system? The answers lie in this chapter, which covers moving both hardware and software to your new computer system.

Moving Over Hardware

If your main reason for buying a new computer is to replace an older computer, consider what really needs replacing. Quite a bit of the older computer's hardware may find a home inside or alongside the new computer. It all depends on the shape of the older system's component. The following sections illuminate what can, might, and shouldn't be moved to the new system.

Antiques: Don't bother

If your early computer is older than four years, then there's probably no hardware in the thing that would serve the new computer well. For example, I have an old, old Macintosh Quadra. There is nothing inside that computer that would work at all with a new G4 or iMac system. Nope, nothing. Ditto for older PCs versus newer systems.

- ✔ If you've purchased any new peripherals or monitors for the older system, then they might be able to be passed on to the new system. Refer to the following sections.

- ✔ So the hardware is crummy . . . but don't forget your data and software! See the sections later in this chapter for moving over your software.

- ✔ Honestly, computers never really go out of date as long as they work. The new computers are faster, but given the choice between using an old clunky IBM PC/AT and WordPerfect 4.2 or a typewriter, I'd take the old clunky PC any day of the week.

Monitors

Monitors tend to fade and fuzz out with time. If your older computer's monitor is doing well, you can consider moving it over to your new computer. Not buying a monitor can shave a few hundred dollars — or more, depending on the type of monitor you presently have — from the new computer's purchase price.

As an example, I purchased one of those new flat-screen LCD monitors for an older computer whose monitor was on its dying days. When I replaced that computer a few years later, I simply bought a new console and moved the LCD monitor over to the new computer.

- ✔ As long as the monitor is in good shape, use it!

- ✔ Moving an older PC or Mac monitor to a new system can even save you money; there's no need to buy a new monitor when you can reuse your older computer's monitor.

- ✔ Even if you already have a monitor for your new computer, you can add the second monitor to the system. PCs running Windows 98 and all Macintoshes (but not iMacs) can easily have two monitors installed. (You may need a second video adapter, though.)

Disk drives

I would not recommend removing older hard drives and installing them into new computers. The hard drive is one of the first things to go on an older system, so relying on it for a new computer would be risky. Even installing the older hard drive as a "backup" is questionable. No, you're better off just getting the information from the hard drive and using a newer unit.

External disk drives can easily be moved to a new computer, simply by plugging them in. Always make sure you have the original installation disks, which helps the new computer recognize your older hardware.

Some internal disk drives, CD-ROMs, or maybe a new DVD or CD-R you added, can be moved over to the new system no problem. Again, remember the original software installation disk so that the operating system recognizes the new hardware.

Memory

Memory is something you generally cannot move from computer to computer. The reason is that older memory is probably a lot "fatter" than your new computer can handle. By fatter, I mean the memory is probably of lower capacity and slower speed; a new computer probably needs higher capacity memory (say 64MB versus 16MB SIMMS) and faster access times. No, moving over memory is a waste of time.

Expansion cards

Some expansion cards may work in the newer system; some may not. The best advice I can offer is that if you've recently purchased the expansion card for the older system *and* it offers some feature the newer system lacks, then consider the move.

As an example, suppose you just bought a USB expansion card for your old PC and the new PC also lacks USB ports. Then moving over the old USB expansion card could be a good move. Ditto for newer network cards and graphics adapters.

- ✔ See chapter 10 for more information on expansion cards.
- ✔ You'll have the best success moving plug-and-play expansion cards to a new system.
- ✔ PCI and AGP cards are the best candidates for transfer to a new computer.
- ✔ Also worthwhile are specialty cards: video input cards for any video editing software you own, sound synthesis, and special waveform cards, as well as anything else you need with your software.

Printers

The easiest thing to move from an older computer to a newer model is a printer. This makes total sense: There's no point in buying a whole new printer just because you have a new computer. As long as the printer is working just fine, keep it!

- ✔ You might need a new printer cable. For example, new Macintoshes require USB printers, so a USB-to-Mac Printer adapter would be in order.

- ✔ Don't forget your printer's original software disk! You may need it to install the software drivers for the new computer.

- ✔ My main printer has been used now with four different computers. It's a robust little guy who's served me well for over seven years!

Modems

Providing that the new computer doesn't come with a modem and that your old computer's modem is fast enough for you, yes you can move it over.

External modems are, obviously, easier to install on a new computer than internal modems. In fact, some internal modems are a real mess to install. And if you have any trouble installing the old internal modem, consider buying a newer model and save yourself some headaches.

Other peripherals

Peripherals can easily be moved from an old computer to a newer model. For example, I'm typing these words on a classic IBM keyboard that I've been using for almost six years now — even though this Micron computer is only two years old. (I'm very picky when it comes to computer keyboards.) This IBM keyboard, should it last, might even find its way on whichever computer replaces the Micron. . . .

Scanners can also be passed from computer to computer, as can most other peripherals. Providing there is always a way to connect the device to the computer and that you still have the software and installation manuals, reinstalling the peripheral for the new system is a snap.

- ✔ No, there is no reason to buy a new scanner for a new computer if your old scanner works just fine.

- ✔ This peripheral keeping and sharing will become even more popular as USB devices take over the world.

✔ As you get more adept at using and upgrading computers, you may find yourself ordering the bare minimum when you buy. Just transplant your favorite items from the old system to the new model and you're off and running in no time!

Transferring Your Software

There are two parts to the software you'll transfer to the new computer. The first is the programs you've accumulated — programs you want to install on the new system. The second part is the data you've created. You might want to keep all that stuff as well — which, in many cases, is probably more important than all that old software anyway!

Reinstalling applications

Being an honest person, you purchased all your software from a retail store, or the software was included with the computer purchase. Whatever the case, you have the original box, manuals, and disks that came with the software. (That stuff is important, pray tell you didn't toss it out!)

When you move to the new system, you need to "move over" your old software. This is done simply by reinstalling each program onto the new computer.

You *must* reinstall the software. You cannot simply copy the program files from one computer to another. These days, software has to be installed properly for it to work. If you copy the programs from the old computer (however that's done), things most likely will not work to your expectations.

I suggest installing the software as you need it. For example, if the first thing you want to try with the new computer is your word processor, install it. Ditto for a game or an "Office" suite or any software you use.

✔ Some software might need corresponding hardware installed. For example, your imaging software may yearn for the presence of a scanner. Better install that scanner first.

✔ Older software may not be compatible with the newer computer or its operating system. Oops! If you see any sort of error message or get a warning about incompatibilities then — *ka-ching!* — you'll need to pay for an upgraded version of the program. Yes, this happens. (I paid over $1,000 to upgrade various programs between Windows 3.1 and Windows 95. Ouch!)

✔ Some applications on your old computer might be "upgrade" or "OEM" versions. For example, that version of Word that came with your old PC may be an OEM-only version (meaning it was supplied by the computer manufacturer), and you might have trouble installing it on a new computer. My advice: Try your best! If it doesn't install, then you will have to go out and buy the program. Yes, I know this is unfair, but it's how it works.

Moving over data

Ah! The tricky part. On your older computer, you probably have lots of files you've created, documents, images, and other information that you need and use every day. I call them "data files." The object is to get those data files over to the new computer — if not all of it then at least the stuff you really, *really* need.

There are many ways to copy data files from one computer to another, but before moving, make sure that you can *find* your data files.

✔ **On a PC:** The data files are generally in the My Documents folder and its subfolders.

✔ **On a Mac:** The data files could be anywhere. Hopefully you've put most of them in a single, handy place. If not, may the hunting begin!

I recommend in all my computer books that you keep your data files in one specific, special location on the hard drive. On my PC, I use only the My Documents folder (plus drive D) for my documents and all the junk I create and want to keep. On my Mac, I created a My Stuff folder, which serves the same purpose as My Documents does on the PC.

Here are the methods you can use to move over your data files:

By disk. This is the slowest and potentially most painful method. It's also guaranteed to work on all PCs because they all have floppy drives. Copy your data files to floppy disks or, better still, Zip or Jaz disks. Then move the files over to the new computer, copying them from the removable disk to the hard drive. Yes, this is a lot of work. (I've done it many times.)

Of course, having the larger-capacity Zip or Jaz disks is a boon; copying with floppy disk is like moving items to your new house in a shoebox. (It really helps you think about what's worth keeping.)

If you have a CD-R, obviously, you can burn a CD with *all* your data files and easily move them over to the new computer in one fell swoop.

By backup. If both your old computer and newer model have tape backup drives, and they eat the same sort of tape, you can back up your first computer's data files and restore those files to the new system. Easy, simple. (I actually buy external tape backup units just for this reason; I simply reinstall the tape backup hardware on the new computer, and I'm in business.)

By network. If your computers are connected by a network, you can easily access the files on the old system and "beam" them to the new computer. This by far is the easiest and most efficient way to do things. In my office, I typically keep the old system up on the network for months to ensure I've pulled off every single file I need.

By cable. Second to the network method is to directly connect both computers using a special serial port cable. You can then use Windows Direct Connection Wizard to force both systems to talk with each other and, after some cajoling, zap files to the new computer. This is slow, and unfortunately, it's poorly documented. I've used this method twice, and it does work when all else fails.

Special transfer software. Continuing the idea of connecting two computers by a cable, but doing it better than Windows Direct Connection Wizard, are special utility programs that get two computers talking directly. Some of these programs even come with the cable you need to connect two computers.

However you make the connection — disk or cable — moving over the files is an important part of making the move. I miss the files I've left behind on various computers over the years.

✔ An interesting piece of software to check out is Miramar System's Desktop DNA. It grabs not only software, but personalized settings and other options, allowing you to move your old computer's "personality" to the new system. Also available is a program called Personality Transport from Tranxition Corp.

✔ Windows has the Direct Connection Wizard, but I am unaware of similar software available for the Macintosh. Since the new Macs all generally come with Ethernet network ports, the best way to move files to them would be to put both Macs on the network.

✔ The newer Macs lack a serial port, so moving files between them via cable is no longer possible. You can, however, hook up new Macs to a network hub and transfer files via the network. Various network starter kits are available for under $100 if you want to try this route.

✔ Another, albeit slower, method is to use your computers' modems to send information back and forth. But you'll need special communications software to handle the file transfer. On the up side, though, you don't need to use the phone lines: Just plug a phone cord into the old computer's modem directly into the new computer's modem. It works!

Eliminating the preinstalled bonus crap

Most computers sold today come with prepackaged *stuff.* I find this most unnerving.

Sometimes the stuff is useful. For example, you get a new computer and a brand new version of Microsoft Office. Or maybe you have your choice of Office verses a home package (including Quicken and maybe Word) or a gamers package with a ton of nifty games. That's fine.

What's not fine are the bonus programs they give you that you don't want and will never use. That's bunk. And it junks up your hard drive. Of course, the question looms as to what is really junk that you can remove versus what programs are valuable and keep the computer running.

 ✔ **Stuff you can freely delete.** I've noticed that most, if not all, new PCs and Macs come with programs to connect you with various online services. If you want to try them, swell! If not, delete them. Ditto for any other offer for online services or Internet connections you do not want or feel you'll never use. Zap 'em away.

 ✔ **Free trials.** Anything you get that's offered as a free trial or demo version of some program you can zap away. Only bother keeping something to check it out if you're interested. If you're not interested, remove it.

Be careful how you remove things! In Windows, always use the control panel's Add/Remove Software icon. Peruse the list displayed and uninstall anything there you do not want. If you're unsure about something, phone the dealer and ask them what it is or whether you need it. Then uninstall!

This problem isn't as pervasive on the Macintosh as it is on the PC. Only Apple makes the Mac, and Apple has not (at least since 1986 when I bought my first Mac) preinstalled junk the way junk is preinstalled on a PC.

Still, you may notice, for example, both Netscape and Internet Explorer available on your Mac. If you use one, drag the other's folder to the Trash. Ditto for AOL and other online service sign-up icons. If you don't need 'em, drag 'em to the Trash.

Chapter 25

Selecting an ISP

. . . .

. . . .

*I*n addition to the basic hardware and software, you should now consider that all computers have a third element: Internet access. In some cases, Internet access is provided by your company, the university you attend, or maybe some local organization. But for the small office or home, Internet service is another purchase you need to make. Just like buying more hardware or software for your computer, there are certain things you should look for when selecting an *Internet service provider,* or ISP.

Your computer probably comes with dozens of offers from national ISPs or online services like AOL, plus you may occasionally find newspaper fliers or junk mail (regular mail) for local ISPs and their offerings. This chapter helps you sift through all that stuff, finding an ISP that suits your needs to a tee.

Getting on the Internet

The Internet isn't a single computer nor a piece of software. Instead, it's lots of computers, all connected with each other. They store and exchange information. To "get on" the Internet, you need to connect your computer to another computer that's already on the Internet. That computer is usually owned by a company that provides Internet access — an ISP.

What you need

To access the Internet you need a computer with the necessary hardware and software, plus an account at an ISP or other Internet provider. Basically it boils down to five things:

A computer. This you most likely have, provided you've worked through the various chapters in this book designed to get you a computer. Congratulations.

A modem. Most of today's new computers come with modems, if not, you can go out and buy one. See Chapter 11 for the details on buying a modem.

Internet software. Again, most of today's computers come with Internet software. Windows (supposedly) *is* Internet software, and the Mac comes with both Internet Explorer and Netscape, which you can use to navigate the Web. E-mail software and other Internet programs might be included with your operating system as well.

An ISP. This is the company that provides Internet access. Unless your computer already has Internet access through your company or the university, then you'll need an ISP to grant you access.

Money. Ah, yes. Nothing is free. Unless, of course, you live in the U.K. where Internet access is really free. But for most parts of the world, you still need to pay your ISP for access.

You probably have three of these five things already. All you need is most likely the ISP and the money. The following section helps with the ISP. The money . . . I'll leave it up to you to figure that part out!

- ✔ A good way to get money is to work. Most people who have money also have a job.
- ✔ Some handheld computers require special Internet software, though if you're serious about Internet access, you'll probably have a desktop or laptop system that serves as your main Internet computer.
- ✔ The pundits predict that eventually *all* Internet access will be free, à la the free system in the U.K. This doesn't seem likely in the U.S., however, where most people are conditioned to pay for Internet service. So if there is a change, it probably won't happen for some time.

What the ISP gives you

In exchange for your hard-earned coin, an ISP should provide you with the following services. Remember, the *S* in ISP stands for service:

✔ **A dial-up number.** You need a number to call so that your computer can access the Internet. This number, along with other basic account information, is given to the Internet connection program that configures your computer for the Internet.

✔ **An e-mail box.** This is very important. As part of your account at the ISP, you should receive an e-mail address and a mailbox for receiving messages on the Internet. This is a must! Avoid any ISP that doesn't offer e-mail as a basic service.

✔ **Some kind of getting-started booklet.** Even the pros need some of the basic, and often technical, information required to connect to the Internet. The booklet should tell you about the ISP's service, what's offered, general information like phone numbers and tech support, plus lots of how-tos and some Q&As.

If the ISP is really on the ball, you might also get some or all of the following. These may be offered at an additional charge or they might be included with the base price:

✔ **Classes.** Not only should there be classes offered on basic Internet, Web browsing, and e-mail, but some ISPs may also offer classes on Web page design or maybe even using a shell account. The beginning classes should be free or included with your sign-up fee. They may charge for the advanced classes, or classes may be offered in conjunction with a local community college. No problem there.

✔ **Software.** Some ISPs may have special software available, including a Web browser, e-mail program, and other programs. The getting-started booklet (see above) should tell you about the software.

✔ **Web space.** This is a location on the ISP's server, reserved for your use should you ever decide to create and post your own Web page on the Internet. Sometimes this is an extra cost; other times it might be included with your account.

✔ **Newsgroup access.** Some ISPs offer newsgroup access (also known as USENET) with regular accounts. Others may offer newsgroup access separately or for an extra fee. Having an ISP that provides *all* the newsgroups is a bonus.

✔ **Shell account.** This is a rather nerdy option for those who love Unix and maybe want to access the Internet and use tools available from the Neolithic Internet period before the Web.

✔ **Personal domain name.** If you're interested in having your own dot-com or dot-org or dot-whatever Web page, ask if your ISP can provide you with it. Some can — at an extra charge, of course.

✔ **Programming services.** Some ISPs also offer programming for Web pages, providing you want such a Web page. This and other services are usually reserved for businesses that need such facilities.

Changing ISPs

Unlike cable TV service, it's entirely possible to change ISPs without moving your house. If you're dissatisfied with the service or somehow feel ripped off, you can sign up to a new ISP and dump the old one just like you can start shopping at a new grocery store.

If you do plan on switching, sign up with the new ISP *before* you dump the old one. Make your connection, and let your e-mail buddies know your new e-mail address. Then cancel the old account. That way you won't miss anything.

Overall, what you really need is the number to dial, basic account information, and an e-mail box. That's really enough to get you started. Having the other options available may help down the road. For example, your home business may blossom into the next eBay, in which case it would be nice to be connected with an ISP that can provide you with the necessary bandwidth.

How much should it cost?

The price for Internet access ranges anywhere from free (like it is in the U.K.) to several hundred dollars a month, depending on which services you're getting.

First there is a sign-up fee. This may be a connection fee or other one-time fee to get you started. Some places have them, some don't. Sign-up fees can also be waived. Mostly, use them for comparison: If one ISP has a sign-up fee and another doesn't, go with the cheaper of the two.

Second are monthy fees. These can range from as low as a couple of dollars to several hundred a month. Typically, Internet access is about $20 a month.

Finally, there are contracts. These are deals whereby you sign up for a large amount of Internet time for a lower price. These can be good or bad, depending on your needs.

As an example, my company buys Internet time one year in advance. By paying for the full year up front, I get a heck of a discount. On the other hand, that's a *big* check I write. It also means I'm stuck with that ISP for a full year.

Avoid long-term contracts at all costs, such as the two- or three-year contracts that come with "free" computers. At $20 a month, that adds up. Besides, you should be getting a hefty discount for a three-year contract. Plus a back-out clause would be nice. Please don't be fooled by these offers.

Always review your billing options. Never assume that the rate you signed up for is eternal. For example, you may have signed on for $20/month service at AOL, but discover that the $4.95 rate will suit your needs just as well. If so, change! Ditto for ISPs: Don't pay more for services you don't use. Refer to the ISP's current rate information or phone up their support crew for information and try to save yourself some money.

Finding an ISP

There are many places offering Internet access: local, regional, and national. Finding them can be as easy as looking in the phone book. Or, if you have friends on the Internet, you can ask them which ISP they use and if they're happy.

My best advice is to shop around. Just as you would buy computer hardware or software, look around and check out the services and their prices before you make a commitment.

Phone calls can be made to the ISPs to see what they offer. Remember that you are interviewing the ISPs as you call for information. If they're rude or appear too busy to care, then you can immediately hang up and phone the next one on the list.

A special type of ISP is the national service provider, like AOL. Personally, I would recommend a true ISP over AOL, which I find slow and clunky for regular Internet access — though AOL has a lot of features that you may find attractive. AOL is great for getting started and wonderful if all your friends are already on AOL.

On the downside: AOL suffers from Internet access that isn't the fastest, phone lines that are often busy, and support that cannot match what you often get from an ISP. (For example, I have the e-mail address of the Nice Support Lady at my ISP. On AOL, there is a general e-mail box for help.)

The "S" Means Service

Finally, remember that the S in ISP means *service*. An ISP should not be judged merely on the fact that they give you a phone number and Internet access. And never buy into an ISP's plan just because it's the cheapest. There should be more.

Beyond classes, I would give high marks to any ISP that offers 24-hour human tech support (that is, a person on the phone). Nothing is more helpful than a human voice when you're experiencing Something Weird on the Internet at 1:00 a.m.

Ensure that the ISP has plenty of phone lines. Ask them how well connected they are; the more connections they have to the Internet, the more likely you'll still be able to use the Internet in the event of a crash (and the Internet does crash from time to time).

And make sure that the *people* at the ISP are those with whom you're willing to work. Having their personal e-mail addresses available is a major plus, almost like having a favorite salesperson in the store.

Chapter 26

When to Buy, When to Sell, When to Upgrade

. . . .

In This Chapter

▶ Knowing when your computer is a geezer

▶ Deciding whether to upgrade your old stuff

▶ Determining whether to upgrade the microprocessor

▶ Upgrading your software

▶ Upgrading your operating system

▶ Selling your computer

▶ Considering used computers

. . . .

*N*othing lasts forever. Well, except for taxes and death. Diamonds, maybe. The things we use have a life span. Rubber spatulas, for example, seem to last about three months before they get all melted and cracked. Cars? Maybe five or seven years (just enough time to pay off the loan). Computers? They have life spans, too.

Expect your computer to last at least four to five years. Although a computer can last longer, technology advances so much and software demands new technology so strongly that after four years, your new computer is seriously outdated. What should you do? Should you sell it? Should you upgrade it? Should you buy a new one? This chapter helps you make those decisions.

Unlike Wine, Computers Don't Age Well

Your computer is outdated the second it rolls off the assembly line. Because those guys in white lab coats are always creating tomorrow's technology today, right now, in a lab somewhere, they have the next-generation microprocessor ready along with a smaller, faster, high-capacity hard drive and more memory. The stuff isn't ready to ship just yet, though.

Nothing is more disappointing than reading a computer ad six months after you buy a computer and discovering that you could have had, for the same money, a much better computer. Don't get discouraged! This situation happens *all the time,* which is why I say "Buy!" when you're ready to buy. You have your computer. You're using it. That's much better than waiting.

When exactly does your computer become a true geezer? Generally, after four or five years of duty. After that time, two things generally happen: The hardware becomes much better and cheaper, and the software starts craving that better hardware. A third thing also happens: Your computer starts to go south. The hard drive may start making a louder noise, especially when the system first starts up. It's a sign that the bearings are starting to go. (It's not an emergency; the drive may still have years of life left.)

Your monitor may also show signs of age. You probably won't notice it — until you look at a newer monitor. Older monitors get fuzzy. The text blurs. The colors bleed. It adds excess eyestrain, which is the perfect clue that it's time for a new monitor — or a whole new computer.

Should You Upgrade?

One of the joys of owning a computer is that you can upgrade or replace any of its components at any time — as long as the computer is turned off when you do so.

Upgrading is an easy alternative to tossing out a fairly good computer and spending more money on a new one. Upgrades are inexpensive. And often all you need is a simple upgrade: more memory, another monitor, another hard drive. A few twists of the screwdriver later, and you have an almost new computer again. Upgrading should come from some serious need: Software demands more memory, you run out of disk storage, or something breaks.

Which hardware to upgrade first

What you upgrade first depends on your needs. Does your software need more memory? Upgrade it. Is your monitor shot? Buy another one. Is your modem just too slow? Get another.

Memory. As long as your computer is properly configured for memory (refer to Chapter 6), plugging in another 32MB, 64MB, or even 128MB of RAM is relatively easy. This upgrade often solves a number of problems you may have with a sluggish computer.

Hard drive. Although plugging in another hard drive is easy, getting it going can be a pain. Hard drives must be formatted, and it's hard to find out exactly how that's done. Better leave this upgrade to your dealer.

The best part about upgrading a hard drive is that you can add a second hard drive of immense size. If you miscalculate and find that 4GB of storage isn't enough, for example, buy an 8GB hard drive! You can install it right inside the console. Upgrading the hard drive is more expensive than upgrading memory. Because humans tend to collect things, however, you'll enjoy the extra space right away.

Monitor. Buying another monitor is cinchy: Buy it! Turn your computer off, unplug the old monitor, and plug in the new one. Done! If you're money mad, you can actually use *two* monitors on the same computer!

Old monitors don't keep their value. You cannot sell them, and you shouldn't toss them out in the trash. Instead, refer to your locality's disposal people for the proper method of tossing out an old computer monitor.

Modem. Quite a few computer experts don't even know that you can upgrade your modem. To find out how, contact its manufacturer. Tell them your modem model number and ask how it can be upgraded. Sometimes, it can be done through software, and sometimes you may have to plug in a new chip. You rarely have to buy a new modem, though.

Other stuff. Just about everything in your computer can be upgraded. You can upgrade, in addition to the preceding items, your CD-ROM player, a floppy drive, a video adapter, or virtually any component in your computer.

Watch your upgrade costs! Sure, it may be fun to buy your computer a present in the form of an upgrade. Tally what you spend, though. If you're not careful, you may wind up spending more on your old computer than it would cost to buy a new one.

My $.02 on upgrading your microprocessor

Another hardware upgrade touted in the computer magazines is the microprocessor upgrade. It's not hard to do: The microprocessor slides or clips into a socket. Most computers are designed that way. I don't recommend it, though, for several reasons:

- ✔ **Cost:** When your dealer buys microprocessors to plug into his computers, he buys them by the truckload. He gets a discount; you don't. You pay top dollar for a new microprocessor, which can be several hundred dollars for the current top-of-the-line model. Spending your money on a memory upgrade may give you better results anyway.

✔ **Compatibility:** Although the new microprocessor may plug into the old one's slot, is all your computer's circuitry geared to work with it? Motherboards are designed around specific microprocessors running at specific speeds. Although the new one may function, it may be crippled or inhibited by the older circuitry on the motherboard. What's the point of having a faster microprocessor when it has to slow down to access your computer's old memory, for example?

✔ **The whole motherboard upgrade:** This upgrade involves another microprocessor upgrade, which directly addresses the issue of compatibility but not price! New motherboards (your computer's main circuitry) are spendy. If you go that route, you may as well buy a new case and a new hard drive and hey! — you have a new computer! You have the old one too, gutted out and not good for anything.

Upgrading software

You'll often be bombarded, more so than with hardware upgrades, with developers' propaganda for upgrading their software. Hurry! Version 4.02 is available! It's only $69 because you're a registered user and *we like you!*

When should you upgrade your software? As with everything else, the answer is "according to your needs." Do you *need* the new features the software offers? Does the new version fix the bugs that annoyed you? If so, buy it.

It's possible and quite common to skip software upgrades. I do it all the time. For example, I had Version 3.0 of a word processor. Version 3.1 was released, but because it didn't impress me, I skipped it. Then came Versions 3.2 and 3.3 and, for some reason, the manufacturer skipped up to Version 3.5. I passed them all by. When Version 4.0 was released, however, I upgraded. I saved money by not upgrading step-by-step (or version-by-version), and I still got the latest version of the product.

✔ If you're using the same software at home as you are at work, upgrade when your office does. If you don't, your older software at home may not be capable of reading the documents the newer software at work produces.

✔ A good argument to eventually upgrade any application, in fact, is to keep compatibile with any new document formats. Eventually you may find that others are using the software and that your older application cannot read those newer document formats.

Upgrading your operating system

Like all software, your operating system eventually will have a new version. In days of yore, this situation caused a real debate: Everything worked fine with the current operating system, so why upgrade? Even if the new version had exciting features, the upgrade may not be compatible. It was a puzzle. Generally speaking, I can give you this advice:

Never upgrade your operating system.

The best way to get the next version of an operating system is to wait until you need to buy a new computer. The new version comes installed on that computer. Otherwise, you risk a great deal by upgrading your current operating system, primarily that some of your older software may not be compatible, which would force you into paying lots of money for upgrades.

You may eventually encounter new software that requires the newest operating system. Traditionally, however, that doesn't really happen until the new operating system is about two years old. Why? The answer is that because software developers don't want to lose you as a customer, they don't write a specific version of their applications until *everyone* has upgraded. So don't panic.

Should You Sell Your Beloved Computer?

I remember when friends of mine in the mid-1980s tried to sell their computers. They had sold cars, so they tried to figure the price of their used computers in the same way. The stuff never sold.

Used computers have no value. If you wait four or five years, the new stuff will be so much better that you'll never be able to recover any value from your original purchase. I have my accountant rapid-depreciate my computers, in fact, because they just don't hold any value.

If you do try to sell your computer, ask only $50 to $200 for it. The best buyer is someone who already has that type of computer and wants to buy another one.

Sell everything when you sell. Make the computer as complete as you can. You can throw in software, too, although that doesn't add to the price of the computer. (Old software has no value.)

Ask for either cash (because it won't be that much) or a cashier's check for your old computer. The last insult you want is to sell something you paid $2,000 for to a guy who writes you a rubber check.

A better thing to do with your old computers is to donate them to charities or schools. Give them as much computer as you can, including a printer. Give them your software manuals and disks. And, ask for a receipt based on the computer's fair market value (see an accountant for more information). You get more from the computer that way, as a tax deduction, and you give something back to your community.

Please give away your *entire* computer and make sure that the thing works! An accountant "donated" her old computers to our local community theatre, but none of them had keyboards or monitors *and* she wanted the hard drives back. That's not a donation — it's a joke. If you want to give away your old computers, do so. Don't be cheap.

Buying a Used Computer

There are many reasons for buying an old computer. The most common is that you have a computer exactly like it and want another as a spare. Or maybe your software just runs better with an older microprocessor. If your software runs fine on an older system, then buying one saves you hundreds of dollars over buying a state-of-the-art system whose power just isn't needed.

Test-drive a used computer before you buy it. Take some software with you, and load it up. Make sure that it runs. Save something to disk. Print something. If it works, then the used computer is worthy.

Used computers, unless they've been used less than a year, are worth only a couple hundred dollars — max. Don't overpay! Check the classified ads to see what's being asked for used equipment. Then check the prices of new equipment and compare. Obviously, paying $200 for an old 386 PC makes no sense when a new Pentium model sells for $400.

Someone may tell you, "Oh, but you also get $2,000 worth of software for only $200!" Just laugh at the person. "Ha-ha!" Old software has no value. Sure, the guy may have paid $2,000 for it originally, but it's worth nothing now. Do insist that the seller include all the boxes (if they're available), original software, and documentation.

Part V
The Part of Tens

The 5th Wave   By Rich Tennant

"GENTLEMEN, I SAY RATHER THAN FIX THE 'BUGS', WE CHANGE THE
DOCUMENTATION AND CALL THEM 'FEATURES'."

In this part . . .

There are always last minute lists that need to be checked off. For example, when you travel by air, the pilot and copilot in the plane check off dozens of tiny items to ensure that the trip will be a safe one, that they'll have enough coffee and that they can actually see out of both eyes. The same types of lists need to be completed when you buy a computer.

The chapters in this part of the book contain lists of ten items (sometimes more, sometimes less) which you should review at various stages in the buying process. It's all good advice. Read it and heed it.

Chapter 27

Ten Common Mistakes Made by First-Time Computer Buyers

• •

In This Chapter

▶ Not knowing what you want the computer to do

▶ Buying hardware rather than software

▶ Shopping for brand names

▶ Shopping for the cheapest system

▶ Being unprepared for the sale

▶ Forgetting the "extras"

▶ Paying by check or cash

▶ Not reading the setup manuals

▶ Forgetting that software is expensive

▶ Buying too much

▶ Not counting learning time

• •

*I*f you've followed this book's advice, you (hopefully) won't fall into the trap of making one of the following ever-so-common mistakes. It's worth putting them in a list, just as a reminder.

Not Knowing What You Want the Computer to Do

Computers are capable of many things — nearly as many things as there are people who own them. Don't make the mistake of buying a computer just because "everyone else is doing it." You must have a solid reason for buying a computer or know how a computer can help you in some way.

Buying Hardware Before Software

Software controls the hardware by telling it what to do. Don't be tempted by marvelous hardware features. Don't be lured into buying one brand or the other by some advertising campaign. Without software, the hardware is next to useless. Buy your hardware to support your software.

Dropping Brand Names

When people find out what I do, they usually want my advice about buying a computer. "Dan," they say, as they puff up their chests about to impress me with some trivial tidbit, "I've been looking at the UltraDork computer. What do you think about it?"

"Big mistake," I answer. It doesn't matter which brand they mention; I always say the same thing. Software is more important than hardware. Most people don't see that, so I'm not rude when I tell them this. But thinking about brand names instead of what the computer will do is a big mistake.

Shopping for the Cheapest Computer System

When you buy a *bargain system,* you will probably wind up with a competent and functional computer. When things go wrong, you'll want the dealer to provide service to get your system fixed. That bargain price often doesn't include service, however. Look for a dealer you can grow friendly with. The dealer's reputation, which is more important than price, is how it stays in business.

Being Unprepared for the Sale

Computers have a different jargon (in case you haven't noticed). Don't expect a computer salesperson to be able to explain to you all the subtleties of things like VRAM, MMX, scan rate, MPEG, and SCSI-3. Some disreputable salespeople might even dupe you into paying more money for obsolete and unnecessary technology.

Forgetting Some Extra Items

The ad says $700, and you have just a hair over that — enough to pay the sales tax. Alas, you didn't read the fine print: That $700 computer doesn't come with a monitor. Oops!

Ensure that you buy a complete computer system! Double- and triple-check the ads for any missing pieces. You need a monitor, a keyboard, memory, and a hard drive to make a computer system.

Not Paying by Credit Card

Never pay for a computer with a check. Never pay cash. Always pay with a credit card. Why? Because credit charges can be put into dispute if anything nasty happens between you and the dealer. Credit card companies support their clients. If someone sells you junk, the credit card company won't force you to pay for it (as long as you've taken legitimate steps to resolve the problem).

Most banks don't let you reverse the charges on a check. If you pay cash to a shady dealer, your money is gone forever. Computer dealer scams aren't as popular as they used to be, but look out for them anyway.

Not Reading the Setup Manuals

As a general rule of advice from a self-proclaimed computer guru: Read things over before trying them. If you make a mistake or something doesn't happen right, read the instructions again and try a second time. Consider it a last resort to make that phone call to your dealer. Don't substitute the phone for the manual.

Forgetting That Software Is Expensive

Contrary to what you may think, computer hardware is only half your cost. The computer software your computer needs will probably cost the same amount as what you paid for your computer (over time, of course). Piece by piece, package by package, software is expensive.

Buying Too Much

Start simple. If you buy too much stuff too quickly, you may go overboard and never find out all about your system. My recipe for becoming a computer guru, in fact, involves starting with a minimal system. After you have that mastered, upgrade slowly and learn as you go.

Not Counting Learning Time

If you've just figured out that you need a computer "yesterday," you're too late. I advise everyone (businesspersons, students, or just the idle curious) to give themselves at least three weeks to use and become comfortable with their computer system before the real work starts.

Chapter 28

Ten Tips and Suggestions

• •

In This Chapter

▶ Your computer's clock

▶ Get a second phone line

▶ Reread your manuals

▶ Put a timer on the Internet

▶ Get Internet software for your kids

▶ Subscribe to a computer magazine

▶ Join a users' group

▶ Buy some computer books

▶ Don't let the computer ruin your life

▶ Have fun!

• •

*N*o one wants any surprises when using a computer. Imagine buying a new car, signing your name, being handed the keys, and then the sales-person saying, "Oh, I forgot to tell you — this thing runs only on 110 octane multigrade" or "Always hold your steering wheel with your left hand because the car pulls to the right." Fortunately, owning a computer doesn't involve many surprises along those lines.

This chapter contains a list of ten tips, suggestions, and warnings. They're nothing major; they're just some last-minute items you may not know about — by-the-way sort of things to wrap up this book.

Your Computer Has a Clock

You may not notice at first, but your computer keeps track of the time. And it remembers the time, even when you turn off the computer or unplug it. The reason is that the computer has a battery that helps it remember the time as well as a few other items.

Someday, in about five years, your computer's battery will die. You'll notice it because not only will your computer have lost track of the time, but you may also see an error message when the computer starts up. When that happens, phone your dealer and get a new battery installed.

A computer makes a lousy clock. No two computers can keep track of the same time. Some are fast; most are slow. You have to reset your system's clock every month or so. If not, your computer could be lagging by as much as 20 or 30 minutes by the end of the year.

Get a Second Phone Line

If you plan to use a computer and a modem at all, do yourself and everyone else a favor and get the computer its own phone line. I tried to phone up a friend one night, and his phone was busy for *three hours.* He was on the Internet and utterly unaware that anyone was trying to call.

Oh, and forget about call waiting. If you have call waiting on your phone, it disconnects your computer from the Internet whenever someone calls. Just be logical and get another phone line.

If the second line from the phone company costs you too much, then consider getting a digital cellular phone instead. Often times the monthly bill for the cell phone (especially a digital model) is much less than buying a second phone line. And you can take the cell phone with you.

After a While, Reread the Manuals

Although computer manuals are horrid, they may begin to make sense a few weeks after you use your computer. Use any program for a while, and try to figure it out. Then go back and read the manuals. Not right away; take some time and do something with the program. Learn how it works. After that, for some reason, the manual tends to make sense. I follow this simple advice, and for some reason, everyone thinks that I'm a computer genius.

Put a Timer on That Internet

If you plan to be on the Internet, set a clock! The Internet sucks up time like a black hole in space. Limit yourself to 30 minutes or an hour for your Internet browsing, or else you'll see the sun rise some morning.

Get Internet Antiporn Software

If you have kids, get some special Internet software that prevents them from wandering into places no sane parent would let their kid wander into. Programs such as Surf Watch and Net Nanny are good at filtering those nasty places from young eyes.

Visit www.surfwatch.com for a copy of Surf Watch.

Refer to www.netnanny.com for information about Net Nanny.

Subscribe to a Computer Magazine

Now that you have a computer, it makes sense to get a computer magazine. That's where you find advice, tips, and information about computer things. The magazine keeps you up-to-date and informed better than dealers and developers, who put their own interests above yours.

Several levels of computer magazines are available, from novice magazines to hard-core nerd publications. Most bookstores have racks full of them, so take a few minutes to browse and pick up a few of the ones that interest you.

Join a Computer Users' Group

Sociologists tell us that injured people tend to cluster after a catastrophe. It's a force of nature. Just like those walking wounded, computer users — dazed and bewildered — gather in small groups in cities across the land. They discuss. They share. They learn.

Refer to your local newspaper events column to see when and where any computer groups meet in your area.

Buy a Great Book

I can't recommend books enough! Some great titles are out there to help you find out about anything you can do on a computer. When your dealer support craps out, when the developers admit that they loathe the customer, and when you've exhausted your friends and computer buddies, buy a good book.

As with magazines, be aware that different levels of books — beginner, intermediate, and advanced — are available for different computer users: You can get reference books, and you can get tutorial books. Buy what suits you best.

Remember That You Are in Charge

The biggest problem most new owners have with a computer is taking it too seriously. Life is just too important to take anything seriously, especially a computer.

Above all, never think that it's your fault when something goes wrong. If you always blame yourself, you have a horrid time computing. The truth is that computers are dumb. They foul up all the time. It's not your fault.

Don't Let the Computer Run Your Life

Computers are *not* a big deal. They're tools. You use them to extend your own abilities. They are not important. Human beings do not live to serve the computer.

If you find yourself overly enamored with your computer, make it a point to take a break every so often. Walk outside. Get some fresh air. Talk to a human being. If the universe has a center, it's not powered by a microprocessor.

Have fun.

Chapter 29

Ten Warning Signs

*1*f all people were good, wholesome folks with high morals, standards, and a strong sense of customer support, I wouldn't have to write this chapter. Because this chapter is here, though, I suppose that you'll have a better understanding of human nature.

Because the computer industry is full of terms and standards that only real computer geeks have a knowledge or understanding of, it's rather easy to pull the wool over your eyes. I don't want that to happen. The best thing I can do is educate you on what to be aware of. Consider this chapter a computer-buying self-defense class.

Hi-yah!

Industry "Standards" versus the Ads

Beware of computer hype! You may read about "groundbreaking" technology, but, honestly, unless you see such a technology available in a computer ad, forget it.

A case in point is the current rage over the DVD disk. Yes, one day all computers will have DVD drives instead of CD-ROM drives. But check the ads! There are still lots of computers sold with CD-ROM drives. More importantly, where are the DVD disks in the software stores?

Any new hardware technology takes time to become accepted. Wait until something "fabulously new" is available on most new computer systems before you decide whether to buy one. *Remember:* Software controls the hardware. You need software in order to use the new hardware regardless of whether every computer has the new hardware.

Out-of-Date Stock

Computer dealers like to sell stuff they don't have to fix. No one — neither you nor the dealer — likes to see you come back with your computer in the box because it doesn't work. I don't mean, however, that shady dealers won't try to sell you old stuff just to get rid of it.

Do your research (like reading this book) before you walk into a store. Be aware of what is appropriate for your needs and what the computer industry suggests as standard (which you determine by reading the ads). You don't want a pushy salesman convincing you that a 28,800 bps modem is a pretty darn fast modem because he has three dozen stacked up in the storage room and the boss told him to get rid of them.

(I worked *one day* at a computer store. During my only sales meeting, we were told to "unload" an ailing computer, to steer customers to it first regardless of what their true needs were. Like I said, I worked there only one day.)

Money Down Required

For what possible reason would anyone need money down on a computer? It's just not necessary. Don't believe them if they pull this bit: "We need the down payment to ensure that you are committed to buying this computer." Computers are selling like hotcakes, so it's not like they would build a computer and be stuck with it forever if you didn't take it. Someone else will buy it.

✔ Never put money down, especially cash, on a computer.

✔ Always pay for your purchase with a credit card.

Missing Pieces

If you open the box and everything isn't there, take it back immediately! Chances are good that you were sold a computer someone else returned and everything wasn't put back properly. Tell the people at the computer store that you want another computer. Don't accept their giving you the missing parts. Unless someone there told you that you were buying a refurbished computer, he cannot legally sell it to you. Check the laws in your state about selling refurbished equipment.

No Address in the Mail-Order Ad

In some cases of fraud committed in the 1980s, fly-by-night outfits bilked hundreds of people out of money on computers the shysters never planned to build or sell. Reputable dealers post their addresses in their ads and not only their 800 numbers but also their direct lines.

Salespeople Too Busy to Help

My theory has always been that if people are too busy to take my money, I don't want to give it to them anyway. Go someplace else, to wherever you find someone who's willing to answer your questions and take the time to fully explain what they have to offer you.

Salespeople in the Store Ignore You

If the salespeople in the store are ignoring you, one of two things is going on: Either no one knows enough to walk up and help you, or no one gives a hoot whether you buy a computer. Apathy and ignorance are two qualities you don't ever want to do business with, regardless of whether you're buying a computer, a car, or some shoes.

(I was ready to plunk down $800 for a new hard drive in a local store, and *everyone* in the store ignored me. The salesperson didn't know what a SCSI drive was. The techie only commented on the SCSI drive, not telling me whether it was in stock or available for sale. It was a nice store, too; it had a classroom in back and competitive prices. Because the people in there were jerks, though, I bought my $800 hard drive by mail order.)

Also, be wary of any salesperson who refers to you behind your back as a "mark" — unless, of course, your name is Mark.

No Classroom

If a store doesn't offer some kind of computer class to help you with your new purchase, the folks there really aren't concerned with giving you complete customer service. They're more concerned with making a sale.

If you are a first-time computer buyer, taking a class gives you a better sense of confidence to go exploring with your computer, and your frustration level will be much lower.

No Software Documentation

All software comes with some kind of documentation: installation instructions, information on how to play or work the software, and maybe even some technical notes. This stuff is all-important. If the software documentation doesn't come with the computer, chances are that the software is stolen. Don't leave the store without seeing that documentation. If someone makes any of the following comments, leave the store!

- ✔ "The software doesn't come with any documentation."
- ✔ "Oh, you'll be able to figure it out."
- ✔ "The program tells you what to do as you go along."

All software must be sold with documentation! Even if it's just a CD, that CD may have a serial number on it — or sometimes the entire manual!

Chapter 30

Ten Other Things You Should Buy

*T*his chapter is dedicated to the ten additional things, whatnots, and items you need to buy that will help with your whole computer-using experience. Buying these things is not optional. You really need them.

Mousepad and Wristpad

Ever try to use a mouse with a dirty ball? No, really, I'm being serious. The mouse has a ball it rolls on, and if that ball becomes dirty, it doesn't roll smoothly and you have a heck of a time trying to get it to point, drag, or do anything.

A *mousepad* is a screen-size piece of foam rubber that sits on your desk and that the mighty mouse rolls on. A mousepad makes the mouse roll more smoothly and keeps that mouse ball clean (as long as you don't drop cookie crumbs all over it).

You get the best performance from your mouse if you buy a mousepad that is slightly textured. Smooth pads don't work as well.

Buying a wristpad is more of a health measure than a technical one. Lazy keyboarders drop their wrists to an unnatural position, which eventually causes stress on their wrists and the infamous carpal tunnel. This condition, of course, can be painful.

The purpose of a wristpad is to keep your arms and hands in a normal, healthy position. It fits right below your keyboard, and your wrists gently lie on it.

Wristpads are also available for your mousepad, sometimes both in one unit.

Neither a mousepad nor a wristpad is expensive, and you can get creative with a mousepad. Kinko's has a process in which you can put your kids' pictures (or pictures of your cats, if you don't like kids) on your mousepad.

Power Strip

Not until you start putting together your computer and all its various gadgets does it occur to you that homebuilders truly underestimate the need for wall outlets.

You have to plug in your computer, printer, modem, scanner, lamp, clock, and answering machine. The list can get pretty long, and you're probably looking at one, maybe two, plugs to accommodate all this stuff.

Power strips are like short extension cords, except that they have several outlets to accommodate your computer paraphernalia.

Kensington SmartSockets is a brand of power strip that has a large, wide area that allows more room for the AC converters that often come on computer peripherals. I recommend this brand.

Surge Protector

A *surge protector* is merely a dooded-up power strip. It's like a power strip with a fuse to even out the electricity in times of power glitches, which can crash your computer and make you lose everything you've been working on.

> ✔ A power strip can also be a surge protector. Some just have extra outlets. Others have surge protection in them, like the SmartSockets mentioned in the preceding section.

✔ Some surge protectors also come with filters for protecting the phone line and network cable.

✔ The more you pay for a surge protector, the better the protection. The highest level of protection is *spike protection,* which protects your computer from lightning strikes.

✔ Sorry — you can't get any "wrath of God" protection.

UPS

UPS (not the delivery service) stands for *Uninterruptible Power Supply.* It keeps the computer on (for a while) during a power outage.

By plugging your computer and monitor into the UPS, you have enough time to safely save and close all your documents before turning off your computer. The UPS also has surge protection, but you don't really have to plug *everything* into it. After all, who cares whether your modem or your printer goes off during an outage? The data in your computer is more important, and that's what the UPS protects.

✔ If you plug too much stuff into a UPS, your computer doesn't have enough power to last long enough to save any of your work. Plug just the computer and monitor into the UPS.

✔ Never plug a printer into a UPS; printing can wait until after the power comes back on.

✔ If possible, try to find a UPS that supports swappable batteries. That way you can replace only the battery should the unit get sluggish and not have to buy a whole new UPS.

✔ Most UPS systems are good for around five minutes, so don't dawdle! Save your work, and then turn off your computer!

Printer Cable

Printers don't come with printer cables, which has always amazed me because you can't get your printer to work unless a cable connects your printer to your computer. It's like buying a television without a cord to plug into the wall. Ugh.

The only thing you need to worry about with printer cables is that your printer can be no farther than 20 feet away from your computer. Information tends to get lost at that distance. The most common length for printer cable is 6 feet.

(Note that the 20 foot limit applies to parallel printer cables. For USB printers, the limit is theoretically 3 meters, or about 10 feet.)

Printer Paper

Paper. Gotta have it for the printer or else the darn thing is kind of useless. Only a few rules apply when it comes to paper:

- ✔ Don't use *bond* paper in a laser printer. Bond paper may have a dust on it, which clogs up the printer.

- ✔ Don't use erasable typing paper. This type of paper is good for manual typewriters, where you have to erase all your typing mistakes, but with a computer the dust on the erasable typing paper can clog up the printer's internals.

- ✔ Buy a whole box when you go to buy paper. You'll use it. Nothing is more frustrating than printing a report, running out of paper in the middle of it, and then realizing that you don't have any more.

More Ink Stuff

Printers, like ink pens, run out of ink — except with a pen, you're more likely to throw the darn thing away and buy another one. You don't want to do that with a printer. That could get costly. Instead, you have to buy more ink.

Printer ink comes in various containers and exists in various states, depending on your printer.

- ✔ Ink jet printers use little containers of ink that are really super-easy to change.

- ✔ Laser printers use a drop-in toner cartridge. These cartridges are fairly easy to install if you follow the directions.

- ✔ Impact (or dot matrix) printers use a ribbon.

Because all these printers require you to handle the ribbon or cartridge, you run a risk of getting this stuff on your hands. Be careful! It's ink. It doesn't come off easily. It kind of wears off more than it washes off. To help prevent that, wear some rubber gloves when you change the toner or ribbon in your printer.

Removable Disks

Even though your hard drive has a huge capacity to store information, you still need removable disks. You use them for transferring information from one computer to another.

For your floppy drive, get floppy disks. Buy a box of preformatted disks for either the PC or Macintosh.

If you have a specialty drive, like an LS-120, Jaz, or Zip, get some of those disks, too.

CD-R and CD-RW drives deserve to have their own media as well. Stock up on those disks, where buying them in bulk is often cheaper than buying them one-at-a-time.

- ✔ Make sure that you get the proper-size disks: 3½-inch 1.44MB floppy disks. Try to buy them preformatted if possible.

- ✔ Jaz disks are expensive. Buying them three or more at a time will save you some money.

- ✔ If possible, try to get the green-gold type of CD-R disks. They tend to be more reliable and compatible than the cheaper CD-R disks.

Backup Tapes

Most tape-backup units come with one tape, just as kind of a tease. You need at least two other tapes, for a total of three. Take the sample tape with you to the store to make sure that you buy the right size and capacity for your tape-backup drive.

Why three tapes? Because you want to rotate them as you back up. Label the tapes A, B, and C. Put your first backup on tape A. Your second backup goes on tape B. The third backup goes on C. Then start over again with A. This system makes it easier to keep track of old data. If one of the tapes goes bad, you have a second and third backup handy.

A Roll of Paper Towels

Paper towels? You're surprised, right? Even though one of the rules for computer use is that you don't eat or drink by your computer, you will. It's inevitable. You'll succumb to temptation and grab a cup of coffee to keep you company.

Paper towels are for those times when you spill your beverage of choice. Spilling liquid of any kind can cause havoc with your computer, so either don't drink and compute or keep those paper towels close by.

Getting your keyboard wet fries the keyboard (metaphorically speaking — it's not like smoke and stuff billows out of the keyboard). You can try to let it dry out or use those paper towels to try to wipe up the liquid before it does too much damage.

Appendix

Commonly Asked Questions and Their Answers

• •

Software

Q: What's the difference between Version 1.2 and Version 1.3 in software?

A: Version 1.3 lacks all the bugs that were in Version 1.2. Likewise, when Version 1.4 comes out, it will have fixed all the bugs found in Version 1.3. Other improvements may come along the way as well, though they're usually presented in the major version releases; in this case, the major version release would be Version 2.0.

Q: I have some old DOS software. Can I get Windows to use my software?

A: Windows runs all older DOS software, or so it claims on the box.

Q: How about integrated software? If I buy one package for $700, isn't that better than buying the individual software applications for $300 each?

A: Only if you plan to use *all* the applications. For example, buying Microsoft Office when you need only Microsoft Word is a waste of money.

Q: I can't get my program to run. Help!

A: Reading the manual helps. You can also get a good book on the subject because computer book authors have more time and are willing to put more into their work.

Q: I don't have the manual because a friend gave me a copy of his disks. Now what do I do?

A: This is theft. You should never use this type of software. You wouldn't think of going into the software store, taking the disks from the package, and walking out the door without paying, would you? Also, this type of "freebie" is how computer viruses are spread.

Q: Should I worry about computer viruses?

A: Sadly, computer viruses are a fact of computing life. They are mischievous little programs that sneak on to your computer to either amuse, annoy, or curse you. Special programs called *virus utilities* can be used to check your system for signs of infection and remove the viruses. If you use only shrink-wrapped, store-bought software, however, you'll never have anything to worry about.

Bits and Bytes and RAM

Q: What's the difference between expanded and extended memory?

A: *Expanded memory* is extra memory for DOS programs. It's rarely used today. *Extended memory* is now just called *memory* because it's the memory Windows and all Windows programs use.

Q: What is virtual memory?

A: It's hard disk storage that's used to help your computer manage memory. For example, your computer may "swap out" a chunk of data in RAM, storing it on the hard disk as *virtual memory.* When the computer needs that information again, it's swapped back into RAM.

Disk Drives

Q: Can I add a floppy drive to my iMac?

A: Yes. Any good USB external drive will do you. Some can even be found that will match your iMac's color.

Q: Can I add a second hard drive to my computer system?

A: Yes. Most computers have room for two hard drives. If yours does, you can add a second, larger hard drive quite easily either by yourself or by having your dealer do it for you.

Monitors and Keyboards

Q: Does a bigger monitor display more colors?

A: No. It's not the monitor that's in charge of the colors; it's your video adapter card. You can plug the card into any size monitor and it doesn't change how the card's circuitry displays colors. The only thing a bigger monitor gives you is a bigger image.

Q: My eyes hurt after computing. The wife says that it's because of my computer's monitor. Is there anything I can do?

A: The problem is caused more by the lights in the room than by your monitor. The lights reflect off your computer screen, and that's what causes eye irritation. I recommend buying a nylon screen for your monitor. It cuts down on the glare and provides more contrast for a better image.

Q: Speaking of my wife, she says that the computer will ruin my eyes. Is that true?

A: Not at all! Using your eyes does not cause them to go bad. Your eyes may get fatigued. When they do, get up and stare out a window for a while. Changing focus is the best way to relieve your tired eyes.

Q: What's a Dvorak keyboard?

A: It's a specially designed keyboard that supposedly enables you to type faster. They keys are laid out in a logical order rather than in the mechanical order on current keyboards. Although Dvorak keyboards never really caught on, some computers allow you to activate a "Dvorak option" if you want to try it out.

Printers and Peripherals

Q: Can I use my typewriter as a computer printer?

A: That works only if the typewriter is designed for that purpose. Normally, a typewriter is a stand-alone device and doesn't talk with your computer. It would be nice, though (and slow as a frozen river).

Q: How can I print 10-foot-long banners on my printer?

A: Banners are normally printed on printers that use continuous form-feed paper. On laser and ink printers, you usually print the banner a sheet at a time and then tape them together. Some ink jet printers do have a special slot for banners.

Q: My printer doesn't print at all.

A: You probably have two printer ports on your computer. Nothing is wrong with that, except that both ports are fighting over which one comes first. Use your operating system to ensure that the printer is connected to the proper port.

Q: Can my CD player play music?

A: Sure, as long as you have the proper multimedia software that lets your computer's CD-ROM drive play a musical CD. Both Windows and the Macintosh System Software come with music CD player software.

Q: If I have a modem, can someone call up my computer and steal information?

A: Only if you let them. First, in order for someone to call your computer, you must run special software that lets them do that. Furthermore, you must tell the software that the person can steal information from your computer. If this ever does happen, it's because you let it happen. Your computer will never answer the phone unless you have software that tells it to do so *and* you set it up that way.

Q: Can I hook up my fax machine to my computer?

A: Only if it's designed to do so.

Q: Will my computer receive faxes if it's turned off?

A: No, your computer doesn't do anything if it's turned off. It can receive faxes if you're not there, but you must have a fax/modem installed, and the software that's required in order to receive the fax must be running. External fax machines can receive faxes when the computer is turned off, but the machines must be turned on.

Computer Systems

Q: Should I buy only Intel microprocessors?

A: If it makes you feel better, do so. Otherwise, no major problems have been found with the microprocessors manufactured by others. If problems did exist, the manufacturers probably wouldn't sell many of the chips — which isn't the case.

Q: Do you recommend IBM equipment?

A: Just like the preceding Intel microprocessor question, if buying IBM stuff makes you feel better, do it! Otherwise, when you peel back the outer wrapper, you'll see that all PCs contain basically the same innards.

Q: I want to write letters and balance my checkbook. Will a Pentium computer fill this need?

A: Fit the computer to meet your needs. Look for your checkbook-balancing software *first.* Then match that software's lust for hardware, and that's how you tell what type of computer you need. This basic method is what this book offers. If, in the end, all indicators point to a Pentium, you can buy it.

Q: Should I pay extra for an "Intel motherboard"? My dealer says that they're better.

A: For a Pentium computer, I would get an Intel motherboard, if I had a choice. The reason is that Intel knows how to make the motherboard for its own microprocessors and for the *PCI bus.* It's worth the extra cost (if any), in my opinion.

Q: What's a "flash programmable BIOS"?

A: It's a special chip that can be upgraded without removing the computer's cover. The *BIOS* is your PC's personality chip, and often manufacturers upgrade the BIOS to make it happier with newer PC components. In the olden days, you had to upgrade the chip by physically pulling out the old one and replacing it. With a flash BIOS, you can do the job by running a program on your computer. It makes the job simple.

Q: I've seen deals on refurbished equipment offered without a warranty but at very low (ridiculous) prices. Tell me what's wrong.

A: You have no warranty, and you're taking a stupid risk. Don't mess up your first computer experience by being cheap.

Q: What's a *clone,* and what's a *compatible*?

A: These terms have no concrete definitions, though they seem to have fallen out of favor as the dominance of IBM fades. Traditionally, a *clone* was a no-name, locally assembled computer. A *compatible* was a national brand. Compatibles are usually more expensive and more reliable, and they come with a better warranty (because it's honored by service departments across the country). The warranty on a clone is usually only good in one place: the store where you bought it.

Q: I want to buy one computer and hook up ten monitors and ten keyboards. Can I do that?

A: Not the way you think. What you really need is a file server and several workstations. However, a properly-configured PC with Linux and a special serial card can get the job done. Again, it's the *software* that makes it possible here; Linux is the software that does that job.

Q: What about those dedicated word-processing machines? Because all I want to do is write, why shouldn't I get one of those instead of a computer?

A: Don't! Those dedicated machines are slower, much slower than similarly priced and equipped computers. Don't let the price fool you. A computer can be had for the same cost, plus you get your choice of word-processing software, a faster printer, and a path to future upgrades and more software options. Those dedicated word-processing machines are a sucker's buy. Don't be lured.

Q: I'm interested in picking up a used computer system. How can I tell whether it's any good?

A: First, I don't recommend a used computer system for your first computer purchase. You're definitely cutting off your service and support, not to mention any warranty. For a second or third purchase, used computers are a deal; most of them still operate and are decent machines. Just take along some software to test drive, and "kick the tires" by trying out the keyboard and monitor and turning the unit on and off a few times.

General

Q: What does $CALL mean?

A: It means that they can't print the price because the manufacturer won't let them or some other strange reason (such as to foil the "we'll beat any advertised price" crowd). It may also be a ruse to get you to phone up the company to see how much the doojobbie costs. In fact, that's the "call" part of $CALL.

Q: Can I set my computer on the floor? Will it leave a grease spot?

A: The only important thing about setting a computer anywhere is giving it breathing space, as discussed in Chapter 22. Make sure that you don't set the computer on carpet that can clog any breathing slats. If you didn't buy a tower-style computer, consider getting a little stand to help stand your computer up on its side. And, no, no grease is inside a computer to make a spot.

Q: Why doesn't someone make a computer that has every processor in it and can use every operating system?

A: They did. No one bought it. It did everything, but, like any jack-of-all-trades, it didn't do everything well. The cost of the computer was more expensive than buying each of the other computers separately.

Q: I have an old PC that isn't upgradeable. Can I do anything?

A: Sell it — if you can. Or donate it to a school or charity. They may grouse about it, in which case you can always find another school or charity that won't look a gift horse in the mouth.

Q: My computer runs hot — sometimes it shuts itself off. What can I do?

A: Buy a new power supply or, better still, take your system to an authorized repair service.

Q: If I want to learn how to program my computer, where should I start?

A: Buy a book about programming. Many excellent tutorials are out there that let you work at your own pace. For a programming language, I recommend BASIC. Sounds easy enough.

Q: Can I play Nintendo game cartridges on my PC?

A: Nope.

Q: I want a question answered that hasn't been covered in this book. Where can I go for help?

A: First, try your dealer (if you have already purchased a computer). You paid him money; he should give you the support and answer your question. He may redirect you to the software manufacturer if the problem is with your software. Second, try a local users' group or a friend who is computer-knowledgeable. Third, you can also try writing away to those "Ask Dr. Computer" columnists in the national computer magazines. You can always find both help available for computers and people who are willing to help you.

Index

Discover Dummies Online!

The Dummies Web Site is your fun and friendly online resource for the latest information about ...*For Dummies®* books and your favorite topics. The Web site is the place to communicate with us, exchange ideas with other ...*For Dummies* readers, chat with authors, and have fun!

Ten Fun and Useful Things You Can Do at www.dummies.com

1. Win free ...*For Dummies* books and more!
2. Register your book and be entered in a prize drawing.
3. Meet your favorite authors through the IDG Books Author Chat Series.
4. Exchange helpful information with other ...*For Dummies* readers.
5. Discover other great ...*For Dummies* books you must have!
6. Purchase Dummieswear™ exclusively from our Web site.
7. Buy ...*For Dummies* books online.
8. Talk to us. Make comments, ask questions, get answers!
9. Download free software.
10. Find additional useful resources from authors.

Link directly to these ten fun and useful things at
http://www.dummies.com/10useful

For other technology titles from IDG Books Worldwide, go to
www.idgbooks.com

Not on the Web yet? It's easy to get started with *Dummies 101®: The Internet For Windows®98* or *The Internet For Dummies®,* 6th Edition, at local retailers everywhere.

Find other ...*For Dummies* books on these topics:
Business • Career • Databases • Food & Beverage • Games • Gardening • Graphics • Hardware
Health & Fitness • Internet and the World Wide Web • Networking • Office Suites
Operating Systems • Personal Finance • Pets • Programming • Recreation • Sports
Spreadsheets • Teacher Resources • Test Prep • Word Processing

IDG BOOKS WORLDWIDE BOOK REGISTRATION

We want to hear from you!

Register This Book and Win!

Visit **http://my2cents.dummies.com** to register this book and tell us how you liked it!

- Get entered in our monthly prize giveaway.

- Give us feedback about this book — tell us what you like best, what you like least, or maybe what you'd like to ask the author and us to change!

- Let us know any other ...*For Dummies*® topics that interest you.

Your feedback helps us determine what books to publish, tells us what coverage to add as we revise our books, and lets us know whether we're meeting your needs as a ...*For Dummies* reader. You're our most valuable resource, and what you have to say is important to us!

Not on the Web yet? It's easy to get started with *Dummies 101*®*: The Internet For Windows*® *98* or *The Internet For Dummies*®, 6th Edition, at local retailers everywhere.

Or let us know what you think by sending us a letter at the following address:

...*For Dummies* Book Registration
Dummies Press
7260 Shadeland Station, Suite 100
Indianapolis, IN 46256-3917
Fax 317-596-5498

™

BESTSELLING
BOOK SERIES